To Larry Shea
Best of the best

Fred North

FLYING
SIDEWAYS

A MEMOIR

Fred and I have had MANY great shoots with you Larry lets have many more
HAWS

FRED and PEGGY
NORTH

DEXTERITY
NASHVILLE

DEXTERITY

Dexterity, LLC
604 Magnolia Lane
Nashville, TN 37211

Flying Sideways is a work of nonfiction. Some names and identifying details have been changed to protect privacy.

Printed in the United States of America.

First edition: 2023
10 9 8 7 6 5 4 3 2 1

ISBN: 978-1-947297-87-6 (Hardcover)
ISBN: 978-1-947297-88-3 (eBook)
ISBN: 978-1-947297-91-3 (Audiobook)

Publisher's Cataloging-in-Publication Data
Names: North, Frederic, author. | North, Peggy, author.
Title: Flying sideways , Fred North : the story of the world's most famous stunt pilot / by Fred North and Peggy North.
Description: Nashville, TN: Dexterity: 2023.
Identifiers: LCCN: 2023900378 | 978-1-947297-87-6 (hardcover) | 978-1-947297-88-3 (ebook) | 978-1-947297-91-3 (Audiobook)
Subjects: LCSH North, Frederic. | Stunt flying--Biography. | Stunt performers--United States--Biography. | Air pilots--United States--Biography. | BIOGRAPHY & AUTOBIOGRAPHY / Aviation & Nautical
Classification: LCC TL540 .N67 2023 | DDC 797.5/4/092--dc23

Cover design, interior design, and formatting by Becky's Graphic Design®, LLC

Wherever available, environmentally sustainable and/or recycled materials have been used in the manufacturing of this book.

PRAISE FOR **FRED NORTH** AND
FLYING SIDEWAYS

"*Flying Sideways* is a captivating memoir, one that covers its authors personal and professional journey to the top of his game and the heights of our industry. In a voice that is as authentic and straightforward as Fred himself, this book hooks you in from its very first pages, sharing compelling details and nuance as it chronicles Fred's unlikely and inspiring path to becoming one of the best there's ever been."

—**SHAWN LEVY**, Director and Producer–
Night at the Museum, Stranger Things,
Free Guy, The Adam Project

"Fred North is the best f*%#ing stunt helicopter pilot on the planet. If you want the impossible shot for your film, call Fred."

—**SAM HARGRAVE**, Director–
Extraction 2

"Fred North is a master filmmaker who helps craft the story with amazing aerial photography. He bends, twists, dives, and contorts his helicopter to get the shots that defy gravity and make audiences cheer . . . He brings a level of expertise and experience that comes from the thousands of hours he has spent flying . . . He's the man."

—**PATRICK NEWHALL**, Producer–
Extraction 2

"I've worked with Fred for over 20 years on my films. Not only do I consider him the best helicopter pilot in the world, but I also regard him as a true artist with his machine. Fred can dance like no other, navigating that whirling bird to help the camera capture the most breathtaking images. Fred and I have developed an unspoken language; when he hears my voice on a ground-to-air radio, he knows it's game on."

—**MICHAEL BAY**, Director and Producer–
Armageddon, Transformers, Bad Boys

"Fred embodies the word 'trust.' I had so much trust in him and his abilities to create an incredible stunt sequence for our film while keeping us all safe. He made us all want to push further than we thought possible. He cares deeply about his work and even more deeply about his family. They keep his number one priority on safety. I literally put my life in his hands on the film and would do it again without any hesitation."

—**CHARLIZE THERON**, Actress and Producer–
Atomic Blonde, The Old Guard, Fast and Furious

"*Flying Sideways* is an exhilarating book, reminding us that sometimes all the wrong turns lead us to the right course. This book is a testament to a life lived in extreme circumstances, adrenaline-fueled chaos, revealing life-threatening danger with each turn of the page. The risks, the danger, the wins, the losses, the agony, and the ecstasy. *Flying Sideways* reminds us to always follow our destiny and live life at full throttle. While we wait to find our own true north, this book inspires us by journeying with Fred as he finds his North."

—**GERARD BUTLER**, Actor and Producer–
London Has Fallen, Greenland, Kandahar

LARRY, YOU ARE THE GREATEST! HERE'S TO MANY MORE, THANKS FOR EVERYTHING, IVAN

"Challenges make life interesting, however, overcoming them is what makes life meaningful."

MARK TWAIN

Table of Contents

Author's Note   1

Prologue   3

PART I

01   Look Up   11

02   The Simple Things Are Enough   21

03   Go Off the Main Trail   29

04   Don't Fit the Profile   37

05   Don't Be a Quitter   45

06   Stay Connected   55

07   Follow the Adrenaline   65

PART II

08   A Deal's a Deal   77

09   Adapt   89

10   Boredom Is the Opposite of Freedom   101

11   Keep Pushing   113

12   BYOC (Bring Your Own Compass)   123

13   Own Your Mistakes   139

14   Read the Signs   153

15   Do Something Different, Somewhere Different   167

PART III

16   Dream Bigger   188

17   Some Things Are Worth Waiting For   195

18   The Landing Is the Hardest Part   207

19   Nothing Is Impossible   221

20   Cover Your Ass   235

21   Go Higher   243

Epilogue   253

QR Codes (Video Links)   258

Photo and Illustration Credits   261

About the Authors   263

Acknowledgments   265

Author's Note

TO SET THE RECORD STRAIGHT, no, I am not a comic book superhero, but yes, my real name is Frédéric North.

In France, my last name is not as cool as it is in English. When spoken, it sounds less like the direction on a compass and instead rhymes with not-so-desirable words like *wart* and *short*. If you really want to do it right, imagine you are German, roll the *r* a little bit, and say "*Norrrte*." As far as my first name goes, only my mother calls me Frédéric. To everyone else I am Fred. Though I am often asked, I did not change or buy my name. Fred North just happens to be a very good name for a helicopter pilot, which conveniently turned out to be my fate.

It is hard for me to say when my life story begins. My great-great-great-grandfather, or so I was told, was Lord Frédérick North, the twelfth prime minister of Great Britain. This would be a very cool fact to start with, but apparently he was a bit chubby and not a great guy. The *actual* beginning, my birth, was not remarkable aside from the fact that I am a twin, and no one in my family seems to remember that day well. So I choose to begin in the first moments I felt truly alive—the birth of a dream that has stayed with me my entire life, through many changes of address, some failures, and the odd success too. But perhaps the stubbornness of that dream is my biggest success of all.

Originally, this book was written for my children at the insistence of my wife and collaborator, Peggy. She wanted a collection of all my crazy stories—the big adventures, the little moments that mattered a lot, and a few of the lessons I learned along the way. The urgency of the project, she said, had nothing to do with my getting older, but I'm not sure I believe her. Anyway, she's very convincing. Then I joined social media, and suddenly, my family members were not the only ones asking me how an odd kid who was held back in school became one of the most famous stunt helicopter pilots in the world. This book is my best attempt at answering this question.

Having spent much of my time on earth in the sky (and a few nights in various jails around the world), and having seen death and life from many angles, my memory is not perfect. Memoir is not perfect. I have done my best to remember things as they occurred. Conversations and sequences of events have been recreated based on my recollections with as much fidelity as possible. Many character names and identifying features have been changed to protect the privacy of the people I love *and* to make sure the people I don't love aren't too pissed off at me. I'm not here to embarrass anyone but myself. All of these "characters," good and bad, have been important parts of my life—a life I am deeply grateful for. Also, to the helicopter pilots reading, this book is not meant in any way to be a manual. As they say on the big screen: "WARNING: Do not try this at home." There is a lot of cool stuff in this book, but I insist that you don't attempt any of it. I am a trained stunt professional, and nothing is more important to me than safety.

So now you know the basics: My name really is Fred North. I am a stunt pilot. I am a husband and a father. Now I am an author. This is my story. It is a story about not giving up.

Prologue

FOR THE LONGEST TIME, I can't bring myself to watch the movie *Extraction*. I see a couple of teasers online before it releases, and truly, that is enough for me. I'm sure the cast is great and the director, Sam Hargrave, is a genius, but the helicopter work is not so impressive. Call me arrogant or stubborn; both of those things are true. Mostly, though, I'm a perfectionist. I'm a film pilot. It's my job to help create and capture the best footage possible. I don't like to see a good aerial shot where there can be a great one. My friends tell me to watch *Extraction*, as do my kids, but I'm not the kind of person interested in sitting down for one hour and fifty-six minutes to think about what I would have done differently. Not until they hire me for the sequel anyway.

My phone rings around nine a.m. on May 10, my sixtieth birthday. It's the producer of *Extraction 2*. The guy is a fast talker. I don't even want to know how much coffee he's had. I listen and respond as well as I can, but all I know by the end of the call is that they're shooting in Australia, the big scene will involve a train and some helicopters, they need a budget yesterday, and they want me on board. He asks if I'm interested. Of course I am.

For a month and a half, I perform intense research, source the best Australian pilots for the scene, figure out what kind of restrictions will be in place at the location, and track down choppers we can use. For a month and a half, I watch *Extraction* over and over again. I have to admit, it's actually really good.

In June, I meet Sam Hargrave on a Zoom call with at least ten other people from his team and the studio. I've studied Sam's work, read interviews, and listened to podcasts. I'm thrilled to be working with him. Sam isn't just a director; he's a stuntman, an actor, and a coordinator. He understands a little bit more about what I do than most directors do, and he seems more character-driven than most of the action movie guys. In *Extraction*, he used a "oner", a single camera, to capture the action and a lot of close-contact fighting between the main actor and the bad guys. He seems to take a more intimate approach. Normally, action directors want things to look as enormous and explosive as possible, and I mean literally explosive.

At first, the call is mostly people from the studio talking about how excited they are. They're excited about the project, excited to be on the call, and excited to see what we'll come up with. Like the producer who brought me on the project, they have all had too much coffee. Sam doesn't say anything at all, and neither do I.

I read the big scene the producer pitched to me, even though I'm not much of a reader and there isn't much detail yet. There's a helicopter, a train, the bad guys, and a good guy. Sure, we have a lot of room to work together and build something, but directors aren't always super open to creative input, especially from a helicopter pilot who can't get through the entire script.

The people on the call continue to be excited for a few more minutes, smiling at me in their little Zoom squares, occasionally asking me a question about the (sizable) budget I put together for them, filling me in on COVID-19 set protocols, and going over the shooting schedule. Finally, Sam jumps in.

"So, Fred, I want to shoot the most epic train sequence in the history of moviemaking."

Heavy words. Not such a boring call after all. If Sam wants epic, we can do epic. This is exactly the direction I was hoping for.

He explains the scene in a little more detail. Three "attack" helicopters will drop a couple of guys on top of a train to go after the main character, a mercenary named Tyler Rake, played by Chris Hemsworth. There will be picture helicopters, the kind you see in the movies doing the stunts, but we'll also be getting aerial footage at the same time. So far, it's nothing revolutionary, but Sam is getting louder, more animated, and talking with his hands.

"OK, Fred," he says. "So the helicopters will come in. They're going to go around the moving train, shooting at it with automatic weapons. There'll be an explosion and the first helicopter will crash. . . ."

He pauses, probably to gauge my reaction. I try to look excited, but there is always an explosion and one of the helicopters always crashes. Sam is undeterred and continues.

"The second helicopter will drop the bad guys on top of the train and fly off. The third helicopter will get shot from the side of the train and leave the frame."

He pauses again.

"What do you think?"

The scene is fine, but it won't be "the most epic train sequence in the history of moviemaking." It's been done. It doesn't need to be done again. I don't want to hurt the guy's feelings, and I don't want to get fired; I want to do something unbelievable.

"Are you open to suggestions?" I ask him.

"Absolutely," Sam replies.

"Give me one week," I tell him, and we say goodbye.

After several days thinking of nothing but the scene, it comes to me when I'm brushing my teeth. And it *is* epic.

"Sam, we need to land a helicopter on top of the fast-moving train to unload the bad guys."

Sam is silent. The entire team is silent. They're all staring at me like I'm crazy, but this is the answer. *This* is the scene.

"The helicopter will enter the frame with speed, fire at the train—*bah bah bah bah bah*—and then fly alongside it super close and aggressively. I'm talking buzz the lead actor! Then I'll flare like crazy, my tail rotor will be only a couple feet from the train, and *BOOM!* We'll land on it. No shaky landing. *The* landing!"

Everybody is still quiet. My breathing is heavy. There's sweat on the tops of my hands. I'm pretty sure I was yelling into my computer mic.

Sam starts nodding. His eyes light up. His face breaks into a smile and he comes back to life. He starts yelling too.

"Yes! Yes, yes, yes! Fred, this is brilliant! I love this idea! Everybody! This is going to be epic!"

With Sam's blessing, the team is now very into the idea too. Suddenly they can't imagine *not* landing on the train. *Thank God.*

We talk a few more minutes about the pros and cons of each type of helicopter and then log off. A fraction of a second later, I freeze.

Why do I always need to come up with the craziest ideas? What's wrong with me?

I know what the scene needs to be, but I have no idea how to do it. I don't even know if I *can* land on a moving train. . . . I'm thinking I can, but how am I going to train and practice for it? A transport truck?

Merde. I got everyone on board for a multimillion-dollar scene, but now I need to deliver. There's no other choice.

Sam calls later in the week. He's even more amped about the scene than before.

"Fred, quick question: Can you fly backward at sixty miles per hour, in front of the train at about fifteen feet off the ground, and fire at the train at the same time?"

Oh Jesus. What have I done to Sam Hargrave?

"Well, Sam," I reply, "I won't be able to go that fast backward because it will stall the engine. The engine could fail, and then I might die, but I can fly sideways. Would that work?"

"That's it!" Sam yells. "I'm going to rewrite the whole sequence!"

Holy moly. I am in so much trouble.

The scene is incredible. Nothing like this has been done before.

What if it's impossible? I think to myself.

Quickly, another voice inside me answers—a voice I've been listening to my entire life.

But what if it's possible?

Part I

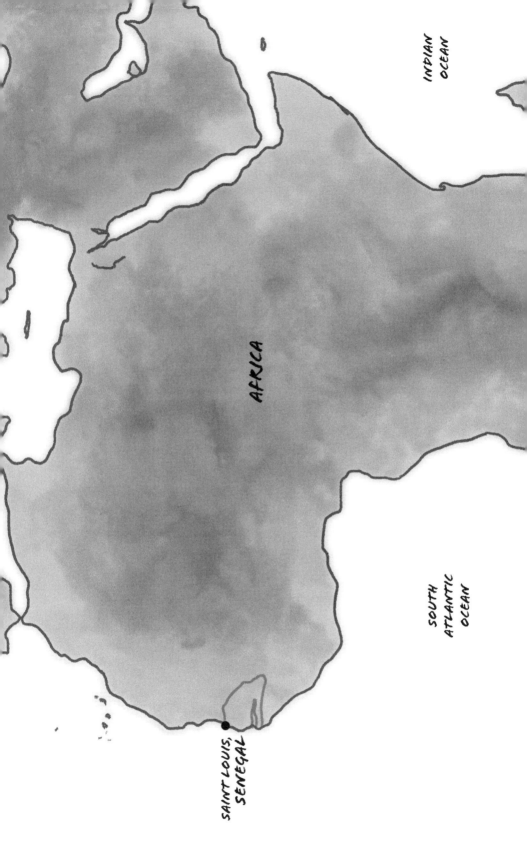

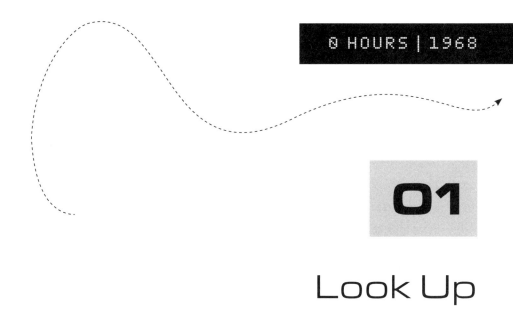

01

Look Up

"FRED! FRED!"

My twin sister, Catherine, is calling me. I have been in the filao tree since we got home from school, pulling my body up, branch by branch, toward the top. I do this every day, and every day Catherine shouts. But I like to be high up. I am not afraid by it, even when my hands sweat and the trunk gets thin. For me, it feels safe and natural to be above, looking down on Saint-Louis. I can see everything—the beige block-shaped homes in our neighborhood, the Senegal River, the strip of white beach where I kick up sand at my friends and try to catch fish. Most importantly, from the trees I can see our neighbor, who is keeping at least four illegal monkeys. I have been spying on him for weeks. The monkeys stare back and seem to notice me, but he never does.

"Frédéric!"

Catherine is standing by the base of the tree, giving me a look. She is skinny, pale, and driven, with freckles on her nose and small wrinkles on her forehead. We are both seven years old, but she is taller and looks older, more serious. I ignore her, which I do often, and climb higher, tearing my shorts on a twig and laughing as a shower of dry needles falls past her face and lands at her feet. I'm not ready to come down yet. The higher I go, the better I feel. I count a few baobabs, watch the monkeys scratch each other's backs, and follow a bird from the roof of our compound until it disappears into the place where the sky meets the sea.

Catherine and I were born in Tunisia but have lived in Senegal since we were one. My parents are French, and they have been teaching in Africa since they were married in 1957. My mom's family is just middle-class, and my dad's parents did not approve of the match, so my parents left France after the wedding. You would not expect them to be adventurous people; they are academics and are always following the rules, but they also like to explore, learning as many things about the world and the people who live in it as possible. My father is a principal, and my mother teaches French. In 1962, the French government gave them a small concrete house across from the armed forces base here in Saint-Louis and hired them to run the military school. For as long as I can remember, this has been our home. If I am French, and I'm told that I am, I have no memory of France. All I have known is yellow dirt, sugarcane, fresh fish, cuckoo birds screaming at me in the morning, and Catherine screaming at me in the afternoon.

My sister is pissed now, marching around the tree and sweating in her school shirt.

"Up here!" I call down to her, swinging my legs and bare feet, letting go of the trunk, and balancing on a branch with just my seatbones. Her eyes go wide and white when she spots me. I wobble, catching myself, but just barely.

"We have to do our homework," she scolds as I hop down. "And you're gonna break your legs one day."

And I probably will . . . break my legs, that is. Not do my homework.

The inside of our home is very European. There are pieces of art, too many lamps, and even more books. There are nice dishes and a tablecloth to set them on. Only the bedrooms are furnished simply, which is fine by me because I mostly live outside. Isabelle, my oldest sister, is in the living room working on her math, too focused and stressed to notice me when I come through the door. Catherine goes straight for her copy of *Le Petit Prince*, which we're supposed to be reading for school. She walks off to her room with her face so deep in the book, I watch her just to see if she'll crash into a wall. Olivier, who is only five, asks Aissatou, the kind local woman who watches us, about dinner, tugging at her boubou and pouting. She tries to calm him with a sweet West African song, and his giant cheeks lift into a smile. Olivier is very easy to cheer up. I am not.

My bookbag is hunched over in the corner of the room like a drunk, and if it had arms, I am sure they would be crossed. All I have to do is look at the bag, and my stomach is sick. I hate school. School doesn't like me much either. I am supposed to be smart, bookish, and well-behaved like my parents, but instead, I am a menace. I don't like being told what to do—especially by the teachers, who treat us like small prisoners. When we have things to say, we're punished for speaking. When we're told to stand up, sit down, or form a line, we're expected to do it, regardless of our bodies' desires. I'm left-handed, but in school they force me to use my right. I could deal with my anger in a kind, calm way, but that would make me a liar *and* a bore, so instead, I throw rocks, speak out of turn, and refuse to complete my assignments. More often than not, I am in trouble, and when it comes to discipline, the teaching staff at the military school are not especially creative.

First, they beat me at the front of the class with the ruler, and when that doesn't work, they beat me in the schoolyard on my bare butt using whatever they can find lying around—which, I suppose, is a little creative after all. They have one move called the four-by-four where the teacher gets four of my classmates to pin me down, holding me by the arms and legs, while he hits me. At first it was a little embarrassing, but the other students quickly became used to seeing my snowy white butt. Now they don't even bother to look. My parents take notice, of course, but they aren't creative about discipline at home either. Most discussions with my father end with a print of his signet ring on my left cheek. My mother, thankfully, is more of a slapper. Isabelle and Catherine are both obedient and good students. Olivier will likely be the same. Nobody really knows what to do with me. My parents prefer the kind of children who read under trees instead of climbing up them, and they make it known to me.

"Fred?" Catherine pokes her head out of her room and lifts her chin toward my bookbag. "Have you started yet?"

She looks at me tired and cross, like a tiny librarian. I shrug my shoulders and walk back out into the heat.

There is a bit of time before my parents get home for dinner, so I leave my work unfinished and go to meet Moussa, Abdou, and Ousmane at the construction site. Moussa and Ousmane are in class with me. Abdou is a little bit older with a tall, stretched-out body. I have never seen any of them with shirts or shoes on. They could say the same about me.

"*Bonjour, mon ami,*" Ousmane says when he sees me walking up. I nod to him, and immediately we begin spying on the workers. A dozen men in white plastic hats march around, mixing concrete and looking up at the bones of a structure. What they're building will be a casino one day, though none of us knows anyone in Saint-Louis with the money to gamble.

Our friendships are simple and not very personal. We play games, go to the beach, steal materials from local builders, and work on our toys. Because there are no stores, we have to make our own gadgets—collecting sticks, searching the roadside for strips of tire rubber, carving bits of acacia wood into slingshots and throwaway fishing rods to use in the river. My siblings and I are not the only white kids around, but everyone plays together. Nobody seems to care who is French and who is West African. Senegal is friendly and very laid-back that way.

"Psst . . . look," Moussa hisses.

We keep our bodies low to the ground like big cats and join him behind a bush, stalking stacks of blond wood and boxes of screws, waiting until the workers pack up, letting our noses drip and throats go dry, allowing red ants to crawl on our wrists and ankles, never making a sound.

"Aye!" The foreman spots us, I'm not sure how, and we scatter barefoot, filled with adrenaline, in all directions. Eventually we wander back home for dinner.

Childhood goes on like this for a while. We steal shoestrings and match-books from our parents and neighbors, and we peek over the walls of the military base next to my house to watch men drop into the big green tanks. We spend hours on the beach trading school supplies for candies and chew-ing Malabar gum, blowing pink bubbles that taste like nothing and deflate on our chins. We build and build and build, once even creating an airplane out of wooden boxes, warped nails, and Ousmane's bike. We bribe the guard at the casino with cigarettes to let us test it on the big concrete slab, and we walk into the site feeling like a team of astronauts getting ready to go to the moon. We push the plane, run beside it, and wait for it to fly, but of course, it doesn't. We're not really bothered though; there are too many other things to do. My parents would prefer me to be inside following the rules instead of outside breaking them, but when they are through giving me crap, they give me freedom—and really, that's all I need. Unless I'm in school, I live shoeless, in a tiny, filthy pair of briefs and nothing else, running wherever I like with my little pack of friends until pitch-dark. I don't know what it is to want anything more from the world until I realize I can fly above it.

The noise is quite strange, like thunder up close or giant swords slashing the air. We are in the street having footraces not far from my home, just me, Moussa, and Ousmane. It is not long after my birthday. I'm sure that turning eight has made me taller and faster, and today I am determined to prove it.

As soon as the sky gets loud, we shrink and cover our heads. Our games come to a stop.

"*Au secours!*" Ousmane shouts over the noise.

I shrug at him and keep my hands over my ears. Moussa won't even lift his eyes.

We have never heard anything like it. There has never been anything like it in Saint-Louis. I look up and the body of a flying machine, smooth and earth green, appears, approaching from inland, making a shadow the size of a freight liner over the neighborhood. It passes over us and leaves us dumb, staring at one another with our hands cupped over our ears. The chopper turns toward the football stadium. Without a word, every child in the city, dozens of us, in one motion, begins to run, chasing after the machine and trying to keep its tail in view.

The stadium in Saint-Louis is brown sand and nothing else. There is not a single piece of buffalo grass or even an anthill, and when the helicopter begins to land, it picks up every bit of dust from the ground and disappears behind a thick, tan cloud. The police are there, and another hundred people, all of them standing stunned in a crowd behind the officers. A few meters away from us, the machine drops down in a straight line, not like a plane or a bird. It's not really graceful at all, but precise. Out of breath, muscles on fire, we watch and wait while the dirt falls back to the ground and the rotor begins to slow.

"Wow," Ousmane says, and I nod.

The air clears, and it's like something from a dream: a glass dome with no doors sitting on two long metal skids, all topped by three sharp, dangerous-looking blades. I look at it and feel embarrassed by all of our inventions.

I'm not sure who I think will step out from the body, but I am definitely not expecting to see my geography teacher, Mr. DuBois, with his huge, ridiculous moustache. He exits the left side of the aircraft in his regular slacks and leather shoes, and I can't believe it. Never in my life have I been so happy to see a schoolteacher. I want to know everything. Without thinking, I duck under a police officer's arm and head straight toward the helicopter. Someone grabs the back of my shirt, but I don't bother looking back.

"It's all right," DuBois tells the cop. "Hello, Frédéric," he says to me, ruffling my hair. I only allow it because I'm in shock. I begin pelting him with questions instead of little stones, which makes him laugh.

The helicopter is an Alouette II, owned by the Senegalese military. DuBois has a simple assignment from the new government: to take photographs of the place where the river spills out to the sea. I don't ask why, but I guess it has something to do with oil. Senegal has only been independent a few years, so it could be anything. DuBois talks a little more about the river and the photographs, but I stop listening and stare at the machine.

"Fred." He smiles. "Would you like to come along with us?"

I'm not sure why he asks—maybe because he's never seen me interested in anything other than causing trouble, or maybe he's just a nice guy when he isn't trying to teach us about the map of Europe. I have two seconds to decide. The pilot, a cool Senegalese guy in military dress, looks in my direction, and I nod.

"Do you want to bring a friend?" DuBois asks.

Moussa and Ousmane violently shake their heads no, looking at me like I'm crazy. They're afraid to fly. I'm afraid not to.

"Good luck, Fred!" Moussa shouts. I slide onto the back seat behind the grown-ups, curling my fingers so tight around the edge of the metal bench that my hands go white and start to ache. There are no seatbelts. Or headsets. Or doors.

The pilot pushes the buttons in a frenzy, as if he's just guessing. The gauges turn, the instruments light up, and all at once the helicopter begins to shake. The engine screams and I feel the skids lift. I start to scream, too, but nobody can hear me. DuBois is fussing with his clipboard and camera, and the pilot is too busy with the controls. The machine rises straight up, and the crowd that swallowed me up just sixty seconds ago is now the size of a pill. My eyes and ears feel like they're bulging out of my skull, and the hairs on my arms stand on end. It is thirty-five degrees Celsius (95 degrees Fahrenheit) all year long here, so this is first time I've seen goose bumps in West Africa. My heart is pounding and shaking inside my chest, almost like a tambourine in a marching band. The familiar treetops, which for years have held me, become little seeds as we climb higher, higher, higher. Soon, Saint-Louis is a collection of specks.

Nobody talks to me the whole time as we dip down low and take our first turn toward the spot where the dark water of the river joins the bright-blue of the Atlantic. I hold on tight to my little seat, sure I'm about to fall, feeling the closest to death and most alive I ever have. I am not afraid; I am awake. I am something I never have been before, someone I have never been. It is as though I am meeting myself for the first time. The Alouette circles several times and then, with my balls and my heart in my throat, we fly back to the stadium.

Everyone is still there when we land: Moussa and Ousmane, the construction crew from the casino, the girls from school. They are screaming, but I can't hear them through my own shock and the sound of the engine. I imagine they are waiting for a story, wanting to clap me on the back and tell me I'm a king, which normally I would love. Today, though, I have no time for it.

The skids touch down and a gust of sand blows through the door, hitting me in the eyes and teeth.

With the engine still running and the rotor still spinning, I step out of the machine in a trance. My legs feel like dead fish. I thank DuBois and the pilot—at least I think I do—and sprint home, forgetting about the filao tree and the milkcrate airplane. Words are my only souvenir. If I don't share them, I worry the entire experience will somehow be lost forever.

I bust through the gate, the door, and into the kitchen. My mother is working quietly, drying the drinking glasses and smiling to herself. Her eyes go wide when she sees me, red in the face and completely out of breath. Between giant gulps of air that sting my throat, I try to tell her about the stadium, the crowd, the helicopter. She doesn't know whether to calm me or scold me for not asking her permission.

"I'm going to be a helicopter pilot," I tell her.

"Oh, Frédéric." She sighs and shakes her head. "No."

But "no" has never stopped me.

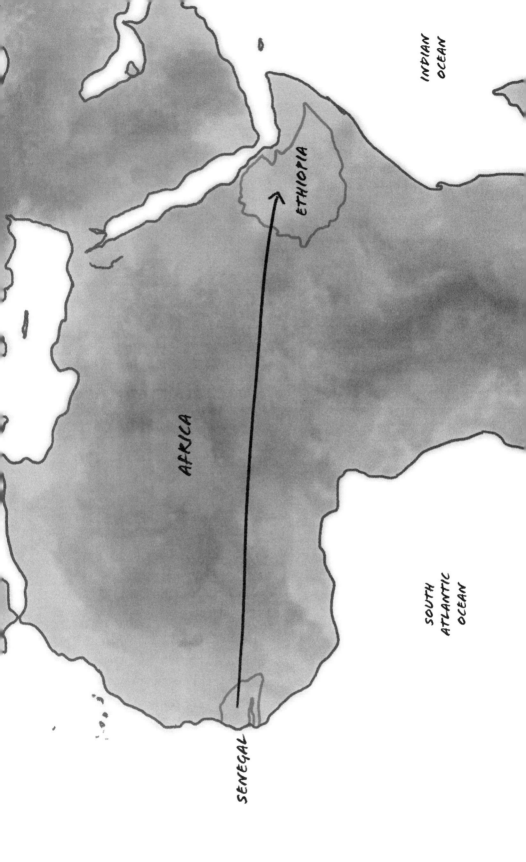

02

The Simple Things
Are Enough

THERE IS A DEAD MAN in the road. At least he looks dead to me.

"Stop staring!"

My dad is in the passenger seat, smoking cigarette after cigarette, reprimanding us while an Ethiopian man drives us to the Lycée Français Guébré-Mariam in a white Peugeot 504. My dad is principal there now. With over a thousand students, three times the number of our school in Senegal, he is stressed. I am fourteen years old and a real prick—stubborn and undisciplined. I don't like it here.

My parents moved us to Addis Ababa, Ethiopia, in September 1974, right after a communist military group called the Derg took control of the government. Maybe they are good or maybe they are bad? Maybe they are Marxists or maybe they are just pissed off? I don't really know. All I know is that *I'm* pissed off. I'm living under military rule. There is nowhere to play, no trees to climb, no construction sites to loot. I still hate school and have lost total connection with my family.

"Frédéric!" he growls. "Eyes forward!"

I glare, right into the back of his skull.

If you don't want your kids to stare at dead bodies, don't move them into the middle of a civil war.

I only think it. If I said it out loud, mine would be the next corpse in the street.

We pass a tank in the main square. A bunch of military officers are smoking and laughing next to an orange bonfire, air wobbly and strange above it. A man collapses next to them.

Catherine tugs on my school shirt and gives me a look, trying to keep me out of trouble. I lean back next to her, trying to find space for my shoulders along the bench seat. With four of us packed tight across, it is not easy. Pretending to shut my eyes, I keep staring until we pull through the front gates of our new school.

Without the war, I might like living in Addis Ababa. Sitting at an altitude of 7,726 feet, the city is surrounded by mountains and filled with cool air. Having come from Saint-Louis, where the sun feels like it is sitting on your shoulders all day, just breathing here is a relief. It is too busy for my taste—Volkswagen Beetles zipping everywhere, long lines at the store, not enough space left for nature—but I like not sweating so much. There are kids around, lots of them, but with the curfew put in place by the Derg, we can't really hang out. Ethiopia lost her freedom and I lost mine. Most days I am unhappy and don't know what to do with myself, which mother blames on teenage hormones. Both of us know it probably has less to do with pimples, though, and more to do with the war. The fact that my father walks around like a military commander doesn't help much either.

My dad doesn't listen, doesn't share. He only instructs and gives orders. Everybody in the family is expected to follow them, including my mom. Of all the people in Addis that are impossible to know under the Derg, he is the hardest to reach. I try talking with him, mostly about sports or memories from Saint-Louis, but we don't get along any better in Ethiopia than we did in Senegal. He wants me to fall in line like the others, but I can't. My grades are still garbage, and the teachers from school seem to think there is something psychologically wrong with me. Sometimes I wish there were. Maybe then he would give me a break. Or maybe he would be too stressed-out to care. I don't know. He's in charge of the education and moral development of over a thousand students in the middle of a socialist revolution, and I am not making his life any easier. I try to remind myself of these things when I fantasize about him stepping in piles of crap.

It's just after my fifteenth birthday, and we're seated around the dinner table with two of my parents' colleagues. Ife, who cooks for us and watches Olivier, sets down a stew and a pile of injera, the thin pancakes they use here instead of spoons. Unfortunately, we've just gotten our school reports. Isabelle is excelling in maths, and Catherine is at the top of her class. She is already one year ahead of me. Though it's never a surprise to my dad that I'm failing, seeing it in print makes it more of a disappointment to him. Academics seem to take things more seriously if they find them on paper.

For a few moments, we eat quiet and lazy, sopping up our stew and not caring much about how it tastes. I don't like the food here. It's hard to like much of anything. The war has taken away our hunger for most good things. I don't think about helicopters anymore. My mom doesn't get excited about art or museums the way she used to. The girls who should probably be crazy about boys only care about schoolwork. Olivier is still happy, but that's just how he is. If I have dreams, I don't remember them. They are bland, like the stew. Just when I think I've escaped a lecture, my dad starts in on me from across the table. He's read my report and he's not happy.

"What are you good for, Frédéric? What are you going to be? Nothing? A stubborn little boy forever?" he says, staring at his soup and not bothering to look at me directly.

I don't say anything back.

Ignoring him works sometimes. It often does with thugs and bullies. Today, though, he is like a fisherman, baiting me and baiting me. Maybe he's trying to impress his guests, but they look uncomfortable.

"Olivier, maybe you will graduate before Frédéric, eh?" he goes on.

My brother's round cheeks go pink.

Dad is laughing now, pushing his dish to the side and rolling up his sleeves. Waiting.

"What's wrong, Frédéric? Nothing to say?"

My mom starts to look nervous, which is nothing new. They are a progressive couple, but not so progressive that she'll stand up to him when he humiliates me. She just sits big-eyed and stiff like a rabbit. Ife comes back to retrieve our dishes, rushing in and out of the tension as quickly as she can.

"What do you want me to say?" I mutter to him, finally giving in. "I don't like school."

His jaw tightens. Now it is my turn to bait him.

"Do you want to hit me? You can hit me as much as you want. It won't change anything."

And he does, walking around the table and laying the back of his hand across my cheekbone so hard it makes the table jump. He stands over me for a minute, panting and shaking his head. One perfect bit of hair falls to his forehead. I smile.

"You have nothing more to say, Frédéric?" he asks, face sticky with sweat and red with adrenaline.

"Nothing," I tell him.

I don't speak to him again for six months. He is right; I am stubborn. I will never know how to connect with him. I would never admit it to anyone, but I worry I will never know him at all.

After months of bloodshed and summer monsoon, the dry season begins. In October 1976, everything is green and blooming like a strange, mixed-up spring. We are still in a war zone, but we are figuring out how to live. We don't jump at the sound of a gun anymore. We make friends in school. Our feet take us home, almost by instinct, an hour before curfew. To me, it is an improvement, and everyone in Addis seems happier. Even my dad.

"It is time to visit the Highlands," he announces one day at breakfast, out of nowhere. I rub my eyes, still waking up, and blink them. I'm surprised he wants to leave the house. It's been ages since we've done anything fun or even something different.

We've lived in Ethiopia for more than a year and a half, but we've hardly seen any of it. It hasn't been possible. Our friends have told us about the country—the angry hippos at Lake Langano, the walled city of Harar, and the Blue Nile Falls—but we only half-believe any of it is real. I am ready to see for myself. I have been ready for a while.

Following my dad's orders without question for once, I jump up from the table, dress, and tie up my shoes. They are hard black leather and not made for exploring, but they will have to do for today. Soon my mother and siblings join me at the door, and we all pile into the Defender. We drive for half a day, most of which I spend sleeping against the window.

Just before lunch, we pull into a vacant lot full of red dirt. I'm groggy. I missed the scenery change, but dozing off seemed like the best way to spend five hours in a warm vehicle full of my brother and smelly teenage sisters. When I open the door and finally step out of the truck, I nearly collapse. I'm tired and my muscles are stiff, but it's the beauty that makes me stumble.

The Highlands are a paradise. Huge mountains and broad plateaus go hundreds of miles in every direction. Massive white waterfalls look like specks across the green valley, rushing so fast and forcefully I can hear them ten miles away.

"*Incroyable*," Olivier whispers to me.

I nod.

Tiny brown deer I don't know the name of pop in and out of the thick forest, making Olivier giggle. My mother raises her ridiculous binoculars to her eyes, but she never catches one in time. Wordlessly, my father collects our things and walks into the green. We know to follow. This is an adventure, sure, but it is *his* adventure.

Our feet get tired quickly, and none of us has the proper clothes for hiking, but there is an understanding that when my dad walks, we walk, even if it means getting blisters. He doesn't have time to stop and explore every little plant and bird and heart-shaped stone, so neither do we. I try to take pictures in my head as we go along, of ferns and rocks and huge bugs. I've never been anywhere like this, and even though I'm marching in a line, at a carefully scheduled and controlled pace, I feel suddenly free. Like I'm myself again. Without gray city buildings blocking the sun and military guys everywhere, the world is big, just like it used to be. It excites me. I can't remember the last time I felt this way.

"Frédéric!" my dad calls. "Faster."

I keep walking. I'm happy to.

When it is time to eat, no one is hungry (except Olivier). We are all too exhausted. The heels of our socks are all worn down, soaking wet with sweat and probably blood too. This is the only time on the expedition when we are free to rest or explore on our own. We have twenty minutes. Isabelle braids pretty grasses into Catherine's hair, and my parents walk to the edge of the ridge to point at and discuss various geological formations in the distance. I walk a little farther on, skipping rocks into a clear stream and then spotting what I think is a kousso tree. I stop at the base of it. I like the way it smells.

Hooking my arm around the lowest limb, I pull myself up the fat trunk and into a mass of shaggy leaves. The higher I go, the better I feel.

I had forgotten about climbing. And my friends, and fishing on the beach, and the Alouette helicopter—all the things I used to love.

My body has not forgotten anything though. I find my way to the top of the tree easily, choosing the best path upward by instinct. Upon reaching a comfortable cradle of branches, I stop climbing and lean back into the bark, watching my sisters at the fringes of the forest, my mom and Olivier by the stream, and my dad standing on the crest of a hill, staring out at the sky just as I am. I still like to be high up, and I think my father does too. I can see the whole valley and beyond. I can see the river and imagine the places it goes.

I can see the sky.

After that first trip, we go on adventures whenever we can to different parts of the country, around the horn of Africa, and even once to Yemen. We're all happier. Living in the city makes us pissed off and aggressive like animals, and when we aren't traveling, we're all just holding our breath, waiting for the next chance to leave. Knowing we *can* leave, though, makes a big difference.

Life under the Derg goes from terrifying to inconvenient to kind of normal. I make friends. The world seems kinder and more accessible. Not as worried that we'll be gunned down in the streets, our parents find ways for us to socialize. Each week, families host parties of thirty or forty kids, and because nobody wants their kids to break curfew and get arrested, everyone is allowed to sleep over, boys and girls together, a mix of Ethiopians and Europeans. I have my first dances and flirtations, my very first kisses. Some kids smuggle in honey wine and cigarettes, though those things don't interest me at all. Too easy. Really, the simple things are enough. I'm just happy to be with other teenagers—to discover that nobody really likes their parents, that everybody thinks school is a prison, and that we are all looking for a little bit of trouble.

Falling asleep on the tiled floor next to my friends with nothing but a thin sheet and pillow, I begin to dream again. Before long I begin to believe that everything will be all right here.

Just as I do, though, my father announces we are moving again. This time to Munich, Germany.

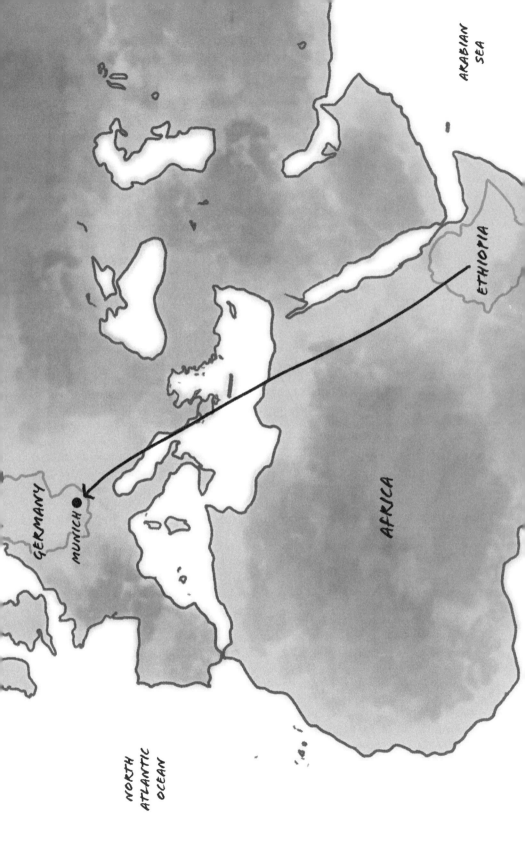

03

Go Off the Main Trail

I AM ANGRY ABOUT LIVING in Germany until I discover girls
and mountains. Luckily, it does not take me long to find either.

During my first week at the École Française of Munich, I lock eyes with
the most beautiful girl I have seen in my life: tall, long legs, blue eyes, au-
burn hair, perfect boobs. She is completely flawless, like something from a
Lamborghini plant instead of a cottage in Giesing.

I'm in love. When she glances up at me from her conversation and hugs
an algebra book to her chest, it's like I've been electrocuted. I didn't know a
person could be so jealous of a book.

Especially me.

The morning bell will sound any second, but instead of heading to phi-
losophy class, I fall into a random line to be near her a little longer. I hope
it looks casual, but I'm not so sure in the end.

All I want to do is find out who she is. Then marry her.

"*Pardon.*"

"*Excuse moi.*"

The kids behind me are trying to get into their maths classroom.

Reluctantly I move away, looking up just in time to watch the mystery girl and her skirt moving from side to side all the way down the hallway.

Mon Dieu, I think to myself.

They say I am impossible to motivate in school. Not anymore. She is all I can think about.

Munich is very simple compared to Addis Ababa. No conflict, no crowding, no dirt. Seriously. None at all. The French government leases an apartment for my family in a neighborhood called Schwabing, where everything is unbelievably clean and organized. A few blocks away from us is a huge park called English Garden with a lake, a river crossing, and a biergarten. Every afternoon when I walk by, the long tables are packed. Germans love beer. They are always drinking but somehow never drunk. They might be the most dignified alcoholics in the world. My dad settles into work quickly, and my mom spends all day talking about whichever museum, exhibition, or library she wants to visit next. The city is perfect for her. There is culture everywhere and absolutely zero threat of war. Really, there isn't even a threat of impoliteness. Catherine and Isabelle are both in university, so just Olivier and I are left at home. Life is peaceful. If it weren't for the beautiful girl walking up and down the hall in her skirt, life would be boring. For the first time in my life, I'm happy to go to school.

Most of September is spent deep in investigation. Even though I am seventeen and most boys my age are sex-crazed and collecting girlfriends like cassette tapes, only one girl interests me. The questions are endless.

Who is she?

Where does she come from?

How can I make her fall in love with me?

After a little asking around, I discover that her name is Hanna.

Hanna. A name is not much, but it's a start.

Hanna, it turns out, is shy. Painfully so. Many other boys have tried to date her, but none have even succeeded in starting a conversation. Hanna's younger sister Claudia (also beautiful), is not so shy, so I make it my mission to talk to her instead. I walk up to her one day in the cafeteria when she's sitting with friends, and I declare that I am in love with her older sister. I am simple and direct, prepared to convince her, pay her, whatever, if she's willing to make the introduction. There is no need for negotiation. Fifteen-year-old girls love this kind of excitement, and Claudia is thrilled to be involved in her sister's romantic life. She invites me over to her house after school that day, and expertly, we put a plan into action.

I show up at their door right when the girls are starting their homework. I make up some story about helping Claudia with geography, which is not believable at all. The three of us sit awkwardly at the dining table, and I sweat through my shirt talking nonsense about population distribution and migration. Hanna is so gorgeous that I can barely look her in the eye. Claudia tries her best to make the whole interaction less of an embarrassment for me, until suddenly and unconvincingly she gets a stomach cramp and disappears. Their mother, Ursula (beautiful as well, of course), catches onto us quickly and goes to check on her daughter, leaving Hanna and me alone with a little wink and a plate of butter cake. I don't even know what I'm saying, but after about twenty minutes of conversation, Hanna is laughing and comfortable. I start to relax too. I am still sweating everywhere, but she likes me.

I had walked into their little Bavarian house with a lump in my throat and am somehow now leaving with a girlfriend. It is a victory for seventeen-year-old boys everywhere.

By November, we are inseparable. I am failing most of my classes, but the most attractive girl in Munich is in love with me, which everyone, even the teachers, seems to respect. I am not successful at anything other than being a boyfriend, but at least I am staying out of trouble. Mostly.

The month begins with ice-covered sidewalks and constant snowfall. It is my official first winter in Europe, and as many times as I prayed for cold in Africa, I pray for sunshine here. The gray goes on forever. Most everyone stays inside, and I understand why. Because she has not had a winter herself in at least twenty years, the only piece of winter clothing my mother purchases for me is a beige puffer jacket, which is not nearly enough to stay warm. I slide all over the streets in my school shoes, and by the time I get home, the edges of my ears are purple. It's miserable, but after Ethiopia, nothing will keep me locked up in my bedroom alone.

Mostly, the other kids at school are reasonable and obedient, but I manage to attract the few who aren't and befriend them. Alexandro Ferretti and I are in English Garden one afternoon when I get a fantastic idea.

"We should go ice-skating," I propose, standing at the edge of the lake.

The ice seems thick enough, and no one else is out on it. The snow is falling at us from all directions. It will be great. Alex agrees. He is not really a rebellious kid, but he's Italian, so he's always up for a bit of fun.

"Give me half an hour," he says.

He fades into the blizzard and reappears thirty minutes later looking like a yeti, with two pairs of hockey skates from home. *Parfait.* We stuff our frozen feet into skates and pull the laces tight.

I feel nothing but excitement as we glide out onto the lake, returning to my "Africa" mentality: *Do whatever you want, just don't get caught.* We skate in big, clumsy circles and fall on our butts, laughing for a full hour and having the time of our lives.

Park management has heated the ice at one end of the lake and made a little hole for the ducks to go in the water. Alex points out a huddle of them, with fat brown bodies and shiny blue heads. We decide to take a closer look.

We skate for a few feet, and the ice begins to groan. I don't have much experience with ice and don't know it why makes noise at all.

Then a splash. Alex disappears under the surface.

There is another groan and I fall in behind him.

The water is so cold it grabs my body. I cannot move or think. I just hang in the water, stunned. For some reason, I *am* hanging. The silly jacket my mother bought me is floating, just enough to pull me up for a breath. I start kicking like crazy toward Alex, reaching him quickly and shoving his body upward toward the edge of the hole. The ducks stand by watching as we climb out.

A German man spots us and yells for us to remove our clothes and run home. Too shocked to question anything else, we do as told. I'm exhilarated, filled with adrenaline, tearing through the clean, orderly streets of Munich naked. It's like nothing I have ever felt before. I almost died but somehow, I am more alive than ever. As soon as the sensation dulls, I want to feel it again.

Next to Hanna, the most beautiful thing in Germany is the mountains, and nearly everyone here can ski. Even Hanna and Claudia. There are several popular resorts only an hour's bus ride away—Garmisch-Partenkirchen, Spitzingsee-Tegernsee, Zugspitze—I cannot pronounce any of them, but I don't have to be able to say the name of a mountain correctly to ski down it. I pick up the sport easily.

Zugspitze is perfectly safe if you're one of the thousands of levelheaded, experienced tourists who visit, but if you're a teenage boy with all the confidence in the world and none of the good sense, things go differently.

My friend Martin and I head for the slopes the first week of January after a heavy snow. Martin is my favorite person to ski with. Aside from the fact that we are both broke, courageous, and easily bored, we don't really have much in common. Martin is short, redheaded, often drunk, and so pale that the glare off the snow has given him a permanent sunburn across his nose. I am dark and tall, taller than my father now (which I think he finds upsetting), and I have never taken so much as a sip of alcohol. After watching Martin try to ski with a wineskin full of Jägermeister, I don't think I ever will.

When the bus arrives at the resort, the sky is blue and cloudless—as perfect as a day can be. The other passengers disembark, grab their skis, and head off to buy lift tickets from the chalet. We don't. It costs thirteen German marks to ride the lift. The runs are slow, tedious, and busy. If you don't mind a little hiking, you can find as much fresh powder and privacy as you want for free. All you need to do is go off the main trail.

The sun is intense on our three-hour trek up the mountain and through a pine forest. We stop to catch our breath, and I unzip my jacket while Martin takes a long drink. Below us is a wide, steep descent covered in powder, totally undisturbed. Our slope is exactly parallel to the resort run, just a kilometer away, and we haven't paid a cent.

"Idiots," Martin laughs, imagining the other skiers. "They don't know what they're missing."

"Idiots," I laugh back.

Martin nods at me and begins carving his way gracefully down the first section. I take a deep breath, preparing to follow. Not believing our luck, I laugh a little more.

Then I hear a roar. I didn't know snow made sounds either.

A gigantic crack forms between my skis, and little pine twigs and pebbles begin to hit the back of my neck and smack against my jacket. Out of the corners of my eyes, I see rocks and branches go shooting by. The entire mountain is shaking. *Merde.*

My instinct is to ski as fast as I can to the bottom, but Martin cuts right instead of down, skiing across the slope to avoid the avalanche. Leaning deep into my right leg, I follow him as fast as my used skis will allow, which is not very fast at all and not fast enough. The ground rises up and throws my body straight up into the air.

Everything goes quiet and sort of gray.

A unknowable amount of time passes, and the next thing I see is a small piece of sky. I hear Martin laughing his ass off.

"Come on," he snorts, helping me to my feet. "Let's go find your gear."

We make it back to the bus with my boots and one pole. The rest is buried, along with the very fancy resort town and the bottom of the mountain. We check the news for days afterward to find out if anyone was seriously injured, but we never hear a word.

After Ethiopia, it's good to feel free—but again, as soon I settle in, everyone else begins moving on. Alexandro is headed to university in some small depressing English city. Martin gets a job in Belgium. My sisters are already gone. Even Hanna is leaving. She models for catalogues on the weekends, as she has done throughout high school. Now agents in New York are calling, promising her the career she's always wanted. I am devastated but do my best not to let her know. In the fall I will start my second senior year, though I'm honestly not sure another semester will do anything to help me graduate. I have never imagined my life beyond childhood, but suddenly, I am living it. I'm eighteen, my grades are trash, and I don't have any interests but skiing and women.

In May, my dad calls me into his office. The office is dark—a small, terrifying room filled with books and wooden mallards. I'm nervous. Outside, Munich is bursting with color, covered in blossoms and precisely two inches of green grass, but there is no evidence of springtime in this room. The curtains are drawn, and my dad looks pissed off. My mom is seated in a small leather chair beside him, looking beautiful and worried.

"What are we going to do with you, Frédéric?" he says.

None of us knows the answer to this question. I am still mysterious to my parents. They are still mysterious to me. They love me, but I feel I am their greatest disappointment. At least I am the greatest at something though.

"Frédéric," My mom sighs, resting her head on her knuckles. "Have you considered military service? You have no skills and no diploma. Really, it is the only honorable option left."

I don't like the way she said "honorable," and I'm not interested in war. The uniforms are cool, but that's really all I know about the military.

My father does not say anything but appears ready to scream if necessary. They are waiting for an answer. I don't have one.

I can't really remember wanting to do any one thing with my life—not since I was little, anyway. I look out the window. The sky is the color of a blue flame.

Then I remember.

The helicopter.

In the military, you can be a pilot.

"OK!" I answer. "Yes! I will do it."

My mother smiles, consumed with relief. I can see it in her face and her shoulders, in the way she is breathing.

"Mom, I am going to be a helicopter pilot!"

She stands up quickly, throws up her hands, and walks out of the room, shaking her head.

04

Don't Fit the Profile

THE RECRUITMENT CENTER is near Tours, France—a university town in the Loire Valley with lots of cathedrals and narrow streets. There is a lot of history in Tours, I'm told, but not much for me to do but sit on my rear end and stare at a river that is like all rivers: gray, slow moving, and filled with fallen leaves. I drive past the Basilica Saint-Martin and straight for the École de l'Aviation at the Saint Symphorien air base. I am going to become a pilot. I must become a pilot.

The air force academy is not an inspiring place. There is no "La Marseillaise" playing when you go through the door, nothing heroic about the room. It is a tiny box on the edge of a hangar filled with heavy metal desks and the kind of guys who look like they were born to sit at them. The only sign of patriotism is a limp French flag in the waiting area where I sit, staring at a brochure they haven't bothered to print in color. It feels exactly like what it is: an airport. There is no danger of dreams coming true here.

A serious-looking officer with a pale face calls me up from my little plastic chair a few moments later to process my paperwork. He isn't bald—yet—but it looks as though it could happen any second. I fill out my height and weight, knowing they will test both later, and note my area of interest. They don't do helicopters here, as it turns out, but I've already made the trip. I choose fighter jets instead. Really, it's not such a bad second option.

Sliding a pair of thick glasses up onto his nose, the officer gives my forms one more look. He smiles (as much as a person who works in this sort of place can) and shakes my hand.

"Welcome, Monsieur North. You must complete three days of testing before you can be accepted into the program."

I knew there would be an evaluation, and I'm not worried. Testing is not something I normally do well, but the air force needs pilots and here I am.

"First they will examine your physical health," he says, still shaking my hand.

No problem, I think.

"Then," he continues, "they will assess your general knowledge, perform an IQ test, and send you for psychological evaluation."

Merde. Not ideal.

"Monsieur North." He stops to make sure he has my attention. "The last day is very important. Our flight instructors will watch you with the simulator to see how you would interact with an aircraft."

I don't know physics or geography, but I know I am a pilot.

All I need to do is get to that machine.

As the officer promised, the first day is simple. Some military guy with a stopwatch and huge arms asks me to do ten pull-ups and sends me to run the perimeter of the airfield. After that, I am asked to strip down to my underwear and perform a series of aerobic movements: touching my toes, moving my arms in large circles, jumping straight up in the air, while a cheerful little doctor looks on and takes notes. The most intense work I do all day is reading letters of varying sizes from a poster, one eye at a time.

"*E, W, E, R, S, F, Q, Q, G.*"

"That's all, Monsieur North. You're done."

The little doctor is pleased, and I pass with no issues.

The whole thing feels more like nursery school than military school. Until day two.

After a long sleep in my dorm and a tartine with mysterious pink jam, I walk into a small, expressionless classroom for the general exam. There are three rows of three desks, each topped with three things: a thick paper booklet, an answer page, and a yellow-bodied pencil sharpened so aggressively you could kill a boar with it. I still hate school. I settle into the desk closest to the hallway while the other applicants find their seats. Suddenly my body feels hot.

"You have three hours to complete the assessment," a thin, long-necked man with a huge Adam's apple says. I didn't even see him come in.

"The first section is identification," he continues. "Mark A for French and B for Soviet. You will have four seconds for each slide."

I have no clue what he's talking about.

The lights go off and he flicks on a projector.

What is going on?

Pictures of planes, all bullet-gray and black, flash onto the screen, then off, then on and off again. I can't tell what I am looking at. They're going too fast. I don't know what makes a plane French or Russian. I just know what makes a plane a plane.

The guy next to me looks like a Zen Buddhist. I'm sweating so hard I can barely hold my pencil.

I can admit: whose planes are whose is a bad thing to screw up in the middle of the Cold War, but identifying an aircraft has nothing to do with flying it. It didn't even occur to me that I should study. Honestly, if it *had* known, I may not have come at all.

About an hour later, the overhead lights come back on, and the instructor collects our pages.

"Now that your sheet is turned in," he tells us, "you may begin the IQ test." That's when things get really bad.

I did not wake up an angry person that morning; I became one. First it was the classroom. Then it was the planes. The other guys working diligently and quietly while I develop a headache at my desk do not help much, but I can tolerate those things. I don't have a lot of tolerance for stupidity, and the IQ test appears to be the stupidest thing I have seen in my entire life.

The questions are absurd:

Find the next number in the pattern.

Unscramble the word.

Sequence the pictures.

There is nothing—not a single question—about airplanes. Nothing on the page could possibly assess a person's ability as a pilot. Nobody else seems bothered by it, but I feel myself beginning to unravel the way I have in dozens of classrooms before this one. I press my ridiculous sharp pencil into the page, and as it snaps, so do I. Instead of answering the questions directly, I explain why they are irrelevant.

It does not matter what number is missing from the sequence. It will not affect my performance as a pilot.

I am choosing not to answer, as I will never encounter any scrambled words inside my aircraft. If I do, I will ignore them.

I don't know how much cheese Theo purchased at the store, but if he is a smart kid, he will choose the Reblochon.

It feels like I have been faced with questions like these my entire life— confronted with things that hold no meaning to me but expected to act as though they do. I suffered through school for twelve years, and I simply cannot do it any longer. Not for my mother. Not for France.

I "answer" my last question:

The speed of the bus is unimportant. I am not training to be a bus driver.

After I turn in my booklet, I am sent on to the psychologist. It is the worst possible time for me to undergo a psychological evaluation.

They allot twenty minutes for the assessment, which to me doesn't seem like much time to get to know a person. This psychologist is not interested in getting to know people, so I guess it doesn't matter. He's in his midthirties and cool-looking, but we have no chemistry at all.

"Sit," he says, motioning toward a row of chairs.

He grabs another dangerously sharp pencil and starts in.

"Do you like being away from home?" he asks.

"Yes," I answer.

"Yes, *sir*," he reminds me. "Do you love your family?"

Merde. I was expecting those pictures of inkblot butterflies.

"Yes, *sir*," I answer again. "I do love my family. But they do not understand me."

He does not take the opportunity to ask why. His face is blank the entire time, through at least a dozen more questions that range from, "How often do you think about death?" (never) to, "What would you do if you are on a tight flight schedule and encounter bad weather?" (Deal with it. Go around the storm or something.)

"North," he says when he's finished, "it will be impossible for you to become a pilot . . . ever. You are not a logical person. You will never be able to follow protocol or respect military guidelines."

I think I am the only logical person here.

He sighs. "I'm sorry. You just don't fit the profile."

I don't want to fit the profile. Everything he's saying is true. But also, he's wrong.

"And," he adds, "you scored below average on your IQ test."

"The test was poorly written," I tell him. "It had nothing to do with flying."

He gets up slowly and looks at me. At first he seems to take a little satisfaction in my failure, but then sympathy appears in his eyes. It is the kind of face people make at a lost dog.

"If you do exceptionally well in the simulator, they may reconsider your application. Good luck," he offers.

I just have to make it to that machine.

Most of my evening is spent in conversation with the dorm ceiling, trying to get comfortable, trying to understand myself and decide if and how I fit into the world. I don't know why I cannot just follow the rules like everyone else. Had I answered the questions instead of rewriting them, I would have passed the test. Had I studied what I was told to study in school, maybe the military wouldn't be my only chance at a decent life. Why isn't it enough for me to just put in the work, collect the reward, and go on with life. *Why?*

Why might be my biggest problem of all.

Why do I have to study things that don't interest me?

Why do I have to unscramble words to fly a plane?

I am not a bad person, but I cannot blindly accept authority. Sure, I am a little prick sometimes, but I'm more curious than disobedient. I question the order of things to understand them, and I'm punished for it again and again. It has cost me family, and it may cost me my career. It seems ridiculous that the air force would turn me away, but if my own father can do it, I suppose they can too.

I am expecting a real simulator—a full Alpha Jet cockpit with control panels, lights, switches, gauges, and guns. What I get is a computer game. I am basically supposed to prove myself with PAC-MAN.

There are three other guys here, and we're all seated in front of giant beige monitors. The room is dirty. Everything in it looks as though it's about to break or start an electrical fire. The overhead lights buzz constantly, and the computer chassis are giving off enough heat to make our feet sweat. For the air force, it all seems pretty low-tech, but I try to embrace it. I have to. This is my last chance.

The instructor, a real math teacher–looking guy, walks into the center of the room.

"Good morning. Today we will assess your reaction time, your ability to multitask, and your accuracy. Your job, your only job, is to keep the plane lined up with the light."

I can do that. I grab the cheap plastic joystick, and all together, like a terrible robot choir, the computers beep and the simulation begins.

Just follow the light. Respond. Stay calm, I repeat to myself

A little green light—one of those Soviet planes from day one, I suppose—appears at the center of the screen. I fix my sight over it, a yellow circle, and stay there. After a few moments locked on the target, it switches direction, so I follow. It's simple. All I need to do is feel, be sensitive, adjust my behavior, respond. Don't overreact.

"*Merde!*" someone says.

The guy next to me is going too fast. He keeps crashing his "plane," which causes his screen to shake and light up with cheesy sounds and graphics. You can't bully a machine. You can only seek to understand it.

About thirty minutes in, when everyone else is still working, my test is over.

"North," the instructor calls.

He waves me up to the front of the room, where a big clumsy printer is spitting out the results onto thin sheets of paper.

"Congratulations." He extends his hand. "We have not seen this in years. You scored perfect."

I have never scored perfectly on anything before. Or even come close. Not many things in this world have come naturally to me, not like this.

At the end of the day, I have a final meeting with the colonel in charge of recruitment to discuss next steps. I'm not too worried. The other guys found out about my simulator score, and none of them can believe it. Everyone, including me, seems pretty sure I'll get in.

The colonel welcomes me into his office warmly and seems like a nice guy—the kind I wouldn't mind working with.

"Have a seat, Monsieur North." He smiles sadly.

I was expecting another handshake.

"Based on the recommendations of the therapist, I cannot accept you into our program. You are not capable of following the protocol."

The room slows down and becomes blurry. I can't believe what I'm hearing.

I leave Tours completely broken. For the first time in my life, I go back home not anticipating my father's disappointment but confronting my own. I am not going to be in the air force. I will not be a pilot. *Ever.*

05

Don't Be a Quitter

"YOU'RE DOING IT WRONG. AGAIN."

Albert is standing behind me with his hands on his hips, looking more like a schoolteacher with a stick up his butt than a twenty-year-old guy in the army. He doesn't like the way I'm folding my shirts. I don't like anything about him. Albert is one of my two roommates at the École Militaire de Haute Montagne (EMHM). We have nothing in common. After the air force disaster, I enrolled in the army proper as a last resort. The focus of the EMHM program is alpine and arctic warfare, skiing, and mountain leadership. There are no testing requirements, thank God. All I needed was a passport and a pair of boots. The military is careful about who they send into Soviet airspace, but they'll put anybody over age eighteen on Mont Blanc and give them a rifle. It isn't flying, but it's as close to the sky as I can get.

"If you don't do it properly, they'll wrinkle," Albert whines.

He's such a cocksucker. He's desperate to please the lieutenant and knows he has a better chance of doing it with a stack of perfectly folded shirts than his performance. Poor guy is built like a scarecrow. He'll kill himself on his skis if he doesn't do it with his gun first.

"Hey, Albert," Guillaume, our other roommate, calls from his bunk across the room. "Eat shit." Guillaume is great. He's a skier who, like me, has no idea what to do with his life other than be here, climbing mountains.

Looking like he's been kicked in the balls, Albert slams his cabinet door and stomps out of our room.

"Such an idiot," Guillaume whispers, nodding after him.

I agree.

I'm bad at folding my clothes, but for once in my life, I'm fitting in well at school.

The first six months of training are hard-core. We get out of bed every morning at four a.m., still halfway asleep, to run ten miles through the snow. In the afternoons, we climb the mountain with our skis strapped to our backs, loaded down with eighty pounds of rocks. The worse the weather is, the harder we work. Whiteout conditions, ice storms, blizzards, extreme cold—we train through all of it. Many of the guys aren't used to that kind of physical challenge, and the altitude doesn't help them much. Even though Chamonix is only situated at 3,400 feet, more than once on the way up Aiguille du Midi, somebody doubles over to vomit in the snow. The regimen is extreme, but it's nothing compared to the working environment. If you are not burned alive by the cold on the glacier fields, then the constant yelling, the failure, the frustration, and the insults will finish you off. We start out a group of twenty-seven, but after the first few months, we are less than half that.

The verbal assaults don't even touch me though. No matter how hard the lieutenant tries, he's not smart or harsh enough to compete with my father. I'm mostly happy here—not because I am unbreakable, but because I have already been broken. I don't take anything personally. The ability to fail feels like my secret to success. Plus, after more than a dozen useless years in formal education, I'm relieved to finally be learning some practical skills: assessing snow quality, predicting weather patterns, and avoiding avalanches (which, given my history, is important). We even spend a few days in class on helicopters.

In the mountain unit, they use the Alouette II, a chubby but sleek machine with a round glassy nose, and the Lama, which they call the "Ferrari of the air." I'm so happy to see them pop up on the overhead projector, I have to work not to smile like a little kid. The instructors don't teach us anything about flying, of course—just how to behave around the aircrafts so we don't lose a limb or cause an accident. Those lessons are fine by me. Besides, I like EMHM. Digging people out of snow in the Alps will not be a bad life for me. These are some of the best mountains in the entire world, and I often remind myself of this when the instructor shows us footage of the pilots flying between peaks and landing in the snow. The mountains are great, but they are not the sky.

Our first rescue simulation happens in March, about nine months into training. It's a bright-blue afternoon, a rarity in this part of the range. Often, blizzards fly into the valley and get caught like birds, frantic and turning suddenly dangerous when least expected. We are lucky with the weather and want to make the most of it. Guillaume and I are working together trying to locate a giant dummy in the snow near the Vallée Blanche with only our compass. We're deep in focus, taking everything very seriously and moving quickly. The lieutenant is yelling anyway, "Go! Go! Go!"

We take no offense to it. By now we know that yelling is just part of his large personality.

"Fred!"

Guillaume spots the "victim" near a stand of trees. We run over, planting our skis on the slope and carefully rolling the dummy onto a backboard. Gently, I put the cervical collar onto the eyeless plastic head and step back. The lieutenant's giant VHF radio crackles, and we hear a voice that sounds like it's coming from a different planet.

Suddenly the sky fills with noise, and I look up.

It's the Alouette. Again. Bright cherry-red against the white mountain.

It turns toward us and instantly, I am eight years old, a little boy standing mystified in Senegal.

I belong up there.

The joy and grief are breathtaking. The dream is as real now as it ever was—just as thrilling, but now impossible. I'm in the mountain unit. I will never, "ever," be a pilot.

The helicopter lands, we load the dummy, and as fast as it came, the Alouette is gone.

I do my best to forget about it, but I can't. The seed is planted. Just a few weeks later, it grows into something bigger, wilder, stronger, more important than I could ever imagine.

Our mornings off are not so different from our regular mornings at the EMHM. Guillaume and I go skiing together, but without Albert complaining and the lieutenant screaming in our ears. Today the resort is busy, as it often is in spring. Stylish men and women from Paris who have no idea what they're doing stand in line in their neon outfits at the lift, talking and going up for the occasional run, but mostly waiting around for the après-ski. Guillaume and I take advantage of the powder they leave for us, but we also spend a good part of the afternoon watching the few brave tourists tackling the slope, falling, somersaulting, then eventually giving up and heading for the chalet.

"At least it will be easy to find their bodies dressed like that," Guillaume jokes, pointing at a man in skintight, electric yellow skating sideways down the hill.

I start to laugh along with him, but suddenly the sky is filled with noise.

A Lama appears in the corner of my vision. It is flying toward us, hauling an enormous pole from its belly. They're building a new ski lift, and I guess the only way to transport materials up here is by helicopter. I have never seen anything like it. I have never seen a pilot at work this way.

Guillaume is talking to me, but I can't hear him. I'm frozen solid, like everything else on the mountain. All I can do is watch the pilot through the open doors as he navigates to the construction site, positions the pole, and communicates with the ground crew. He works easily with the machine, delicately. It's a dance. I feel myself adjusting my body, maneuvering and responding, probably looking insane, as I look on. This man, whoever he is, is a god to me.

"I'm going, Fred." Guillaume shrugs. He's been trying to get my attention for the last few minutes.

"Yeah." I nod.

He shoots down the side of the hill, but I stay right where I am.

The pilot sets the pole down with crazy precision, and it hits me.

This guy is not in the army.

This is a civilian operation.

Flown by a civilian pilot.

I don't need the military to fly a helicopter. I have never needed it. It may not be the "honorable" path, as my mom would say, but I can find the training all on my own. The future opens up in front of me. The world is new, full of possibility. *I have my dream back.*

As fast as possible, I ski to the bottom, ready to pack my bags, ready to get out and get on with my life. Smugly, Albert reminds me I have a contract. For the next five years, France owns me. But I don't have five years or another second to waste.

I have a week off between the end of training and the beginning of my post, so I visit Hanna in New York City. I'm depressed and need cheering up; Hanna is lonely and misses having her boyfriend around. The timing is perfect for both of us. She's settled into a brand-new two-bedroom apartment in Greenwich Village overlooking the busiest streets I've ever seen. You can see the very top of the Empire State Building from her bedroom window and smell the Chinese place nearby, the *dozens* of Chinese places nearby, all through the apartment. She is ecstatic to see me, which feels nice after sixteen months with Albert.

"Do you like it?" she asks, looking around, worried.

"It's great." I smile.

The place is incredible. She's one of her agency's top models, a rising star living the dream day in, day out. I'm just a soldier who wants to be something else.

"I have to work this afternoon." She frowns, squeezing my hands. "All week, actually, but it will give you a chance to explore New York. I know you'll love it."

That turns out to be the understatement of the century.

In Europe, it feels almost juvenile to want something—but there is ambition in America, a sense that anything is possible, that nothing is off-limits. Everyone has a dream—hot dog vendors, accountants, fashion models, me—and nobody is too shy to chase a dream down. The energy of the city is totally different, totally free: people wear what they like, do what they like, go to bed with whomever they like. . . . There's no judgment. I spend most of my time (and money) buying Ray-Ban sunglasses, pilot suits, and jackets with tons of badges from the Avirex store. Hanna introduces me to the music of Jimmy Cliff, and I like it so much, I go out and get a yellow Sony boombox to carry on my shoulder through the city, which seems to be the fashion here. I tell everyone I meet, anyone who will listen, that I'm going to be a pilot, and each afternoon I roller-skate down to the West 30th Street Heliport to watch the machines land and take off, hoping that since I'm dressed like an aviator, somebody will offer me a ride.

I love New York. Here, I am closer to the life I want than I have ever been before. Since I'm having such a good time, I decide to extend my trip by two weeks. It never occurs to me as I do it that I'm deserting from the French Army.

My return to the mountain unit is not discreet. After three perfect weeks of vacation, I show up on base in full American style: short shorts, a too-tight "I Love New York" T-shirt, sunglasses, and of course, roller skates. I glide through the security gates on a Monday morning with "I Can See

Clearly Now" blaring from my boombox, thinking it will put everyone in a good mood. It does not.

The whole unit is gathered in the center square of the base for morning flag ceremony and announcements. The entire personnel, about five hundred people, is lined up perfectly with arms motionless at their sides, standing at attention. The horns go quiet as soon as I skate onto the concrete. Everyone and everything comes to a stop, except for me. (The concrete is slippery.) I lean back, trying to slow down, but instead, I fly through the middle of the ceremony and straight through to the dorms. The only face I catch is my lieutenant's, and judging by the number of veins popping from his neck and forehead, I know I'm in deep trouble. Before New York, my behavior was questionable, but now those questions have been answered. I throw on my wrinkled uniform and walk as quickly as I can to his office to apologize. For once, he is not yelling.

"Frédéric North," he starts, "you are under arrest. You are a deserter. This is a felony punishable by military law. All of your personal belongings will be collected, and you will be sent to jail."

Two military officers enter the office. Each grabs an arm and they escort me to a cell where, after a hearing, I stay for a month.

Thirty days of detention gives me a chance to think. I cannot buy or work my way out of the contract, and I cannot wait five years. Maybe, though, I can talk my way out. To do that, I'll need a meeting with the general. To meet with such a high-ranking officer, your lieutenant must approve the appointment. Mine refuses, which is not a surprise. One of his men rollerskating onto base looking like Magnum, P.I. did little to help his reputation, and he's not feeling sentimental about my hopes and dreams. So I take matters into my own hands.

The very next morning I wake up, press my uniform so it has exactly seventeen creases, and drive to Grenoble, the administrative center of our region. If nobody will help me get a meeting, I'll get one myself.

The general's office is what you would expect. All the patriotism that was missing from the air force base is in this man's waiting room. There are plaques on the wall and photographs of various military men and politicians. Of course there is a flag, and next to it, a wood carving with the words *Liberté, Égalité, Fraternité* in golden text. It is like a movie set.

The sergeant at the desk is in full uniform, and his shoes are even shinier than Albert's even though all he does, I assume, is answer the phones.

"You cannot be here," he says to me. "The general's office is open by appointment only."

"Yes, sir, I know, but I need to speak with him. I have tried to get an appointment."

He is quiet, first looking angry, then sad.

Maybe it's because I am pathetic, or maybe it's because after decades of military service, this guy has just ended up as someone's secretary. Either way, he allows me to stay.

"You can sit. But it will take hours, and I can't guarantee anything," he cautions.

He motions toward the one chair they keep for visitors.

"I'll wait all day if I have to," I promise him, and that's exactly what I do. I don't eat. I don't drink. I don't take a piss.

Just after five p.m., the general emerges from behind a door that must be ten feet tall. He's in his fifties, with sandy-brown hair and kind eyes. I don't know why or how, but I get the sense that he's been to war, that he's done more in his career than run through the snow and play with dummies.

"And who are you?" he asks me, intrigued. I can tell he doesn't have many unexpected visitors dropping in.

I stand up and start rambling like a maniac. The sergeant does the same, both of us trying to explain why I'm there uninvited.

The general holds up his hands, asking us both to quiet.

"How long have you been waiting?" he asks me.

"Since ten o'clock," I reply, short of breath. "I really need to talk to you. I promise I won't be long, but my life depends on it."

He smiles. "OK, Monsieur North. Come with me."

We go back into his office, and I start right in. There's no sense dancing around it. He sits in his chair, and I stand in the middle of the room like I'm auditioning for something.

"I don't belong in the army, sir. I want to be a helicopter pilot, which is something I can't do here. I've tried and they won't allow it."

I am using all my energy to be succinct and stay focused. The general is totally silent, listening fully and leaning back in his chair.

"Why did you join the army in the first place?"

Suddenly all my focus goes out the window.

"Sir, I love the mountains, the adventure, even the training program—but I am not a solider," I tell him. "I can't follow protocol. I question all the orders. The army isn't who I am or who I ever will be. I don't fit here."

"I can see you have a dream," he says, "but how are you sure you won't quit that one as well?"

I look him right in his eyes. "Sir, I am not a quitter. I have never been. I have always wanted to be a pilot."

I'm terrified he's going to think I'm full of crap, but I feel a connection with him, so I tell the truth.

"When I enlisted," I confess, "the army felt like the only option left for me. I was a bit lost."

My heart is beating through my shirt, and I'm sweating like a pig.

"If this is really what you want to do, then I am not going to stop a smart young guy from living his life. I will sign your release. Just write everything you just told me down in a letter."

I shake his hand, and he reminds me, "Fred, don't be a quitter."

I nod. Then I take off running and dancing into the parking lot.

One week later, I am on my way back to New York City, free as a bird and ready to fly.

06

Stay Connected

"I LOVE NEW YORK," but it does not love me. For five months, I wake up in the morning, put on my Avirex jacket, and hustle, visiting every flight school in the city and trying to convince someone that I belong in the sky. Sadly, my pilot outfits, roller skates, and broken English don't get me very far. The sunglasses may help a little, but not enough to get me in or even near a helicopter. My visa is going to expire, yet I'm still watching people take off and land at the West 30th Street Heliport like a little boy. Hanna misses Europe. We're both burned-out and sick of American pizza, so we decide to move back to Paris. Hanna is successful enough to live anywhere; I'm enough of a failure to do the same.

We settle into a little apartment in a Haussmannian building on Rue Becquerel in Montmartre. There is a patisserie on the corner and a dingy metro station only a few blocks away. It is nothing like Greenwich Village. People are quiet and sophisticated. They move along the sidewalk more with elegance than determination, not rude necessarily but not exactly stopping to say hello either. If Paris is hungry for anything, you never know it. I hope my ambition will be enough of an oddity to interest people. Even if they are interested, though, getting my commercial license will cost close to $30,000. I only have a few hundred in my bank account, most of which is left over from a Dorotennis campaign Hanna convinced me to shoot with her in America. I wasn't so bad at it—even I can admit I have great legs—but I had never felt less like myself than I did pretending to be John McEnroe.

The first place I go for money is my parents, who are living outside Le Mans in a small little castle that used to be the hunting pavilion of King Louis XIV. Or something like that. It smells like a library and fits them like a glove. They're far prouder of *it* than they are of *me*—something that becomes crystal clear after I casually mention that I quit the army.

"What do you want, Frédéric?" my father says coldly. "Money? That is why you are here, yes?"

For a third time, I explain to my parents that I'm going to be a helicopter pilot. For a third time, my mother looks tortured and my father scolds me. I don't want to be petty, but I remind them that they funded my siblings' career training. Why not mine?

"Absolutely not," they agree.

"Frédéric," my mother pleads. "It's too dangerous. Please. Anything else."

I shrug. "I understand, but I'm doing this. I have to."

For a moment I consider getting clever and threatening to move back in with them, but really, I came for more than their money. I want their support. I'm heartbroken to leave without it.

But two weeks later, a $10,000 check arrives in the mail. The rest I try to make by fixing up damaged cars and selling them, which is more trouble than it's worth and probably not even legal. I decide that if I can't pay my way into flight school, I'll talk my way in.

According to a brochure from the student career counseling office by Pont de Bir-Hakeim, ten different helicopter companies conduct training around Paris, but I am only interested in HeliFrance. They have the best ads, and I've spent dozens of hours watching their sightseeing tours take off and land at the Paris heliport. They're popular—*so* popular they must need a young, driven, charming guy like me to join their team. I put on my pilot suit and Converse—perfect for a Monday in spring, perfect for becoming the poster boy for the biggest helicopter company in town—and ride the subway to Balard station in the 15th arrondissement. Then I walk right into the office and introduce myself.

"Hi, my name is Fred North. I just came back from New York, and I would like to become a helicopter pilot."

I'm expecting a bit of a sour response, but the young Moroccan man at the desk smiles at me. "I'm sure we can help you, Mr. North. Where are you from?"

"Well, I was born in Tunisia, . . ." I begin.

He lights up.

I go from "Mr. North" to *"mon frère"* in an instant, and before I know it, he's taking me to see his boss with an arm on my shoulder.

Monsieur Bastien sits behind a large wooden desk, in a suit looking like American actor Ed Harris and smelling like too much cologne. He's exactly what I hoped a helicopter company CEO would be: handsome, cool, and laid-back. There is a fat Rolodex in front of him and a few of those paperweight awards they make from large bricks of frosted glass. I try not to stare at them, or him, too obviously.

"Monsieur Bastien, I have wanted to be a helicopter pilot since I was eight years old. It's the *only* thing I want to be. I was released from the army to become a helicopter pilot. . . ."

I'm in front of the one person who can give me the shot I need, and I'm not leaving the office without it, so I tell him everything. He listens closely, even though I can feel myself ramble.

"I'm sorry, Fred," he says after my speech. "HeliFrance is not set up for training at the moment. We're too busy, and we would need a new helicopter."

Now I need to convince him to give me a chance *and* buy a new helicopter.

"You don't understand," I plead. "I'll do anything—sweep hangars, file paperwork. Whatever! Whenever! You can count on me for anything, sir!"

I refuse to surrender even the smallest amount of hope. If I do, it will be over. I need 150 hours of training to get my license, and I have no problem cleaning toilets for each one of them.

"After," I promise, raising a finger in the air, "I'll work for HeliFrance *for free!*"

I don't know how that would be possible, but I will find a way to make it true.

"Fred, you need fifteen hundred hours to work here," Bastien sighs.

Tapping on his giant desk, he thinks for a moment. My Moroccan friend and I steal a quick look at each other. He seems to want it to work out as badly as I do.

Monsieur Bastien sort of laughs a little after a few moments and throws up his hands.

"OK, Fred." He shakes his head. "Your first lesson is next week."

I walk out of the office ready to kiss the first person I see—my heart beating like crazy and my eyes filled with tears.

Time moves unbearably slow the next week. By Sunday, the waiting is physically painful. I can't eat or sleep, but when the next morning comes, I'm ready. Wearing my Levi's jeans, a white T-shirt, Ray-Ban sunglasses, and the Avirex flight jacket with all the badges on it, I walk into the subway proud as a rooster, looking around at all the smug businessmen in their suits.

In less than one hour, I'll be in the sky, flying above all of you guys, I think to myself as the train arrives.

All the way to the airport, I picture what it will be like: the machine, the smells inside the hangar, the feeling of the pedals under my feet, and the instructor—a man I imagine as God in a leather jacket.

Pascal is not God.

And he doesn't have a leather jacket.

I don't think he's been watching any of the same pilot movies I have.

He's wearing an ugly green jacket and shapeless jeans that he's had to roll up at the ankles. His mustache is the only thing that connects my fantasy to the reality in any way. I look like a fighter pilot. He looks like Dustin Hoffman in *Kramer vs. Kramer.*

"Did you study the books?" he asks, sticking a big blue stick of gum into his cheek. I can tell right away he's a books guy.

I nod, telling only some of the truth.

I had wanted to read the books, but everything in them felt like Chinese to me—so I *kind of* read them, fast.

He smiles. "Good. Then you're ready."

We walk out onto the tarmac, and "Back in Black" by AC/DC starts playing in my head. It isn't particularly windy, but I imagine a breeze blowing through my hair in slow motion. It isn't particularly busy, but I pretend a fleet of fighter jets is parked nearby.

I look over at Pascal, chewing his gum with his short pony legs carrying him forward. If there's anything playing in his head, it's easy listening, something like Gilbert Bécaud.

An F280 "Shark" Enstrom is sitting outside the hangar. It's small and silver with a blue stripe, only able to hold two or three people.

"Fox Golf Delta Alfa Fox," I whisper, reading the tail number and promising to remember it.

It isn't the kind of helicopter many people would brag about, but to me, it's a rocket ship. Pascal says there are only a few of them left in France.

"They keep on crashing. Not enough power." He shrugs. I follow him around like a little puppy as he goes over the preflight and pats the helicopter on the nose. Then he stops, opens the door, and waves me inside.

The Enstrom is like an old barn. It smells of mildew and motor oil—part antique tractor, part rental car. Pascal makes a face.

"Jesus," he says, sniffing hard. "You take the pilot seat," he says, shifting his little body out of the way. "You want to be the pilot, right?!"

This is Pascal's best joke of the day.

I settle into the seat, and my body fills with adrenaline.

"OK, so it's very easy," Pascal assures me. "The stick in front of you, you put your right hand on it. This is called a cyclic, and it's your basic steering. It goes forward, backward, left turn, and right turn. On your left, you have the collective. You put your left hand on it, and it's your power. It allows you to go up and down. Now put your feet down, one on each pedal. Those control your tail rotor and allow you to steer left and right. Simple stuff, yes?"

I nod.

"You're doing great, Fred," he says, slapping me on the thigh.

But I haven't done anything.

"I'll do the takeoff, and then we have about a ten-minute flight to the training area." Pascal grins. "There, I will teach you how to hover. Keep your hands and feet on the controls and follow my lead."

I put on my headset. *Here we go.*

It takes us three tries to get the Enstrom started, each one smelling worse than the last, but finally, it kicks in. Pascal is talking as he prepares to take off, but I'm not really listening. All I want to do is connect with the machine on a deeper level, understand what it feels like just to exist in and with it. The noise, the vibrations, the voice in the headset from the control tower—altogether they cover me in chills. It all makes sense. *I* finally make sense. It's like I was born knowing the difference between the cyclic and collective. I never say it out loud because in 1982, it isn't the kind of thing a guy like me declares to the world, but I have just met my soulmate. Not Pascal, obviously, but the machine. We speak the same language. Slowly we begin to rise, taking a right turn above the Seine and over the city streets. It takes only a few minutes.

"OK, Fred," Pascal says. "You take the cyclic."

I grab the cyclic and he removes his hands from the control.

"Now you have full control," he announces.

The higher we go, the better I feel. The higher we go, the more I can feel. The next hour is the best of my entire life, another fact I choose to keep to myself.

I learn quickly. By the end of my second lesson, I can hover, controlling the cyclic only. At 4.5 hours, I can hover, controlling all three commands. I can land the helicopter, pick it up, and hover again. It is the first time in my life that I'm succeeding at something with ease. After just six flight hours, Pascal says I'm ready to fly solo. He can't dress himself, but he believes in me. He might be the first person in the world who does. I'm his best student, he says, but I'm also the first one he's ever had.

Soon I walk into HeliFrance for a lesson, and Pascal is more excited than I am. He has a stupid grin sitting underneath his mustache, and he's bouncing around like the family dog. Finally he reveals his (and my) big news: "Fred, today is the day. You're ready to fly alone."

I don't really take it too seriously. I need at least ten more hours.

"OK, Pascal. Whatever you say."

But something tells me he isn't joking.

Normally a solo flight doesn't happen until a pilot has logged at least seventeen to twenty-five hours. He should be able to fly the machine, read all the gauges, demonstrate spatial awareness, communicate with the control tower properly via the radio, and have a solid understanding of navigation. I can't reliably do any of those things. I'm not sure why Pascal decides it's time to send me up, especially in the Enstrom in August when it's hot as hell outside and the air is thin.

Per usual, we fly to the training site—a vacant, dust-filled field near Versailles—and I begin to absorb that my geeky instructor is about to let me do something totally insane. I have to decide if I *am* ready. Truthfully, I'm not sure. I try to remember if I said goodbye to Hanna in the morning and wonder when I last spoke to my parents. I could die doing this—something I never really considered when I was at the store buying pilot clothes. If I do die, Hanna will marry some awful banker. My mom will never forgive me.

My dad will have the satisfaction of being right about me, which I definitely cannot allow.

We land in a cloud of dirt and shut down the engine. Pascal unbuckles his harness.

"Fred, it's easy." He smiles. "You're going to hover and go for a little circuit pattern around the field at around five hundred feet. Then just come back and land here. I will talk to you through the radio."

By the time he finishes his last sentence, he's already out of the Enstrom.

The helicopter looks gigantic and empty without him. I feel like I shouldn't even be inside it by myself, let alone flying it. Pascal is standing about sixty feet away in his terrible green jacket and the most boring sneakers he could find. I start the rotor anyway, and he motions for me to go up. Today, AC/DC is a no-show. All I can hear is the machine.

We are having a conversation, I remind myself. All I have to do is listen to the helicopter, respond to it, instruct it, and adjust.

Stay connected, I think.

I raise the collective nice and easy, but suddenly the Enstrom shoots up like a bullet, banking hard left and scaring the hell out of me. It's a different animal when I'm alone, two hundred pounds lighter and fifty times more temperamental. It needs balance that I don't know how to create. I'm fifteen feet off the ground, panicking, nearly blowing over the trees that border the field.

Pascal is yelling at me in my headset: "Up, Fred! Up!"

I'm yelling back at him. Or at least I think I am.

He never taught me how to activate the microphone, so I'm screaming into the abyss. Everything feels wrong. I'm losing the nose, fighting with the wind instead of dancing with it. I can feel the helicopter going down. If I'm going to be a pilot, it's now or never.

Then I raise the collective again and climb fast to five hundred feet, then seven hundred feet. The fifty-acre field begins to look quaint, and I realize I'm flying *by myself.* There are about ten seconds when time feels like less of a monster and I'm not afraid. Instead, I'm a pilot. I'm everything I knew I could be. The Enstrom has given up bucking and bolting, and I'm able to balance it all: torque, direction, and speed. I easily complete the little circuit Pascal planned out, and it feels amazing. Until the last turn.

My final approach is supposed to be long and simple, but I forget again that the machine has just lost two hundred pounds. I take the last corner too tight and set myself up for a steep and complicated landing. Pascal is waving his arms and looking terrified, begging me to go around again. I can't though. It's too late. I'm headed right toward him. The Enstrom starts vibrating hard—hard enough to make my teeth chatter and blur my vision, blending the sky and earth and trees into a blue-brown puddle. I'm going to crash, pass out, kill Pascal, or all three.

When it's time to slow down, flare, and get the machine level, the nose refuses to cooperate. The skids smack hard into the earth, and the Enstrom and I both make a series of terrible noises. I shut my eyes so I don't have to see Pascal crashing into the windscreen. When I'm able to open them, he is alive, standing a foot from the machine with his hands over his face. We are both shaking and in shock. When blood returns to his face, Pascal starts screaming.

"Are you completely insane?" he cries. "You want to *kill* me?"

I have no answers for him. The two of us just stare at each other breathing hard for a moment, trying to understand how nobody died. There is nobody to blame but the both of us. He was crazy to send me for a solo flight at six hours. I was crazy to let him do it. Pascal climbs into the Enstrom, probably the last thing he wants to do, and we fly back to the airport in complete silence, covered in cold sweat. Agreeing wordlessly to tell no one.

Still, for ten glorious seconds, I was a pilot.

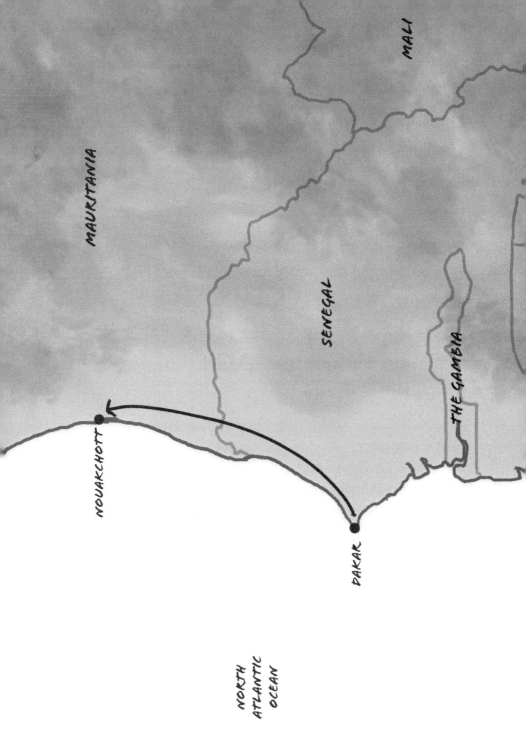

07

Follow the Adrenaline

I MAKE GOOD on my promise to work.

Ten hours per day, five days per week, for three solid months I live and breathe HeliFrance—hauling luggage, sweeping down the hangar, and washing the helicopters with liquid car detergent so they look and even smell brand-new for every single trip. Anything and everything Monsieur Bastien could possibly need, I try to anticipate. Most days, because I'm friendly and dress like an action figure (it's all part of the experience), he has me working the counter at Orly directing VIPs to the bathrooms. Even though they're only a meter to the left of me at the check-in, nobody can seem to find them on their own.

HeliFrance serves a range of customers, from sightseeing clientele— mostly foreigners who want to look down at the gardens of Versailles before visiting gargoyles at Notre Dame and the dancers at the Moulin Rouge—to celebrities, businesspeople, and politicians. The tourists come to see Paris; the others to flee it. One remembers flying in a helicopter for the rest of his life; the other forgets the trip the second the skids hit the ground. I get along great with both types of people, but I only understand one. I earn six minutes of flight time per day for ten hours of work and come home filthy, sore, and broke. Still, to me, it is the deal of the century. I go to bed at night next to Hanna dreaming of the next day, feeling as rich and as cool as a person could ever be. But then, when winter comes, I meet my new instructor.

Michel Anglade is a legendary French pilot and the teacher Bastien selects to train me for my commercial license. He's incomparably cool—long dark hair, leather jacket, movie star friends, and probably more women than he knows what to do with. He's an icon, but for me, the connection is deeper. Michel Anglade is the first person I meet who sees flying, maybe even the world, the way I do. Nothing is by the book; everything is about feel. Working with the helicopter is sensual and smooth, guided by instinct and sensitivity, not force. He's also kind—very confident but not full of himself. There is no hiding the fact that I can still be a bit cocky that way, so I couldn't ask for a better mentor. Under his guidance, even the technical information comes alive. In the summer, after a few tries, I manage to pass the written portion of my certification. All I have left to complete is the medical exam (easy) and the flying test. I am two steps away from living my dream.

In the winter of 1984, things are busy at HeliFrance. Bastien is prepping to supply helicopters for the famous Paris–Dakar Rally, a two-week car race that takes teams of half-mad motorists from France to Senegal, from one home of mine to the other. Michel is the chief pilot; he pretty much has been since the race began in 1979. It isn't the kind of work I think about helicopters doing much, but I'm willing to do anything. Plus, with all the gasoline fumes and travel and prestige and adventure, it appeals to me immediately. The choppers assist with transport, medevac, filming, and orientation, making sure none of the teams ends up lost in the middle of the Sahara—which is basically a sandbox with an area of 3.6 million square miles, looking the same in every direction.

I walk into the hangar on a Thursday. Michel is there checking over a JetRanger, the machine I have been flying since Bastien got rid of the Enstrom death trap.

"Fred!" He smiles. My name comes out in a visible puff of breath. It's mid-December and the hangars aren't heated.

"*Ça va?*" I smile back, rubbing my hands together. It's freezing cold, but soon I'll be too busy sweeping to notice.

Michel nods and smiles again, returning to the machine for just a moment to wipe a bit of bird crap or something from the windscreen. I grab a rag and get to work on the Dolphin, an eight-seater we use for tours.

"Fred, I've been thinking," he goes on. "Would you like to fly back with us from Senegal?"

I am totally frozen.

"It would just be the flight back with me, but it's an incredible trip, about twenty-seven hours."

I can't believe it. Michel begins drawing on an imaginary map with his index finger.

"So we go from Senegal, then over Mauritania, Morocco, the Strait of Gibraltar, and Spain. OK?"

"OK." I nod at him, in complete shock. In a few weeks, I'll learn what many do in a year. It's the opportunity of a lifetime.

As soon as I finish up in the hangar, I go to the Avirex store in Paris and buy a new royal-blue pilot suit. I wear it for the next three days along with my red Converse sneakers, my Ray-Bans, and a fanny pack. I'm not fully licensed, but at least I'm well-dressed.

I fly commercial to Dakar a couple of weeks later, mid-January 1985. The race is over, and though the excitement has died down for many, for me it is just the start. My body is buzzing. The Dakar airport is packed when I deplane, and it feels like more of a homecoming than I expect. The sticky heat, the crowd, the chaotic traffic, the happy messy way people move—it all throws me right back into my childhood. I have had many homes, but *this* is where I am from. I want to get onto a bus headed straight for Saint-Louis, but instead I pull down my sunglasses and prepare for the most important flight of my career.

There are three HeliFrance pilots waiting at the hangar. They look like they've been flying for two weeks straight. Their faces are dry and sun-chapped. They have big bags under their eyes. Everything about them is thirsty from the desert. I am the only one dressed like a fighter pilot. The passengers are waiting around making bored conversation, talking about the race and whether it was worth it to come all the way here. There's a businessman, Gabriel, a kid about my age named Pierre, the son of one of Michel's pals, and a couple of VIPs I can recognize but not name. Some of the company's big clients pay to be part of the ferry flights going down or returning from the race, just to do something a little different from Nice or Mont Blanc, I guess.

I set up my travel bag in Michel's helicopter, an A-Star B, and do the preflight with him. As much as I want to slow the moment down and absorb everything, we need to get back to Paris and the passengers are making no secret of it. I get the engine running, and Pierre settles into the seat behind Michel on the right. Suddenly Gabriel opens the door on my side.

"Get out," he says. "You'll go in the other one."

I look at Michel, stunned. He shrugs. He's not much into drama and is more used to these people doing whatever the hell they want.

"Just go, Fred. It's fine," he says.

I grab my stuff and step aside, quietly pissed off and disappointed not to be making the trip with my mentor.

Settled now into the copilot seat of the second helicopter with an instruc-tor named Charles, we take off and begin flying in formation like birds—a first for me, something I have imagined since childhood. When my father called me an imbecile, when the teachers said I was a deviant, I dreamed of sitting in the middle of *this* sky, looking down on the shapes and struc-tures of a perfectly organized world. A world that never understood me or cared to try. After just five minutes, Michel leads the choppers close to the coastline, deviating from the flight plan. Before I can even question what he's doing, I look down and see the island: Saint-Louis. We fly over the football pitch where the Alouette landed, the concrete pad where they were supposed to build the Casino but never did, our plain little house, and the tree I used to climb to get closer to the sky. Now, here I am.

La boucle est bouclée, I think to myself. *The circle is complete.*

As the sound of the blades goes and goes and the sun warms my face, I feel nothing but joy.

Our plan was to take off late morning, keep going north, and land for the night in Nouakchott, the capital of Mauritania, about 350 miles from Dakar. With favorable winds and only one stop to refuel and clear customs, the trip is supposed to take about five to six hours. Things can change quickly though. Twenty minutes after entering Mauritanian airspace, a thick haze begins to form around us, smoke and dust trapped by the desert heat. Michel leads us away from the coastline and through the Sahara to try and find a safer, more direct route to Nouakchott before visibility gets worse. Everything in the choppers goes quiet. I look down and out at the desert, and it is the first time Africa looks vast and dangerous to me.

"Guys, I heard something," Michel's voice sizzles through the radio. "Big noise. I need you to check my cargo door."

He slows his machine to about sixty knots, and Charles gets ready to pull up behind him. Before we can check anything, Michel's helicopter flares, makes a hard right turn, and drops from the sky in a slow-motion, uncontrolled descent.

When a plane crashes, it glides. When a helicopter crashes, it falls straight down like a rock.

Time no longer exists for me. There is just instinct, action, and lots of sand. I'm divorced from my own breath, my feelings. I follow the adrenaline. It is all I *can* do. Before I can process anything, Charles has landed and my body is moving over a dune toward the wreckage, about a hundred yards away. It's a disaster. The main rotor head is gone with all three blades. The top of the cabin has been pulled off and tossed upside down—no more roof, no windscreen, no nose. If I hadn't been flying beside it, I wouldn't know it was a helicopter at all. The instrument panel is bent forward, electrical wires bleeding from somewhere behind. I don't see any people.

I stop.

Then, about thirty yards in front of the carcass of the A-Star, I spot Michel.

He turns his head toward me and looks at me confused, like a little boy—not like the hero, the icon, the man I know. His ankle is twisted backward, and his tibia bone is sticking out through his jeans. There's blood everywhere, but he doesn't say a word. He just stares at me, calm with shock. About forty feet away from him is Gabriel.

Damn Gabriel, I think, not thinking it on purpose, not yet understanding that his spot on the helicopter was meant to be mine.

He's lying down in the sand with a huge gash on the side of his face, his left eye hanging by the optic nerve. He's still alive but completely motionless. Both men had been wearing their seatbelts, but they'd been shredded on impact, just like everything else. The shock was so intense that they'd been ejected from their seats, which are sitting totally exploded just beyond the wreck.

The only passenger we can't locate is Pierre. The pilot of the third chopper finds the strength to call his name a few times, but there's no response. We walk slowly around the wreckage. And then I notice a hand, colorless and limp, hanging from the cabin. I frantically grab for the wrist and beg for a pulse. There is none.

Dead. Overcome by the brutality, the reality, the other pilots begin vomiting.

Dead. I don't know whether I'm thinking it or saying it out loud.

Michel begins groaning, giving us some purpose, some sort of compass in the void. Gabriel says he can't feel his legs. He goes to scratch his eye.

"No!" I yell, lunging forward to stop him.

We restrain both men and lift them into our helicopter. The third chopper will stay with Pierre's body while Charles and I find help. We have no idea where we are or how to get back. Michel had been our navigator.

With no GPS and nothing but a paper map, our wristwatches, and our best guesses to guide us, Charles and I take off with the men bleeding out and screaming behind us, finally awake to pain. We try to find the city of Nouakchott, a single light even, in the middle of the desert.

The city appears like a constellation in the pitch-dark after twenty minutes of agony, of frantic prayer, of numbing ourselves to the men's cries just to survive them.

"We need to land at the hospital immediately," Charles yells to the controller over the radio. "There are two men on board who are dying."

It isn't real to me until the words are in my headset. The controller gives us instructions, and Charles cuts sharply to the right toward a small brown building about a tenth of size of what a hospital should be. We land hard and fast on a dirt lot, and within seconds, a small army of men in scrubs load the bodies onto stretchers and run them inside.

The hospital is small and understaffed. There is no access to modern technology and—judging by the flies circling the overhead lights—minimal sanitization. Neither Charles nor I can sit, so we pace the halls for hours, no food, no drink, no words spoken. We're completely exhausted. A French surgeon visiting to train doctors meets us by the nurse's station and gives us an update. The men are stable for now, but they don't know if Michel or Gabriel will make it through the hour, let alone the night.

"If you can," he advises, "find a way to get them home and then get some rest yourselves."

I call Bastien from the international line in the surgeon's office. He arranges a medevac for Michel and Gabriel and a hotel for Charles and me where neither of us sleeps. The next day, we fly to the crash site with Mauritanian and race authorities, who begin the process of transporting Pierre's body and the wreckage back to France. The only way to prevent an accident like this one from happening again is to investigate everything. Pierre gets a funeral; the A-Star gets an autopsy. A week later, we discover that a tiny piece of plastic, smaller than a bottle cap, was found inside the fuel system. It clogged the filter and cut off the fuel, stopping the engine. That was the noise Michel heard. *One small piece of plastic.*

I try to make sense of life afterward—still flying, still working for Bastien—but not understanding how I'm able to do any of it, or why the machines that wake me up in a horrible night sweat are still able to bring me such comfort. In the three months following the race, I lose half of my hair and hardly talk to Hanna. She doesn't know what to do with me other than try to act normal and cheerful. I wouldn't know what to do with me either. Both Michel and Gabriel are still in the hospital, and I have to decide if I still want to be a pilot, knowing deep down that even if I wanted to, I couldn't be anything else. Flying may kill me, but *not* flying would kill me worse.

On September 16, 1985, ten months after the crash, I show up at the heliport, meet my examinator, and fly to the site near Versailles where I trained dozens of times with Michel to pass the check ride.

After two and a half years of hard work, I am holding my commercial license in my hand. I am a professional helicopter pilot. I made good on my promise to myself and to my mother. What I can't promise her or anyone is that I won't end up like Michel, the pilot I still want most to be. Over the next week, Hanna and I celebrate, telling the news to every single person who will hear it. Except for my parents.

Part II

08

A Deal's a Deal

I AM TWENTY-FOUR YEARS OLD, and I have my pilot's license. I have accomplished what I set out to do. The very thing that seemed totally unreachable for most of my life is folded up in my wallet, a little bent at the corners already. For two and a half years, I lived and breathed this dream. It has been oxygen to me. I wake one night around two a.m. totally breathless. Suddenly there is nothing left to chase.

I always imagined that once I was fully certified, I would go to work as a pilot for Bastien; but one week after my test, he still hasn't said anything about hiring me as a pilot. I'm still sweeping hangars and hauling Louis Vuitton handbags around the heliport like a bellboy.

One afternoon after loading cargo into an A-Star AS350, I decide I've been patient enough. I walk straight into Monsieur Bastien's office and ask him for a promotion. He could not look less surprised to see me.

"You remember our deal, yes?" I ask him.

"Fred, of course I remember." He smiles. "I was very clear. You need at least 1,500 flight hours before you can work here."

I only have 150 hours, and it's taken me years to get them.

My disappointment is hard to miss. A little bit of sweat forms on the back of my neck, and my jaw is tight.

"Why don't you knock on a few more doors?" Bastien suggests. "There are only so many hours I can give you here, but I'm sure plenty of other companies could use someone like you. Then we can talk about a job."

Yet again I'm knocking on doors, washing helicopters, and helping people find the bathroom, but now I'm doing it with a pilot's license burning a hole in my pocket.

One evening at Toussus-le-Noble Airport, after scrubbing down a particularly messy A-Star, the maintenance guy mentions that a company called HeliTours is hiring. He doesn't know much about them, he says, other than that they need a pilot for their spring and summer activities. I take one look into my bucket of cloudy water, squeeze out my slimy rag, and run straight over to their office. I don't want to wash helicopters. I want to fly them.

HeliTours is run by Claude and René. The office is a mess and totally empty.

"Hello? Anybody here?" I call out a few times.

Eventually I find them, both fat in the middle and bald on top, sitting at an old green card table in the hangar, chain-smoking dark Gitanes cigarettes, and counting envelopes full of cash. They look like a pair of cheap assassins, like something straight from *The Godfather.* Two dirty Bell 47s stand behind them, one with a layer of dust an inch thick on the windscreen.

"I'm here about the job," I announce to them.

The brothers look at each other, then me. Claude stands up, fixes the buttons on his shirt, and extends his hand.

"*Mais très bien, mon petit, très bien!*" He grins, revealing two rows of yellowish teeth.

"*Oui,*" Rene agrees. "*Très bien.*" More yellow teeth.

They offer me a job on the spot, and I accept.

"The position," Claude explains, "is a little . . . uh . . . different."

I don't care. I just want to get paid to fly.

"Can you start tomorrow?" he asks.

"*Oui!*" I tell him.

The next day I show up in my orange pilot suit, and they pin a badge that says "Captain Frédéric North" above my heart.

The position, it turns out, is a little different indeed. Monday through Thursday, I drive a Citroën van through little villages in Western France, yelling, "*Tours en hélicoptère! Ce week-end!*" through a bullhorn and scaring the heck out of little ladies on their way to buy vegetables at the market. Friday through Sunday, I fly.

The sightseeing "adventures" are about four minutes each, and we fly tours for seven to ten hours, or as long as we have daylight. I have no mechanical assistance. I have to add oil every day and grease the transmission bearings myself. The pace is exhausting, *and* I must be prepared to answer questions about every little castle, village, and river we fly over. The only "help" I get is a guy named Cédric, who collects the cash from the customers before they step onto the helicopter.

The whole thing runs more like a mob operation than a helicopter company. It takes two weeks before I have my first engine failure. It's a miracle it doesn't happen sooner.

I'm ready to go for the last flight of the day when a twenty-year-old girl approaches the helicopter pushing her father in a wheelchair. He is missing both his legs, and though I try not to stare, he's quick and proud to explain that he's a farmer who lost them in a tractor accident a few years back. The sightseeing thing, he confesses, was his daughter's idea.

We manage to lift him into the chopper and position him in the middle seat. His daughter, who is sweet and more enthusiastic than the both of us put together, sits to the right side.

One minute after we take off, rising up and over brown-green fields and patches of bright-yellow flowers, my oil pressure gauge is indicating zero.

Merde. We're in the middle of the sky, in the middle of nowhere.

Reducing the collective pitch, I manage to initiate an autorotation. The engine cuts out, and the rotor is being driven only by lift, drag, and pure luck. As I panic, the old farmer taps me on the shoulder as quietly as possible. He knows exactly what's happening.

"Hey, kid," he laughs, "I went to war. I lost my legs. We're going to be fine. Just don't kill us."

His daughter, rightly so, is freaking out. The engine is off, and we're descending fast.

I spot a field full of dairy cows and dairy cow poop and manage to land us safely. The daughter is silent now, and her father is getting impatient. I step out of the helicopter to see what happened and find that the clamp connecting the oil cooler hose to the engine is gone. All the oil emptied itself when we took off, something a mechanic (if Rene and Claude hired one) would have noticed in an instant. I'm still shaking from the landing, and I don't know what to do.

The sky is getting dark and there's nobody coming to help us.

"We'll need to hike to the road," I tell them. "I'm sorry."

Thankfully, they're just happy to be alive. It's a miracle we didn't smash into a bunch of cows and explode.

As I get ready to make the long, disgusting walk, I remember the man has no legs. And he's not a small guy. I shrug at him, and he shrugs back. To him it's just another part of the adventure.

"Sorry," I say again before hoisting him onto my back. It's like carrying a grizzly bear.

The mud does its best to suck my shoes off as we walk slow step by slow step toward a little dirt road. When we get there, I don't feel like captain of anything. I almost lost my Converse and my life in the same day, and I smell like a farm animal.

Thankfully a little Fiat spots us as soon as we reach the shoulder. The driver takes us back to base.

"No refunds," Cédric warns me, but I grab the purse and give the passengers their money back. Then I call my bosses.

Claude and Rene don't care that the passengers are safe. They care about sending a truck to remove their crappy helicopter from the landing site before the police can arrive to inspect it and confiscate it. They're crooks. The whole operation is reckless, and I'm reckless to be a part of it. I threaten to quit, but they promise to hire a mechanic if I agree to finish out the season.

"Things just got a little mixed up," Claude reasons. "Come on, Fred."

For pennies, they hire a young guy just out of school, and he does his best with the knowledge he has.

It's better than washing helicopters, I remind myself.

For a while things are fine, but after a gearbox failure sends me flying sideways through the clouds, the mechanic confesses that Rene had asked him to disable the machine's dashboard warning lights so I would "not get worried and keep flying."

I'm done.

I leave the HeliTours hangar and drive straight back to Bastien's office with my tail between my legs. With nine hundred hours and two near-death experiences under my belt, he hires me on the condition that I fly copilot until I complete my hours—which I do.

"A deal's a deal." Bastien smiles, handing me a new badge.

I am officially a pilot with HeliFrance.

The work starts out very simple and, honestly, very dull. The city sponsors helicopter rides for the elderly over Paris (for a little feel-good PR, I'm guessing). To me, the proposition seems kind of crazy. Taking little blue-haired ladies with pacemakers fifteen hundred feet in the air in one of the most dangerous machines known to man could go badly in a number of ways, but I don't ask any questions. I have the job I want with the company I want—at least, I think it's what I want.

Within a week of running the tours, I'm bored. I find myself weaving through the skyscrapers on the north side of the city, taking interesting routes, and making turns a little tighter than I should. Most of my passengers love it and seem to need the excitement as badly as I do. Only one smacks me on the back of the head with a rolled-up copy of *Le Monde*, the newspaper, and calls me crazy.

I'm not trying to be crazy though. I'm trying to stay sane, trying to find a new challenge—a new goal to keep me going, keep me feeling something, anything, exciting. Hanna is constantly in New York working, and despite my having a very respectable job, my parents are still completely unimpressed with me. They hoped I would grow into a lawyer, marry a doctor, and have a proper family. Instead, I'm a helicopter pilot with a model girlfriend. I'm a total disappointment. Nothing has changed. Hanna is still quiet, still proud of me, still beautiful, but nothing has changed. I spend my days flying over Paris again and again, wishing it looked less gray and hoping to see something new, any sign of magic. A few weeks in, I do.

Just in time for Christmas, HeliFrance signs another contract with the city. Some politician decides that he wants Santa to deliver Christmas gifts to schoolchildren in a lower-income district just outside Paris, but he doesn't want some cheesy guy in a cheap beard showing up in a first-generation Renault 5; he wants Santa and his bag of toys hanging from a helicopter, like Rambo in a red suit. *Top Gun* came out in the fall, and since then everything has been a little more "high-octane," including Christmas. It's an advanced operation, and everyone is excited about it. The pilot will need experience with sling work, lifting, carrying, controlling loads—the kinds of things they do in remote construction sites—but in this case the cargo is a human being, and not just any human being, but Père Noël. When I see my name on the board to take on the job, I'm thrilled. I'm channeling Maverick. Honestly, I'm surprised Bastien has that much faith in me.

One week before Christmas, with an assistant on board, I land in an empty parking lot less than a mile from the schoolyard. The principal and a small committee from the city of Paris greet me. Everyone is excited, deep in the holiday spirit. I keep waiting for somebody to call the whole thing off because it's dangerous and I'm inexperienced, but other than *"joyeux noël,"* nobody says a word. And as long as the pilot has a license, they can do pretty much whatever they want.

The guy chosen to be Santa Claus is probably about thirty years old. He has bright-red cheeks and a bit of a belly, which is good, but I'm thinking he got them at some bar on Rue Saint-Denis, not the North Pole.

The assistant secures a line underneath the helicopter on the sling hook. Then he fixes it to Santa's harness, which thankfully looks sturdy. I watch the rigging process closely, having never done or even seen anything like this before, and it's much more intense than I imagine. It starts to sink in that I really don't know what I'm doing.

"We're ready!" the assistant declares, giving me a thumbs-up.

I start the machine and off we go.

Santa is dangling about sixty feet below the helicopter, and everything is going great. I can see the landing area, the schoolyard right up ahead. The weather and visibility are perfect. I fly like I always do and set up for a long, easy approach.

But the perimeter of the school is surrounded by a wall about eighteen feet high.

With the doors on, and without a mirror to check on the distance down below and properly account for the load, I'm relying on my own spatial awareness. In my head, I'm sure Santa will have plenty of room.

People are yelling down below. They seem agitated, but I can't really hear them and assume they're just cheering us on. By the time I realize Santa is trying desperately to climb up the rope, it's too late. I fly him straight into a brick wall, at full speed, with hundreds of children watching at the windows. All the gifts explode on impact, shredding the toys inside, dumping headless dolls and broken Transformer action figures into the schoolyard.

When I set Santa down, he has two broken legs and not very much

Christmas cheer at all. The teachers make the kids turn away from the windows. It's a complete disaster.

Afterward, the chief pilot admits that I shouldn't have been assigned to the operation. It was an "internal miscommunication." It was also a complete lack of training. Sure, you learn the protocol, but the protocol doesn't cover flying around Paris with Santa Claus attached to a rope. It doesn't cover any education on adapting, reacting, or split-second decision-making. I'm so ashamed that I take two months off. I pack my bags and head to New York, where Hanna has been shooting a campaign. There, I make another quick decision.

On February 3, 1987, Hanna and I go to New York City Hall in our street clothes and get married. She's been travelling a lot for work, and we don't spend much time together. New York loves Hanna, but she does not love it back. The American people are too loud for her, the food is too greasy, and the campaign directors are always asking her to show more skin and making her feel like a prude when she refuses. She's angry and burned-out, and because of it, I can't seem to do anything right. I feel like I'm losing my connection to the helicopter and to Hanna, the two great loves of my life.

We hold hands in front of a clerk, me in my Levi's blue jeans and Hanna in a cropped sweater and giant clip-on earrings painted gold. We repeat simple vows they read off to us, neither of us speaking good enough English to understand the promises we're making, both of us desperate to do something that feels good, moves us, wakes us up a little.

She tells me she loves me; I tell her the same. We take a picture, collect our marriage certificate and receipt, and walk out into City Hall Park as husband and wife, a heavy snow falling down on our shoulders. Again, I forget to tell my parents.

I go back to Paris with stars in my eyes. I'm ready to fly again, ready to learn more, ready to be the best pilot I can be. Bastien sets me up with a student, a good-looking guy named François, who drives a motorcycle like me. He's the heir to some crazy champagne fortune, and Bastien says he could use a friend. I'm not ready to be anyone's teacher, but I can be a friend. I share my experiences with him and we hit the gym together—stuff like that. When Hanna is in town, we all go to dinner, and he brings along whatever beautiful girl he's sleeping with at the time. He's just an OK pilot, but he's passionate, and I love the guy. I haven't had a friend in years, and for a while, it makes things around HeliFrance (and France itself) a little more interesting for me. By spring 1987, I've flown over Paris every single way a person can. I'm bored again and need a change.

With Hanna working in the US most of the time, Bastien sends me to Blois, a village in central France, for the summer. There, I'll be taking people on tours of the Château de Chambord and working standby as a medevac pilot *if* the hospital ever needs me.

To most people, Blois is nothing more than a day trip. People stroll around, take photographs of the castle and the perfectly square-shaped hedges in Jardins du Roy, and then get on exploring the rest of the Loire Valley. It's a pretty, quiet, and simple town with quaint Tudor buildings and cobblestone streets. To a medevac pilot, Blois is the Wild West.

I've been in my new apartment for one week when the hospital calls around eleven o'clock at night. A young woman has crashed with her glider in the dense, humid forest near the château. The towplane's rope broke before the glider was stabilized, and she plunged nose-first into the trees. I've never done anything like this before. My only instinct is to move as quickly as possible, so I grab my map and a flashlight and race to the helipad, where the doctor and paramedics are waiting. Without a word, we throw our stuff onto the floor and take off. The adrenaline is insane.

The A-Star AS350B is a state-of-the-art helicopter, and it's made for this job. It's reliable, agile, and big enough, which is a real concern when you have a medical team and patients on board. About twenty minutes into our forty-five-minute journey, I hear a strange sound. The map, our only navigation tool, is being sucked through a half-inch gap in the doorway.

There's no autopilot, and it's pitch-black outside, so I can't move my hands from the controls. Before I can ask for help, the map is gone. *Merde.* Again, I've made a stupid mistake.

Relying on the lights of the highway and the shape of the roads, a technique called "navigation by default," we're able to locate the accident site, but it takes us thirty minutes and probably should have taken two. Narrowly missing a power line (a detail the dispatcher forgot to mention), we land and pour out of the helicopter.

The woman is eighteen years old and covered with dirt, debris, and sweat. She can't feel anything from the waist down; her nerves are retracting. The doctors move quickly, stabilizing her and lifting her into the chopper.

When we take off again, the doctor gets a radio message from the medical team in Blois.

"She needs to go to the hospital in Tours," he tells me. "I think I know how to get there."

My brain and body return to Mauritania. I feel the intensity of every single second passing, of human life in my care. I have no map, low fuel, and nothing but hope and city lights.

I don't think I take a breath until I see the ambulance lights at the Tours airport.

They get her into surgery just in time, and I don't get into a helicopter again without two maps in my pocket.

I'm not expecting to find a sense of family in Blois, but I do. The doctors, medics, and I see everything: car accidents on the highways, lonely people doing weird things with their farm animals (really weird things), gliders in trees, birth, death, all of it. One day we're treating and transporting a young burn victim; the next, it's a Swedish girl hemorrhaging because she's shoved a vibrator too far up her vagina. No day is the same. The little hospital team are the only people I've ever met who understand the thrill, the adrenaline, the waking up a person does when he is just a few breaths away from death.

When summer and the tour season come to an end, I can't go back to Paris. I need a change. I remember hearing about a cool French guy named Jean Pujol living in Miami and running helicopter tours. The other pilots all know him and convince me I should go visit, get my US private license, and fly for him.

"You'll love it!" they say. "Jean is up for anything."

It sounds like a good idea to me. America and the beach always sound like a good idea.

It does not sound like a good idea to Hanna, though. Again, she plans to stay behind, and I don't blame her. We're growing apart. She doesn't understand why I *have to* do the thing I love, and I don't understand how she can bear to do something she doesn't.

Before I leave, we have a couple of weeks together. She's obviously unhappy, but I want the relationship to work. I'm still in love and I'm worried about her, something I confess to François at the gym the afternoon before I take off for Florida.

"Would it make you feel better if I check in on her?" he offers.

I tell him that, yes, it would.

I'm in Miami for three months. When I return in January 1988, I decide to surprise Hanna, but she surprises me first. I walk into our little apartment in Montmartre, set down my bags, and find her in bed with François.

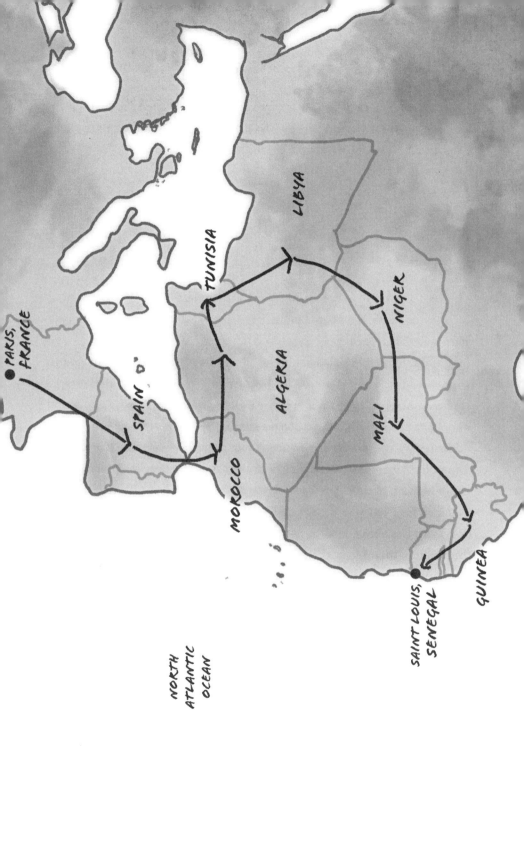

09

Adapt

ALL I CAN THINK ABOUT is things going wrong: Hanna and François, Michel and Gabriel, the impact one small decision can have on human life.

When Hanna and I separate, I throw myself into work, taking on any operation HeliFrance is willing to assign me, spending as much time in the air and away from life on the ground as possible. Flying is a comfort to me. My connection with the machine is not something I can explain, but helicopters make more sense to me than people. And after opening my bedroom door to see Francois's naked white butt, I certainly have more trust in them. Accidents happen, but machines are not capable of betrayal. I have no fear of flirting with death, so long as I'm in control of my destiny. I'm afraid of losing the one thing in the world I understand. I live with the risk because I can't live without it.

All anyone at the pilots' lounge can talk about is the Paris–Dakar Rally. Rumor is that they'll be running it again this year and need even more helicopters. I try not to get my hopes up. In 1986, the race's founder, Thierry Sabine, was killed along with four others in Mali. Their helicopter got caught in a sandstorm and crashed into a dune. It has always been a daring race, but since then, there have been major questions about the race's safety and conversations about whether it should still exist when the man who built it is gone. At the same time, anyone who knew Sabine or knew anything of him considers the race his legacy. Helicopters are dangerous, mostly because people are in control of them.

Even though I wake up at night on my friend Marc's couch remembering Mauritania, thinking about the near disastrous engine failures in Normandy and the power lines in Blois, I would do anything to fly the Paris–Dakar Rally. To me, it is the ultimate dream.

In fall 1988, HeliFrance gets the contract, and Michel Anglade, who is fully recovered and still flying, announces that I've been selected as one of the pilots and will be flying the Bell 206 JetRanger. I can't believe it. Of course, I've already picked out a light-blue pilot suit from the Avirex store with a NASA badge on it. There are no toilets in the desert, and the zipper is in the front. If I have to go to the bathroom, I mean *really* go, I'll have to undress completely. It isn't practical, but it's cool.

Helicopters have always played a big role in the race, whether to help keep drivers on course; to transport VIPs, doctors, and media; or simply to film the cars as they speed through the most extreme and beautiful landscapes in the world. For every leg of the rally, a gigantic village called "the bivouac" comes to life with thousands of tents, trucks, and stations to host the drivers, team members, journalists, and pilots. The atmosphere is almost as exciting as the race itself, and the entire setup travels along with the drivers. It is like a moving city in the desert.

The day before the departure, two helicopters arrive from Monaco to be part of the support team. One of the pilots, Phillippe Tondeur, is thirty-one years old, close to my age, and fresh from the Belgian army. He's cracking jokes with everyone right away and is the only one other than me who seems to want to have a bit of fun with the operation. Everyone else is older and taking things very seriously. Phillippe and I are listening to reggae on my yellow Sony stereo.

The role I'm assigned for the race is "assistant helicopter." Phillippe gets the same kind of gig. We'll be flying the doctor to the scene, getting drivers back on track, transporting diesel and tools, and doing a little bit of everything else—which, truthfully, is the best kind of job you can get. The race lasts fourteen days, and you don't want to be doing one thing the whole time. Assistant helicopter is never boring, even in a JetRanger. It's not exactly the machine I was hoping to pilot. Basically it's the helicopter equivalent of a Dodge Caravan, but I'm sure the only reason I end up with it is because they know how excited I am. I would go to Dakar on a bicycle if they asked me.

On December 31, 1988, just as the sun rises and the sky becomes orange, we all meet at the heliport. Everyone is quiet and feeling the electricity of the moment—the machines are impeccable, the pilots are the best in the world, and above us is the promise of a clear day. Surely some people are nervous, but more than anything there is the feeling that once our skids leave the ground, we will be taking part in something epic.

There's little to no briefing or safety protocols given, which surprises me given what happened two years ago. The only advice I receive is from an older British pilot, about my dad's age, just as we're walking out to load up and leave.

"Hey, mate," he says, jogging up to me. "If you see a sandstorm approaching, just land and wait. Don't even think about doing anything else. Get ready to spend the night wherever you land."

"Got it." I smile back at him, pulling down my Ray-Bans and getting ready for the adventure to begin.

My radio technician, Paul, meets me near the helicopter. He's in his forties and, like Michel, has been with the race since it began. He'll oversee all communication and get me information on where to go and what to do once the race is underway. We shake hands, he climbs on board, and I start the engine.

"OK, Fred." He nods. "Let's go."

The tower gives us clearance and we take off, beginning a route that will take us from Paris through Spain, Tunisia, Libya, Nigeria, Mali, and Guinea, finishing in Saint-Louis, Senegal. This time, I've brought a dozen extra maps.

Flying in the desert is a unique experience. First, between the hours of eleven a.m. and three p.m., you have zero reference points. The sun is high and hot, and it's near impossible to see any kind of change in the terrain. From above it appears totally flat, but it's not; the dunes play tricks on your eyes, so you don't want to fly too low. Second, you don't know where the wind is coming from. There are no trees, no grasses, and normally, no clouds at all. The JetRanger won't have the power to forgive me if I have to land with a tailwind; we'd end up with crazy ground speed and plant ourselves in a sandbank. To be safe, I decide there will be no landing at noon whatsoever—not when the sun is at its highest and the wind at its lowest. We'll piss in our water bottles if we have to.

Refueling in the Sahara is also a challenge.

There's supposed to be a fuel truck roughly every hour along the route, but the trucks often get lost and miss the rendezvous points. If you do find them, there's also no way of knowing exactly what you're going to get.

The first part of the race goes smoothly. Flying through Europe and the northernmost part of Africa is easy because of cities, towns, vegetation, and great spots to land. But by the third day, the spaces between geographical markers and villages are growing wider. One day in Libya, maybe the hottest day of the whole race, Phillippe and I decide to meet a truck to refuel. The guy—a tall, thin man with a huge smile—seems nice and speaks great French. While we fuel up, Philippe and I put some music on and catch up.

"I had to help dig a guy out in Tunisia," Phillippe tells me. "The car was, like, drowning in sand, and the more we dug, the deeper he sank. It was crazy."

Only about seventy of the 182 cars that begin the rally ever make it back.

People are dropping out every day. Paul and I were doing medevacs as early on as Spain.

"The desert *is* crazy," I laugh, shaking my head.

When my helicopter is fully fueled, we say goodbye to Phillippe and head out to help a pair of Italian drivers who missed a crucial turn. Twenty minutes later, Phillippe is on the radio.

"The guy filled me up with water, took the cash, and just sped off! Unbelievable!"

The trucks each have a few drums, some with water and some with fuel. They're independent contractors. The race does not pay them, we do. Maybe it was an honest mistake and the guy just forgot which hose was which. Or maybe, he wanted to hang onto a little more of his valuable fuel, take the money, and run.

Phillippe and his tech, Andreas, end up having to camp for the night, sleeping under the A-Star and hoping the vipers leave them alone.

Thankfully, most of the people we meet on the course are great.

Sabine was careful to make sure every farmer and villager he encountered felt a connection and sense of pride in the race. When we land near a little town, people are happy to see us. Hundreds of curious local people come out to look at the helicopter, to talk to us, and to bring us water and food if they have anything at all to spare. There is nothing better to me than landing outside a village and seeing a crowd of curious children gathering and slowly walking toward us, totally wonderstruck, experiencing the helicopter for the first time just the same way I did. The joy in their faces, the warm welcomes, the excitement—it's all a part of Sabine's legacy. He cultivated something truly special. At the time of the crash, he and Daniel Balavoine, a popular French singer and one of the passengers on board, were working on a project to provide better access to clean water for the people in North Africa. I begin to think that, one day, I might like to do some good here too.

Around the tenth day of the race, we cross into Nigeria and approach a small town in the middle of nowhere. There are probably about fifty one-room houses, about one hundred square feet each, made of red clay and brush. We're flying very low, the way we have to in the desert, following the cars as they stir up dust on the main street of the village. I'm focusing more on my instruments than my surroundings, making sure to not over-torque or draw too much power from the main rotor. We make a quick turn, and though I don't realize it at first, one of my skids clips a tiny cable that was running from house to house. *Merde.*

I assume it's an electrical wire, which is irritating but fixable, but I'm very wrong. In a fraction of a second, one of the little homes crumbles completely, creating a pile of heavy dust. The cable was holding the entire thing together.

"Fred!" Paul gasps. "What if there's someone in there?"

Worried I've squashed an entire Nigerian family, I land and run at top speed over to the shack, or whatever's left of it.

Because everyone is outside watching the race, no one is hurt. With help from the one person in the village who speaks English (better English than we do), we manage to find the villager whose house we just destroyed. He doesn't look like he's in great physical shape, and seeing his home flattened doesn't do much to cheer him up.

"Tell him I'm sorry," I beg the interpreter, who nods and passes along the message. "And here, give him this."

I hand over every dollar I have, about six hundred, promising myself to somehow get back here as soon as the race is done and help rebuild the house one handful of clay at a time.

The man looks down at the cash in his hand, and his eyes go wide. Suddenly he starts dancing. Then his family starts dancing. He hugs and kisses me, laughing so hard he has tears in his eyes. Everybody else kisses me too. This was not the reaction I expected, but we seem to have made things right somehow.

Later at the bivouac, one of the medics tells us we'd given the man the equivalent of one year's salary. The houses take about two days to build and cost thirty dollars. Accidents happen, but some accidents are happy. Sabine would have loved it.

The race is going along smoothly, and everyone from the racing drivers to the guys who make the food seems cheerful. Phillippe and I have fun messing around and pranking the older pilots, and like always, it feels good to be back in Africa. Flying the rally is exactly what I hoped it would be. By the time we enter Mali, I feel the sadness of the ending hanging over me.

Mali is huge, the eighth or ninth largest nation in Africa, and the monotony of the desert makes it seem even bigger and emptier than it is. Paul and I are flying over some of the deepest, remotest parts of the Sahara. We hardly see a village or any sign of life, just dust from the cars and the occasional fuel truck. With any luck, we'll cross the border into Guinea by sundown. Aside from keeping racing prodigy, twenty-four-year-old Stéphane Peterhansel, from driving his motorcycle toward Mauritania (a place I do not want to visit anytime soon), the day is uneventful.

At about one p.m., things change. The air is trembling so hard it looks like it's melting. Paul and I are listening to *Hanging Fire* for the fourteenth time, suspecting nothing. Suddenly I look up, and the windshield of the JetRanger is yellow. I have zero visibility. A wind comes from nowhere and grabs us like a fist, pulling us one way and then jerking us the other. Right away, I know it's a sandstorm. We're all alone, buried in the sky. I remember what the Brit told me back in Paris—"land and wait"—but I don't even know how I would land. It's like nothing else on earth. This is what killed Thierry Sabine. My instincts (or maybe my fears) are telling me to find a way out as quickly as possible. Paul's face is white.

"I can do this," I tell him.

"Fred," is all he can say back to me.

You've done impossible things before, I remind myself, but I know this is stupid.

First, I try to fly over the storm by taking the machine about five thousand feet up. I feel it losing power and see the sand stretching up another ten thousand feet. It's dense as a brick wall. Next, I try to outrun it, but it's like racing the ocean. There's no way to know where it begins and ends. After about a minute, we feel intense turbulence and sand in the cockpit. I'm losing control. We're totally turned around and have no frame of reference. We're screwed.

Paul starts praying or crying or something. With no other solution, I go straight ahead as fast as possible, with no idea whether we're going further into trouble or out of it, or whether we're flying high enough or into a dune. I ask the JetRanger for as much power as it has left and close my eyes. I can't see anything anyway.

In just seconds, there's a feeling of release, as if the storm has decided to toss us aside. The tension falls like a weight from my body, and I catch my breath. Paul starts laughing. The storm is still raging about a half-mile away from us, but we manage to land on a dune just beyond it. It takes the JetRanger a full two minutes to shut down, and when it does, the blades are still spinning at about a hundred miles per hour because of the wind. We wait four hours for the storm to clear up. When it does, we're completely lost. To be safe, we make camp in the desert for the night.

When the sun disappears, it takes the heat of the desert with it. We have a tent, but with the high winds, it's totally useless. We lay our sleeping bags under the helicopter, using half a pack of baby wipes to try and freshen up so we don't have to smell each other all night long. In Mali, I fall in love with baby wipes the way I fell in love with maps in Blois. Paul falls asleep quickly, but I stay awake. My body is still humming with adrenaline.

We could have died.

We probably should have.

On the other side of disaster, I see gaps in my training. I made every stupid choice possible. I need to get better. I need to learn to adapt to my conditions; they're never going to adapt to me. Flying in the Sahara is not the same as leading sightseeing tours in the French countryside. If I want to be a great pilot, I have to do more of this and less of that. I don't really know how I'll do it. Île-de-France isn't known for its extreme terrain.

We make it to the bivouac safely the next day, but I can't stop thinking about what happened, going over how I responded, wondering if more training and work under pressure would have made any difference.

"I need something new," I tell Phillippe.

We've been drinking paper cups full of water and deciding which guys we're going to mess with over the radio during the last leg. Probably Guy, who came with Philippe from Monaco. He's thirty-five going on seventy and a real pain.

"What do you mean 'new'?" he asks. "We're in the middle of Africa. This isn't new?"

"I need more of this," I explain. "More challenge. I'm not good enough."

I tell him about the sandstorm and the village and how I want to be a truly great pilot. It feels good to open up about all of it. The last good friendship I had was with François. It ended poorly.

"Also, I want to do something good in the world, you know?" I go on, losing him a little.

One of the few helicopter books I read argued that the helicopter is one of the only human inventions that actually saves more life than it costs. And I want to be part of that. I miss being part of that.

I'm not expecting Phillippe to have a solution, but he surprises me.

"Come work with me in Monaco!" he says, super excited.

I make a face. Serving the people of Monaco isn't the kind of community service I was talking about. I don't think flying rich ladies to Nice is going to sharpen my skills.

"Look," he explains. "Héli Air Monaco has a French subsidiary doing work in the Alps. Crazy stuff. Longline. You'd love it."

I *would* love it. Flying in the mountains is the highest standard for helicopter pilots; only the very best can succeed there. It entails the hardest environment and the most complex operations: medevac, search and rescue, utility work. *Parfait.*

The rest of the race, I'm thinking mountains, not deserts.

In February 1989, when the ink on my separation agreement with Hanna is still wet, I hop on my V-Max motorcycle with my duffle bag—pretty much the only thing I have left—and drive south to Monte Carlo.

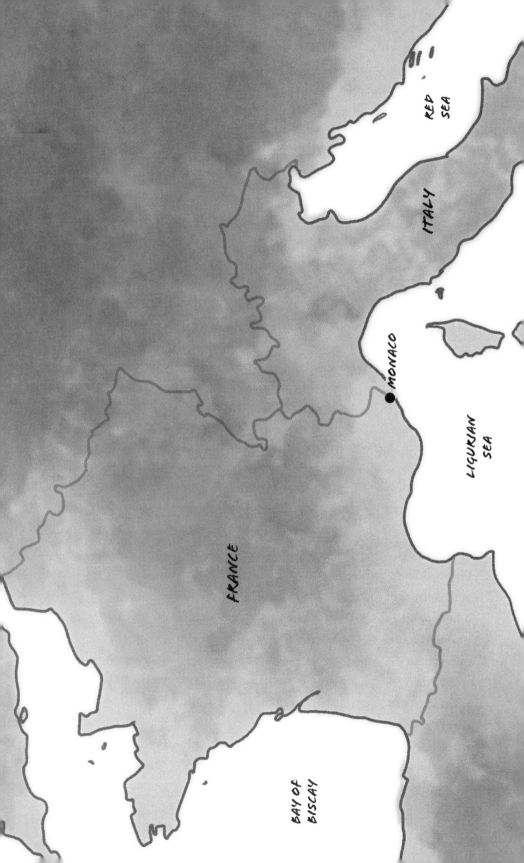

10

Boredom Is the Opposite of Freedom

MONACO IS ONE OF THE wealthiest places in the world, and Philippe and I are the poorest people there. We live together in a *chambre de bonnes*, a one-hundred-square-foot room at the top of an old building with only a sink to wash ourselves and a shared toilet in the hallway. Years ago, rooms like ours were used for maids and household staff, which in Monaco, a helicopter pilot may as well be. Both of us are broke, but we're young, passionate about aviation, and willing to do anything to succeed. Sleeping on the floor doesn't bother us. The communal toilet is another story though.

Living in a seaside tax haven less than a mile in area is a little different from living in Paris. There is no litter on the sidewalks, and most everyone is wearing an outfit worth more than my motorbike. The sun shines three hundred days a year, and you can't turn around without hitting a superyacht. Working at Héli Air Monaco is different too. The pilots are mostly older and take things quite seriously, not prone to making conversation with their passengers as they shuttle them to the Alps, Saint-Tropez, or Nice. The relationship is stiff and formal.

On our first day at work together, Philippe gets dressed in his white pilot shirt, navy-blue pleated trousers, and a freshly polished pair of black leather shoes, just as it's written in the "dress code" paragraph of the company handbook. I don't own any clothing like that, and I don't see how shining my shoes and dressing like I fly a 747 is going to make the experience better for anyone. Besides, it's summertime, and people are on vacation. I wear my red Converse, blue Bermuda shorts, and a white button-down open halfway to my belly button, Miami-style.

Phillippe laughs. "Fred, you can't just do whatever you want all the time, you know."

A little fashion never hurt anyone.

Jacques Crovetto, the CEO, is an old-school, straightforward guy. He doesn't seem to care if I wear a tuxedo or Speedo to work; he just wants me to fly my routes, be of use, and prove myself. He starts me on the rotation between the Nice airport and the Monaco heliport, which is a super quick six-minute flight along the coast. On lucky days, I'm allowed to take clients to Saint-Tropez, a twenty-minute flight. I try to remind myself that Monaco is just a stop on the way to the Alps, learning how to fly through blizzards, and doing longline work. By the end of the first week, I'm bored out of my mind. I have seen so many beautiful people and so much beautiful scenery, I could do without seeing a blonde or a palm tree ever again. I'm dying for something, anything, different.

One afternoon after I take a woman and her poodle to Nice, the dispatcher requests a helicopter to transport a couple from Monaco to Isola 2000, a ski resort in the Alps about forty minutes away. I wait for somebody to take the call. Nobody does. Jacques has given me a very specific route, and the weather isn't looking great—but I would rather fly through a sandstorm than look at Cap-Ferrat one more time.

I accept the call.

"It's not a good idea, Fred," Phillippe warns. "The visibility is going to be crap, and you don't have any idea what you're doing up there."

Phillippe is a great guy but not exactly a rule breaker.

"Plus," he adds, "Jacques is going to be pissed if he finds out."

"*If* he finds out." I shrug.

After flying the rallies, I'm not worried about a few big rocks and some snowflakes.

I pick the couple up from the airport, navigate easily through the clouds, and drop them at the pretty mountain village. Drama-free. No big deal.

When I make my approach back at the heliport, Philippe is waiting for me, pacing around, and looking panicked. I get out of the A-Star, and before the blades stop turning, he's shelling me with questions.

"Fred, where are the passengers? What happened? Where were you? The car service won't stop calling, and everyone is freaking out!"

Phillippe is sweating through his perfectly pressed uniform, breathing heavily. Maybe he should have worn shorts?

"The passengers are fine," I answer. "I dropped them off at the village thirty minutes ago, just like I was supposed to."

Phillippe stops walking suddenly.

"Oh my God." He starts to laugh. "Fred, you took them to the wrong village."

Merde.

Still laughing, Phillippe puts a hand on my shoulder. "Don't worry, I'll call the car service."

Monaco isn't exactly riveting, but Phillippe and I manage to have a good time anyway. He becomes a brother to me. My parents and I only really speak on Christmas. My mother still thinks helicopters are too dangerous, and my dad thinks I'm nothing more than a flying taxi driver. Phillippe is the closest thing to family I have. We're a perfect balance: He does a good job making sure I don't have too much fun, and I do a good job making sure he has at least a little bit. We don't do anything too bad—just spying on couples having sex in the marina, illegally crossing the Italian border to throw flowers at his friend's wedding, or playing the occasional prank—but it's enough to keep us amused. When I break my right clavicle on my motorcycle, a sexy black Yamaha V-Max and the love of my life, it's Phillipe who takes it in for repairs. When I break my left clavicle on the same motorcycle just three weeks later, it's Phillippe who helps me in and out of bed. When he's trying to find a girlfriend, I give him a makeover and lend him my Breitling watch. (It turns out to not be that impressive. Everyone in Monaco has one.) For the first time in my life, I have someone I can really count on.

Logically I know I am living a good life, even if I am sleeping on the floor. But I can't fly shuttles forever. I don't know exactly what kind of pilot I want to be, but I know that *this* isn't it.

Jacques comes to me in May with an interesting assignment. Phillippe and I have just come back from flying the Rallye de l'Atlas, another crazy race through the desert, but this time in Morocco. I had the job of film helicopter and spent the week chasing cars, collaborating with the cameraman, going in close for the best shot, and flying the best I ever have. There's no way I can go back to flying shuttles after. I know it, and Jacques knows it too.

"So, Fred," he says, "one of our VIPs needs a new pilot on his yacht."

In Monaco and Saint-Tropez, it isn't uncommon for a wealthy yacht owner to have a helicopter on call 24-7, someone living on the boat with them to provide transport whenever needed.

"The last pilot wasn't so good at landing when the sea was rough, and they need someone who can handle the changing conditions."

I would do almost anything for changing conditions.

"You understand this means you will have to stay on the yacht for a three-week rotation, right?" he explains.

Considering I live in an apartment the size of a broom closet with another guy, staying on a million-dollar boat doesn't exactly sound like a death sentence.

"I understand," I reply. "I'll do it."

The next day, I pack my bag and fly out to sea.

The Lavigne family yacht isn't a boat; it's a ship. It has three separate decks, a jacuzzi, bedrooms as big as hotel suites, a helipad (of course), and separate crew quarters at the front of the vessel that are pretty luxurious as well. The food is fantastic, prepared by a world-class chef, and I have a lot of downtime to do whatever I want: tan on a lounge chair, swim, exercise. . . . It's the best vacation I've ever had.

The first three-week rotation is great. Once or twice a day, Monsieur Lavigne needs transport for work or just wants to go for a ride and see what the helicopter can do. I fly low over the water and land him any-where and everywhere he asks, which he loves. We get along great, and I can tell he's happy to have me there. Until his daughter arrives for a visit from university.

Danielle is extremely pretty and extremely flirtatious. She has long dark hair that goes almost to her waist, as well as golden, tanned skin that she suns daily on the deck underneath the helipad. Of course I'm not supposed to flirt with her or anyone, but I'm single, in my twenties, looking down, and totally incapable of resisting the smallest bathing suit I've ever seen.

One morning I'm on the upper deck cleaning the helicopter when she shows up in a white tennis dress. She tells me her parents have left for the day on the speedboat, and if I want to, we could hang out for a bit.

"Maybe we could go for a little swim?" she suggests.

I smile. "Yeah, that would be great."

I try to be cool, but I run down to the crew quarters and jump into my swimsuit so fast I pull a muscle in my butt. When I go back up to meet her, she's fully naked.

"Let's jump from here," she says. "No clothes."

At this point, she could ask me to sing like Charles Aznavour while standing on my head naked and I'd do it. She's fun, free, and looking for adventure. She came to the right guy. My swimsuit is gone in an instant.

Throwing her head back and laughing, she grabs my hand. We count down—*un, deux, trois*—and then go flying through the air, screaming until we splash down hard into the water.

We come back up to the surface, wipe our eyes, catch our breath, and see her entire family and some close friends staring at us from the dining deck. They have decided to come back early to have brunch on the boat.

Danielle gets grounded, and Monsieur Lavigne fires me on the spot. Jacques, thankfully, is amused but decides that maybe I'm not cut out for VIP services after all. He transfers me to their sister company in the French Alps. I'd hoped to work my way there eventually, but I didn't expect to have so much fun doing it.

The guy who runs the mountain unit is called Marc Grellet, and he's a notorious jerk. Everyone is afraid of him. He goes through young pilots like sticks of chewing gum and is known for his ability to make anyone with any sort of confidence feel like a complete piece of garbage. He's a brilliant pilot and a bit of a legend in the southeastern region of the Alps. He does longline work—hauling construction materials and equipment on a thick steel cord—better than anyone else. And what he does isn't easy. Line work requires incredible precision, a steady hand, and total focus.

Grellet is in his fifties with a face full of wrinkles set in a permanently dissatisfied position. He's a smaller guy, but when I meet him, I get the feeling he could kick my butt pretty quickly if he wanted to.

"North?" he asks, walking up to me at the tiny Alpine helipad.

I extend my hand.

"Hello! I'm—"

"Get in," he says. "Let's see what you can do."

Grellet flies Lamas, so now I do too. The Lama is the perfect machine for the mountains—small, agile, responsive, and incredibly fun too.

With Grellet in the copilot seat grumbling, we take off into a gray sky and fly around for a little while. I land and take off from what I think are some tough spots and weave through the rocky outcrops and snowy peaks. He gives me no instructions, so I just keep going until he tells me to return to the helipad.

"Your flying is crap," he barks. "You're going to kill yourself out here."

If he's trying to insult me, he'll have to work a little bit harder. He's never met my dad.

"OK." I shrug. "What should I do differently?"

He shakes his head and gets out of the helicopter.

"Do a better job," he sneers, then walks away.

The first week, all I do is watch him work and discover that his observations about my flying are true. My style isn't right for this type of aerial work. I'm not focused enough, and my spatial awareness is pitiful compared to his. I have a lot to learn, but Grellet has no desire to teach me. Our training days are a complete disaster.

"I'm going to test you some more to see if I can use you for anything," he says one afternoon after returning from a logging operation. "But I doubt I can."

I shake off yet another insult, and we fly to a plateau with a little thirty-by-thirty-foot stone house sitting on it. There's no roof, just four walls and a dirt floor. We get out and Grellet attaches two large, heavy drums full of cement to the belly of the helicopter.

"If you can't place these drums inside the shack, you're out," he states with no emotion.

I've never done any longline work at all, unless breaking Santa Claus's legs counts. I have no idea what I'm doing.

I nod. "OK. Got it."

I take a deep breath and fly the drums toward the house, taking a long, easy approach like always.

Then, I fly *into* the house, taking out the entire thing in about thirty seconds.

The sound is terrible, like an avalanche, and a giant cloud of wet dust fills the windscreen.

"Imbecile!" Grellet screams. "You imbecile! You're like all the other shuttle flight idiots." Suddenly my dad looks like a choirboy.

He berates me for another five minutes. I want to tell him to go to hell, but instead, I tell him he has to give me another chance. I want to be a better pilot, and he's the only one who can teach me this stuff.

"You're treating me like trash, not training me." I stammer a bit. "You can't expect me to fly like you if you don't show me how to do it."

"You should already know how, you little twerp," he spits back.

I don't say anything for a minute and neither does he. Finally, when we're ready to fly again, he gives me some insight.

"OK, your approach is all wrong. You need to come steeper. *Then* you need to fly the load. Don't put yourself in the helicopter. Put yourself in the load," he explains, shaking his head at me.

It's basic information, but it's enough for me to use, think about, and later, master.

Naïvely I thought I would have a couple of weeks to train and practice on the mountain before starting any complex aerial work, but because there aren't exactly a bunch of pilots lined up to fly with Grellet, he's forced to put me to work immediately. The day after the shack incident, he asks me to go drop a weather station—a small box, probably five feet by five—on a ridgeline at about five thousand feet elevation. I've never flown a helicopter that high before. There's less air density, so it lowers the engine performance. It's all new to me, and Grellet does nothing to prepare me. Of course, I mess it up.

A technician comes along to set up the station and direct me where to drop off the box, which is attached by a short line underneath the Lama. It's not too heavy, maybe about fifty pounds. I set it down no problem and feel pretty impressed with myself.

But I have to drop the technician off too.

The ridge is steep and full of snow, and I have *no* idea how I'll get him out safely. I go back and forth about where exactly to let him out and how to make the approach. Just as I decide on the higher, clearer side of the slope, the guy jumps straight into the snow and disappears completely.

I wait for him to resurface, but he doesn't.

There's no possible place to land so I fly back to Grellet as quickly as possible.

He's furious.

The tech turns out to be totally fine, but this doesn't stop Grellet from calling Jacques, begging him to take me back.

"Sorry, Grellet," Jacques says calmly. "Fred is your guy, and you will have to make it work."

Grellet grounds me for the next couple of days and tells me to "watch and learn."

Mostly what I watch is him screaming at his crew and almost beheading an engineer with his tail rotor on purpose. More than anything else, Marc Grellet is teaching me about the kind of pilot I don't want to be.

After a couple of months, I begin to get better. I do little jobs and start to fly the load instead of the machine. I fall madly in love with the Lama. It's an incredible helicopter—soft, sensitive, and perfect for a more intuitive pilot like me. I only have twenty hours in it and am still learning the controls, but I'm beginning to think that putting up with Grellet is worth it just to fly something so amazing.

On a freezing cold day, as winter is kicking into full gear, I walk into the heliport to check the board for my assignments.

Frédéric North: swimming pool delivery, Monaco

It can't be.

I'm doing better than I was, but I'm not ready to be delivering any swimming pools.

A flight assistant standing nearby watches the color drain from my face and explains that I'll be picking up an empty fiber pool, about fifteen feet by forty, with a long line from a flatbed truck then setting it inside a hole outside a villa. The line would be about three hundred feet. The most I've ever worked with is fifty.

I nod. "OK. That doesn't sound too bad."

It's worse than bad.

I fly back to Monaco with a lump in my throat. The villa is tucked into the side of a steep slope overlooking the sea. Every bit of the estate is shining bright and brand-new. The pool will be the cherry on top.

After a brief conversation with the ground crew over the radio, which I barely hear because I'm so nervous, the line is connected to the pool. I raise the collective to lift the load, and that pool starts swinging from left to right, left to right like a trapeze artist preparing for the dismount. I can't control it, and it would be impossible to set down on the truck, so I hover for twenty minutes straight with a pool attached to my helicopter, trying to figure out what to do next.

The wind starts to pick up, and each gust is like a giant hand pulling me all over the place. I ask the ground crew if there's any protocol for this kind of thing, and we all agree that the safest thing is to try and get the pool into the ground.

"OK," I tell them over the radio. "Let's do this."

My first attempt is almost perfect. Then a gust comes at the wrong time, and I miss the target by a few feet. When I go back down for my second approach, another gust hits, and this time the pool swings right into the house, crushing the newly installed sliding windows and taking all the furniture with it. The overhead porch collapses, the pool cracks in half, and the villa is totally demolished.

Grellet doesn't talk to me for ten days afterward. It turns out, again, that assigning me the "pool delivery" was a miscommunication. I was clearly not the right person for the job. I was the only person available.

I get better and better at the aerial work, but working for Marc Grellet gets worse and worse. He treats everyone like dirt and takes no responsibility for his mistakes. When he causes damage to a helicopter during a logging mission and tries to put the blame on me, I know it's finally over.

"You're gonna say it was Fred," he screams at the engineer standing under the busted rotor. "If you don't, I will make your life a living hell, you understand?"

The engineer, looking terrified, nods.

Jacques pulls me out of the longline operation, and I'm so relieved not to have to see Grellet's joyless face every morning, I'm practically singing as I fly the Nice to Monaco shuttle.

At the end of 1989, Philippe and I cover another Dakar and our second Rallye de l'Atlas. By the end, Phillippe is missing Monaco. He wants to get back to his routine and his new girlfriend, but when I'm in the desert filming the cars, sleeping in the bivouac, and filled with adrenaline from morning until night, I can't imagine doing anything else. The nine-to-five rotation isn't my style. I need to find more freedom, and for me, boredom is the opposite of freedom.

On my last day in Morocco, I meet with Jean-Pierre Le Cerf—a businessman turned commercial helicopter pilot. I ask if he'd consider letting me lease one of his A-Stars for the rallies. We make a deal: I'll lease the machine over the summer and do some rotations in Saint-Tropez. If those couple of months go well, I can have it for the races.

I rent a little counter at the heliport in the spring of 1990 and start North Helicopter, my first company.

11

Keep Pushing

IF MONACO IS THE UPPER EAST SIDE, Saint-Tropez is the Hamptons. From a distance, it's a typical Provençal-style village with sunshine-colored stucco buildings, narrow walking streets, and tiny cafés. But if you look closer, the money is everywhere. Just beyond the cobblestone alleys and marchés sit modern estates and luxurious villas. All along the bay you find exclusive beach clubs, superyachts, and movie stars in Patek Philippe watches as big as wall clocks. In Saint-Tropez, I'm not shuttling people to the heliport but to their helipads at home. Nothing on earth is unreachable or unownable, but still, everyone is reaching. This is the one thing a tycoon and a shoeless kid from Senegal have in common.

My little desk at La Môle Airport is immediately busy and stays that way. I am not excited to be doing shuttles again, but I like working for myself—and if I can impress Jean-Pierre, I'll be able to fly the rallies independently in fall. Besides, Saint-Tropez isn't so bad. The customers are pleasant, though most of them are not romanced by the helicopter. Honestly, some of them probably have as many hours in the chopper as I do and are just looking for the quickest way from the airport to the yacht. I do try to make the experience special, though. I want to be more than a ride home.

One afternoon in June, the middle of the high season, I have a shuttle scheduled from Nice for a new client named Laura. I get there early and wait in the arrivals area with my little sign, trying to guess who she is before she finds me. The terminal, like always, is looking like a Brigitte Bardot costume party. Beautiful, barely dressed women wait pouting by the empty luggage carousel while men in linen shirts mill around them—staring, I'm sure, from behind their sunglasses. Laura is not a tourist, though, and I don't expect she'll look like one. I'm flying her alone to a private property.

A tall, elegant brunette comes around the corner carrying a small Louis Vuitton duffle bag. She's effortless and graceful, gliding across the floor in a pair of wide camel-colored pants and a white button-down shirt.

Hello, Laura.

She looks so much like Hanna's mom I can't believe it.

With nothing more than a handshake and a few polite words, we walk through the airport and out to the helicopter.

Right after takeoff, Laura takes a book out of her bag and begins to read, which seems a little rude at first. She's in the copilot seat beside me and could at least pretend to be interested in the trip for a few of the twenty minutes. I am glad to not have to make conversation for once, or to point out every geographical feature of the Côte D'Azur. If Laura is comfortable just being herself, I decide I can be myself too.

Since it's obviously not her first trip in a helicopter and I don't think I'll scare her, I fly the way I want to, fast and close to the water. I can smell the spray from the sea, and the water starts to look like blue glass underneath us. After a minute, Laura closes her book, places it on the glove box, and smiles. There is nothing better than reminding somebody who has forgotten about it that they can fly.

She doesn't say anything until the skids touch down on the roof of her compound, a series of white contemporary block-shaped buildings—the kind of place a James Bond villain would go on vacation.

"I didn't know a helicopter could do that," she says, leaning back into her seat, staring out at the sea, and relaxing her body with a long breath. "I've never had so much fun in one before. I've always thought they were boring. Thank you."

"You're welcome." I smile back at her. "Anytime."

I'm happy when her office calls two days later and asks me if I can take her to Cannes.

"Sure," I say to her assistant. "Do you know if she needs me to wait or she will get a different ride back?"

He clears his throat a little awkwardly. "I'm sorry, you misunderstood. Mme. Clair wants you to go shopping *with* her. Are you available?"

"Uh, yes. OK."

I hang up confused but intrigued at the same time. Laura is married. She's beautiful. She can have anything she wants. Why does she want to spend time with me?

For the rest of the month, I spend my time flying Laura as quickly as the A-Star will go, as close to the tops of the waves as possible. I take her shopping in Nice, to dinner in Monaco, and to her yacht in Capri. Not once do I see her husband or hear anything about him. I don't ask, either, mostly because she's beautiful and I'm doing everything I can to make sure we don't end up in bed together. Even more because she's lonesome and brokenhearted, and because she has everything and seems to feel nothing at all. She comes alive in the helicopter, when the coastline goes blurry out the window and the adrenaline hits. She doesn't need me to be her therapist; she just wants to feel alive. And she's not the only one.

With all the money, beauty, and influence in the world, it seems crazy that my clients would be bored—but many of them are. These are people who have surpassed their goals, amassed their fortunes, and traveled the world. They want for nothing, a thought that terrifies me. I can't imagine what it would be like to live without *wanting*. For months I'm hired to take passengers home, but for many, home seems like the last place they want to be. So I do my best to transport them in a different way, maybe help them see the world from a new angle or give them a little thrill. Nobody has seen everything—not even a movie star or a CEO, and not even Princess Stéphanie of Monaco (who, actually, is one of the more down-to-earth people to step into my helicopter).

One day, as I'm working on my schedule for the week, a red Ferrari pulls up at La Môle, growling to a sideways stop in the parking lot. A bottle blonde in a tight dress and high heels teeters out the passenger side, followed by a nouveau riche guy. He's dressed in a cheesy tropical shirt unbuttoned to the middle, exposing a shocking amount of chest hair. He looks like he sleeps in a tanning bed.

He doesn't bother to open the girl's car door but grabs her butt when she walks around to his side. It's like watching chivalry die all over again.

"We want to go for a ride," he asks, walking up to my desk. The girl giggles. They both smell like sunscreen and booze.

"Where would you like to go?" I ask.

He shrugs. "We don't care. Just take us . . . somewhere."

"Well, I have several sightseeing routes," I begin. "We can go over the bay, out to Monaco—"

"Sure, that's good. Let's just get going," he interrupts. Then he winks at me.

We agree that I'll fly them around for an hour. Price is never a part of the discussion. We walk out to the chopper, and I watch him laugh to himself as he gives the girl another little spanking.

I open the door of the A-Star, and they both immediately take the seats behind mine. Usually the guy wants to sit up front with me. Especially a guy who looks like this one. It's all a little bit strange, but I put it out of my mind, take off, and begin talking into my mic, telling them little stories about the Saint-Tropez Bay.

They don't say anything back.

Suddenly, out of the corner of my eye, I see a flash of blond hair on the seat. The girl is lying down, her chin is tilted back, and she's breathing heavily.

No way. No, no, no. They can't be doing what I think they are.

I check my instruments and see in the reflection on the glass that, sure enough, the hairy guy is on top of her. He's pulled her dress up to the tops of her thighs and is unbuckling his belt. I freeze and stop talking. I don't know what to do. They're so close to me I can smell their sweat.

She starts panting softly.

If they want to get crazy, I decide, *then we'll get crazy.*

Richard Wagner's "The Ride of the Valkyries" begins playing in my head, and I dive straight down toward the Mediterranean. Then I raise the collective and we go up, just as sharply, imitating a boomerang move.

The girl is moaning and screaming. He's grunting like a boar.

I fly super low on the ocean and give them the ride of their life. They finish somewhere over a lavender field outside a medieval village called Bormes-les-Mimosas, but I keep that information to myself.

Before landing back at the heliport, I call the radio and tell the guy at the tower that I have a *very* satisfied couple ready to come out of my machine. The poor girl looks a mess. Her bangs are stuck to her forehead, and her lipstick is smeared all over the bottom half of her face. The guy is sweating and his fly is undone, but it's obvious he's feeling like the king of the world.

I'm not sure whether it counts as a threesome, but when the guy gets out, he pats me on the shoulder and gives me the biggest tip of my life.

North Helicopter is here to provide whatever it takes to help you feel alive.

By the end of summer, Jean-Pierre is satisfied with my care of the A-Star, and he agrees to let me rent it for the Pharaoh's Rally, a 1,900-mile motor race that begins and ends at the base of the Giza Pyramids. I know how to fly a rally race, but I have no idea what it looks like to run one and no idea if anyone will hire me. I team up with Bernard Seguy, a legendary race pilot I know from the Dakar rally, to supply the helicopters and secure the contract. Neither of us has much business sense, but Bernard brings a sense of legitimacy to the operation *and* knows the race director. I bring a sense of adventure, but Bernard's reputation is the only reason we get the job.

Normally the races hire big companies like HeliFrance, and for good reason. The preparation is more than a two-man job. First we must obtain permits to bring the helicopters into Egypt and fly them during the race. There is a mountain of paperwork to sort through, and much of it is in Arabic. I have no idea what I'm doing. The only time I've ever dealt with bureaucrats is when they've needed rides from Nice to Monaco.

I manage to get a permit to follow the race, but not to fly from the airport *to* the race. Then I get a permit to fly over the race, but not to *land* anywhere. Eventually the right paperwork comes through, just in time for me to move on to the maintenance preparation: creating an inventory of the parts most likely to break, sourcing them, and hiring competent engineers with the balls to follow us through the desert and sleep in the bivouac. When I finish that task, I need to find a couple more trustworthy pilots to fly the race with us. Thankfully, Phillippe is available. By the end, we're all astonished that I've managed to pull everything together. All I need to do is keep it together, be responsible, and complete the operation.

The day before the race, the producers ask me to film the host hotel, an enormous white tower in the middle of Cairo. It's an easy assignment: Make the hotel look cool. Get the shot. Keep it simple. And really, when I take off from the heliport, that's what I intend to do.

I approach the building just as the sun begins to set over the city, decorating the sky with spectacular beams of orange and purple. The light shines down on the Nile, which snakes through Cairo, splitting it in two. The A-Star feels incredible and the weather is great, so I slip off my shoes and fly barefoot, thrilled to be dealing with a machine and not a customs official. For the first time in weeks, I feel alive. I hover next to the rooftop pool deck to get an epic shot of the space. They're hosting a welcome party, so the racers, sponsors, and VIPs are all drinking champagne and chatting between the potted plants and lounge chairs. If I come in at the right angle, I can almost make it look like I'm going to land.

But what if I did land? I think.

The deck *is* big enough. If I put the A-Star on the other side of the pool, away from the reception, nobody would even notice. Plus, I wouldn't have to drive out to the airport in the morning.

I know it's illegal, I know that civil aviation will have a fit, and I know I'll almost certainly lose my job—but before I can stop myself, the adrenaline takes over. The skids touch down, I step out of the machine, and I watch the sun as it falls into the Sahara.

"Frédéric!" the race director calls from the other side of the roof. "What did you do?"

"Look, I'm sorry," I say. "I know it was a stupid move, but the footage will be unbeliev—"

"I love it," he cuts me off. "I love it! It's so daring! My heart is like . . . *babababa!*" He laughs, slapping his hand to his chest.

I thought I was going to lose my job.

"Can you do it again?" he asks. "It was amazing! Everyone says it was amazing."

For the rest of the race, both with and without permission from management, landing on top of hotels becomes the norm. Maybe people don't even need to be *in* the helicopter to feel something from it?

During the race, I keep pushing the limit. My job is to fly the "reporters helicopter" and get footage of the cars, collaborating with the film crew to get the most exciting images possible. The camera operator I have on board is Vincent Regnier, a kid about my age who works for La Cinq, a French television network. He's audacious, imaginative, and up for anything. One of the few people on earth willing to push the limit about as far as I am. Instead of keeping fifty feet from the cars, we go fifteen feet away. I fly close enough to trade cigarettes with the drivers, toss packs of Marlboros from the chopper through the car windows. The racers love it. We get close enough for Vincent to piss on motorsport legend Hubert Auriol's Citroën while flying sideways at ninety miles per hour. I think he might have preferred the Marlboros. If it hasn't been done before, we try it, coming in at different angles, manipulating the light, defying the rules. And the race directors and producers have a hard-on for all of it.

With the camera, I can bring people, *all* people, into the helicopter—not just rich guys and their girlfriends wanting to have a good time. Everyone. The race ends and the other pilots go back to their lives and families. Phillippe goes back to Monaco and Bernard goes back to Paris. The thrill begins to wear off, and I start to feel restless.

I go looking for my next adventure. Adrenaline will make a junkie out of anyone.

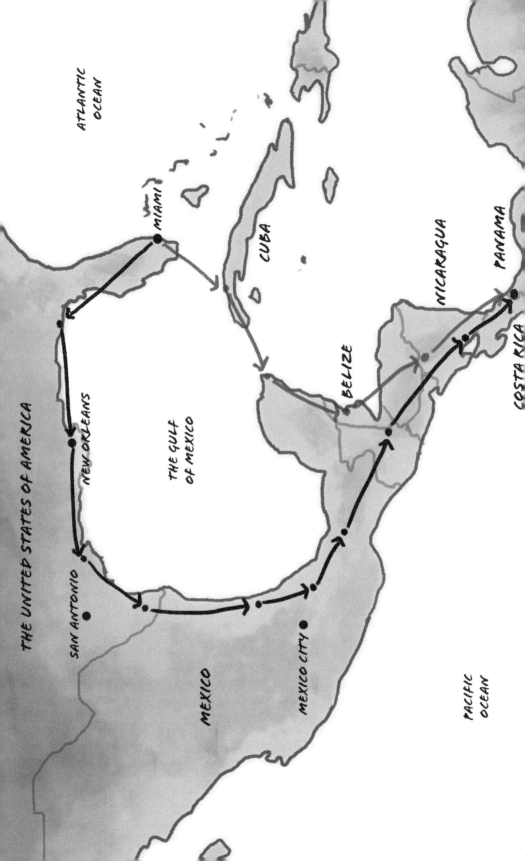

12

BYOC (Bring Your Own Compass)

THE CALL COMES IN around noon.

"Fred! It's Gérard Fusil. Listen, I got your info from the Dakar team. I would like you to fly with us for my next race in Costa Rica."

I am standing at my little Formica desk in the Saint-Tropez airport and talking to my hero. I'm also ignoring a banker with an unlit cigar between his teeth. He is ready for me to take him to the Italian Riviera, but I'm trying very hard not to say anything stupid or embarrassing while Fusil goes over the details.

Gérard Fusil is known by the media as "the French Indiana Jones." As a journalist, he has covered the Tour de France, the Paris–Dakar Rally, the America's Cup, and basically every major sport race imaginable. Now he's created a competition of his own, the Raid Gauloises—the most grueling modern adventure race known to man. No main roads. Bring your own compass. Get to the finish using only canoes, horses, and your own two feet. In the first installment, just nine teams out of twenty-six were able to finish. Fusil is a legend. This man pisses adrenaline.

"*Pardon.*" The banker is playing with his thumb ring and sweating through his linen pants. If I had to guess, I'd say he pisses Dom Pérignon. I smile and hold up a finger, turning away from him as politely as I can. I don't like to make clients wait, but this is Gérard Fusil!

"Fred?" Gérard asks on the line. I can practically see his panama hat and chest hair. "Can you do it?"

I think I can, but he doesn't just want me to fly. Fusil wants me to coordinate. The race is four months away. I would be handling all the helicopters, providing support and transport during the ten-day race. I'd have to be organized and responsible at all times.

My history with responsibility hasn't always been so good, but apart from landing on top of hotels without permission and jumping naked off yachts, I have made some very good choices. I did well during the Pharaoh's Rally, and in December, I'll be the chief pilot for the Paris–Dakar Rally. I can do this. I don't know where Costa Rica is, exactly, but I can do this.

Static buzzes in my ear. I pull the phone away. The reception sucks, but he needs an answer. "What do you say?" he asks.

"Of course!" I reply. "It would be an honor."

I hang up the phone, fly the rich guy to Italy, and wonder how I'm going to pull off the hardest job of my life in a country I can't find on a map.

If the Raid Gauloises is an adventure, preparing for it is an odyssey. Sixteen weeks to get everything together will be possible, but tight. I don't speak Spanish very well, and I've never set foot in a jungle, let alone flown through one. From the other side of the Atlantic Ocean, I'm in charge of sourcing helicopters, hiring pilots and engineers, organizing fuel, and purchasing maps and equipment, all in a nation I had to look up in the atlas they keep in the lounge at La Môle.

How on earth am I going to do business there? I wonder, looking at the atlas entry. It is mostly pictures of coffee beans and poisonous frogs.

Right away, I discover that sourcing helicopters in Costa Rica isn't an option. They have a half-million kinds of animals there (something I also learn from the atlas) but only a few kinds of helicopters. We need the right machines. The race is four hundred kilometers from the Atlantic to the Pacific side of the country. When you're following an inflatable raft down river rapids in a cloud forest, you don't want to be doing it in an antique.

It isn't ideal and certainly isn't in the budget, but the only choice is to source our little fleet from a different country and ferry them over. I don't know anybody in Mexico or Central America, so I call my old friend "John" in Miami.

Jean Pujol is from the South of France. Nobody is really sure how he ended up in Florida, but he is a successful businessman. Nobody is really sure what his business is either, but he lives on a yacht in a marina off 5th Street with a rotating group of big-breasted women. Also, he really does prefer if you call him "John" now, not Jean.

By day, he runs helicopter tours, romantic sunset flights, and Everglades adventures. That sort of thing. He is also involved in "nightlife" in some way, but I don't ask too many questions. He's a passionate pilot who may have even more in-flight hours than I do, and he was kind enough to host me on his boat while I got my American private license. John is a great guy—laid-back, generous, and always up for some fun. Exactly the combination I'm looking for. He also happens to be the proud owner of a Gazelle and an A-Star, which I imagine would do quite nicely in Costa Rica. The Gazelle is small and fast, often used in the military for scouting and surveillance missions. The A-Star is like a Ferrari—slick, agile, and versatile. In an emergency, it's also big enough to accommodate a medical team, a patient, and gear.

I call him at his office at the beginning of October, and it takes about thirty seconds to convince him that ten days of flying through the rainforest with me will be more exciting than sitting at his desk in South Beach. He signs on as a pilot that day and agrees to lend us his machines.

"Ah, Fred! This is going to be insane!" he laughs into the receiver.

I laugh back, though I'm hoping we can keep the insanity to a minimum.

To round out our team, I pick up two guys from the Dakar crew, Marc and Christophe. I've worked with them before, and I like them. Plus they're available, and since they're student pilots working toward their licensure, they're desperate for the hours and will help pay for fuel. Marc is an accountant, and Christophe works in real estate. They don't have a ton of experience, but they've done Dakar, so I know they'll be up for an adventure.

The four of us meet in Miami one week before the race is set to begin. The ferry down is probably going to be as much work as the race, so I get to work planning the journey with John. As far as I can tell, Marc and Christophe are just sitting by the pool. We'll fly down to Key West, then over Cuba, Mexico, and Central America, all the way to San José in Costa Rica. Fusil calls to check in every day and is not thrilled when he hears we have to ferry the machines from America.

"Was there not an easier way?" he asks.

Truthfully, there may have been. The ferry is eighteen hours one way. The important thing, though, is that I found people and machines I could trust.

"Gérard, I've got everything covered," I assure him.

But I still need to arrange customs clearances, secure permits to fly above Cuba, Mexico, El Salvador, Nicaragua, and Costa Rica, and figure out how to find fuel.

Even though most of the English I have is from *Top Gun*, I manage with John's help to work my way through the necessary forms and get us all the permits we need over the course of five days. The route is mapped out. We have money in several different currencies for food and fuel. The machines are in top condition. Somehow, with two days left to spare, I've managed to pull everything together.

"Come for a drink on the boat. We can celebrate." John smiles.

"Not tonight, but thanks. Have fun without me," I reply.

I don't drink or do any of the other things John probably does to celebrate on his boat. I have to stay focused. I'll celebrate when the job is done.

It's five o'clock in the morning, the day before our set departure date, when the telephone in my hotel room starts to ring. I try to ignore it, but the whole thing lights up like a dashboard and the phone rattles so hard in its cradle it practically answers itself.

"Fred North?" the caller asks.

"*Oui* . . . yeah . . . yes," I reply.

"Miami Police. We need you to come down to the station. Your friend Marc is accused of a felony. He needs you to bail him out."

"Wait, what?"

My English is not great at any time, but at five a.m., it is especially bad. I sit straight up in bed and start to sweat, trying to remember what the word *felony* means from *Miami Vice*.

"Sir, can you please repeat the last sentence?" I ask.

The officer hangs up. Right away I call John (who is with at least one female visitor), and together, we drive to the station where Marc is waiting in a day cell.

Miami is a fun place. The weather is great, the clubs are open until sunrise, and the number one hobby of the entire city is to Rollerblade down Ocean Avenue in a Day-Glo thong. Miami is a good time, but not the kind "good time" Marc was looking for last night at 11:56 p.m.

The police station smells like window-washing chemicals and is floor-to-ceiling beige—nothing like the one on *Miami Vice*. Officer Diaz, a small man with coffee-stained teeth, explains that Marc was arrested for trying to pick up a prostitute on the way home to the hotel, romancing her with an irresistible "How much?" from the opposite side of the road. As if that line shouldn't be enough to put a man behind bars, he also happened to try it on the one prostitute who was an undercover cop.

"Jesus," John says, taking a long drink of police coffee from a Styrofoam cup (the only courtesy we're offered). Then he laughs. "His wife is going to kill him."

"I hope so," I breathe sharply. We're supposed to leave tomorrow. I'm losing time that I don't have. I briefly try to explain that we're flying the Raid Gauloises, but nobody in the US knows what that means.

"Like Gauloises cigarettes," I try.

They only sell Marlboro, Camel, and Newport here.

"What do we need to do to get him out of here?" John asks Diaz.

One stack of paperwork and $5,000 later, Marc is following us like a lost dog to the car. We make sure he doesn't talk to any women in the parking lot. Fusil calls an hour later to check in, and I say nothing.

"So far, so good, Gérade." I smile, no longer sure whether I'm a liar or an optimist.

The permits are complete, the maps are organized, the schedules are set, and everyone is out of jail. There is only one more problem left to solve.

The helicopters have a three-hour fuel capacity, and there's no way we can cross Cuba to Mexico in less than three hours. I figured there would be an island or something we could land on in between, but the Gulf, it turns out, is much larger and emptier than the atlas at the airport made it look. I thought we were home free. For hours John and I sit in our small gray hangar going over the options, which include hiring a boat, rerouting, and finding helicopters in Venezuela—another country I've heard of but couldn't locate. Then he gets an idea.

"I've got it, Fred! Give me twelve hours!"

I nod.

Twelve hours will put us past our planned departure time, but it's our only chance. I go back to the hotel and try to sleep, but I mostly think about how I'm going to have to tell Fusil that everything is a mess.

John calls the next afternoon while I'm drumming my fingers on the nightstand.

"We're ready."

When I get to the hangar, John is standing proudly by the A-Star. Inside the machine, he's rigged up homemade auxiliary fuel tanks—two drums with a battery, a pump, and a long hose to stretch all the way to the tank. The setup looks crazy. After twelve straight hours breathing in petrol, John looks a little crazy too.

"It should work." He shrugs. "I think."

I don't even think to question the legality of the tanks. We don't have the time.

"Let's do it," I say. "It's our best shot."

After some testing, some fixing, and a few hours of avoiding Fusil's calls, we get the system functioning around midnight. Exhausted but short on time, we decide to leave at three thirty a.m.

Thankfully, I added two extra days onto our ferry trip as a buffer when planning, but we've already lost one of them.

After a quick nap, John gets in the A-Star with Marc and I get in the Gazelle with Christophe and we take off over the lights of Miami Beach, flying south into thick layers of swamp fog.

Just as the sun starts to come up, we approach our first fueling stop: Key West. I take a deep breath, lower the collective, and land at a tiny regional airport, completely relieved. We're finally on our way.

Our rotors are still spinning when three cars approach from behind. Two gray sedans and a yellow Pontiac Trans Am come barreling toward us in a cloud of smoke and dust. In a quick motion, they flare the back ends of their cars and stop a few meters from the helicopters. Blockbuster movie–style, six guys and a woman, all in denim and regular T-shirts, badges hanging from chains around their necks, get out of the cars and point their guns at us. It's exactly like *Miami Vice*.

"Shut down your engines!" one of them yells.

I look across the tarmac at Christophe, who looks at Marc, who looks back at me, like, I swear it was only the one hooker. Then we all look at

John. He's sweating. Before we can say a word, the cops cuff us, slam us face down onto the hoods of their car, and read us our Miranda rights, which I recognize from American television and Marc recognizes from being arrested a few days ago.

"You have the right to remain silent. Anything you say can and will be used against you in a court of law. You have the right to an attorney. If you cannot afford an attorney, one will be provided for you. Do you understand the rights I have just read to you? With these rights in mind, do you wish to speak to me?"

"*Oui*," I reply. "I mean, yes."

There is no time for lawyers.

After a couple of hours of detention and harassment in the airport, somebody finally tells me what is happening. John bought the Gazelle at an auction. In her former life, she was used for transporting cocaine to Central America and had been seized by the DEA at least once. There's even a weird trap door in the cabin floor, which I'm realizing now was used to ditch drugs midflight. When we started rigging our helicopters with the drums and pumps, someone at the airport had reported the activity and we'd been placed under surveillance. Then we decided to take off in the middle of the night with flight plans crossing Cuba and Mexico. *Merde.* Even I can admit it's not a good look.

We go to jail for a few hours while John's lawyer puts together enough evidence to get us out. The helicopters, though, will be locked up for two to three months. The four of us drive back to Miami in a rented Ford Taurus, and I get ready to call Fusil with the news. But I can't. We still have a few days before the starting gun goes off.

I think about the race all night in my tiny Best Western hotel room. Without the support of the helicopters, the race will probably need to be canceled. There are six hundred people involved. The financial consequences are catastrophic. Exhausted but desperate, I call John's lawyer.

He sighs. "The helicopters are with the DEA, Fred. Your only option left is to go to Washington, D.C. I can get you an appointment with a judge first thing in the morning, but I am telling you right now, your chances are one in ten."

One in ten is better than zero.

"Make the appointment," I tell him.

For every Frenchman with an American dream, there is an American man with a French dream. Judge Harrison is one of those men. He is about sixty years old with a pink, chubby, serious face. I'm worried about communicating this impossible situation to him, but the worse my English is, the more he likes me.

As soon as I open my mouth, his eyes brighten.

"Oh, you're French! *Comment allez-vous? Je m'appelle Judge Harrison.* Not bad, right?!"

He chuckles at himself for a moment and goes on. "I love France. I just got back from a two-week vacation there with my wife. Where are you from?"

I tell him I live in Paris. He gasps.

"Ahh, Paris! Paris! The most beautiful place I have ever seen!"

I start to breathe again, and in the Frenchest way possible, I explain what happened. He has never heard about the Raid Gauloises or Gérard Fusil. I have no contract to show him; everything had been agreed upon over the phone. He listens intently, nodding along, and more than once, raising his eyebrows (understandable). By the end of my story, we're both in disbelief.

He smiles. "I think I can help."

If we pay a $15,000 fine and promise not to fly above Cuba, the helicopters are ours.

I don't have $15,000, but John does. He makes a call to his bank, and like magic, a little elf in an Armani suit shows up at the courthouse with the money. I don't really want to know, but I thank God for whatever it is "John" Pujol does to make a living. I make a call to the guys and tell them to get a good night's sleep. We leave in the morning, and since we now need to go around the Gulf of Mexico, we'll be flying and refueling for forty-eight hours straight.

The Raid Gauloises begins at nine a.m. Our skids touch down at eight thirty. Fusil, in his hat and khaki shirt, is completely breathless when we show up—so relieved we made it, he doesn't bother to ask why or how we were held up for two extra days. There are at least three walkie-talkies attached to his body, all making noise, and his skin is sunburned and looking like pink leather. Racing teams in matching gear check their packs and retie their shoes. Medics fold reflective blankets and stack IV bags into large plastic bins. The camera crews wipe their lenses, something they will do millions of times in the wet of the rainforest.

The jungle is thick, green, and all around us, and everything except the mountain peaks is covered by a layer of mist. Even though I'm half-dead and delirious, I can see that Costa Rica is a beautiful place. It inspires and worries me. I can see why they don't fly a lot of helicopters here. Instead of one or two breathtaking obstacles, this country seems to have all of them: mountains, humidity, storms, forest, coastline, and probably volcanoes. In my experience, the most beautiful things are also the most difficult.

"Be careful," I tell John as we watch the racers stretch and walk down to the river for the starting leg.

The first day isn't too bad, even though all we have time to do when we arrive is refuel, piss in the bushes, and drop off our bags. The weather and the terrain are both erratic, which isn't a surprise, but when you're trying to locate a competitor with a potentially venomous snakebite sitting on a rock between a two-thousand-year-old mahogany tree, patches of fog, and a waterfall, things get a little tense. There is a lot of pressure and plenty of opportunity to make a stupid decision: overload the machine, misjudge the air density, or misjudge the landing area or your own capabilities. All we can do is stay aware, react quickly, and keep ourselves and our machines in good working order—not easy considering the four of us have slept about eight hours combined in the last three days.

The Gazelle is an awesome partner, small and agile like a flying cat, but it doesn't have a ton of power. It's perfectly suited to transporting cocaine in South Florida as the DEA suggested, but probably not designed to cover a race like the Raid Gauloises.

A few days in, the competitors are set to climb Cerro Chirripó, the highest elevation in the entire country. We're supposed to meet them at the summit with medical supplies and support staff. Chirripó is over twelve thousand feet high with temperatures in the mid-nineties. The air will be thin, a big contrast from the jungle, and a big pain in the neck.

Helicopters don't really fly; they fight themselves into the sky, continuously pushing down against the air with the rotors to create lift, like treading water. I'll be able to take off down at sea level, but when I get to the top of the mountain where the air is thin and there's not much to push against, the landing will be tight. If I don't show up at the top of that mountain with electrolytes and doctors, though, nobody will make it down.

After waking up early and staring out the window at Chirripó for over an hour, I know I need help. I call an engineer from Turbomeca in France, the company that manufactures the engines for the Gazelle, and he tells me to remove the shield hat, a thin metal cover, from around the engine and turn off the generator. Maybe, he guesses, it'll give me two or three percent more power when I hit the higher altitude. I'm not feeling great about attempting the flight, but the alternative is telling Fusil I can't do it, which at this point would kill him. I get rid of the cover, put on my sunglasses, and hope for the best.

I walk up to the Gazelle around ten a.m., and a group of passengers is waiting to climb inside. These are not ballerinas. These are big, heavy guys with big, heavy gear: safety equipment, food, medicine, water.

There goes the three percent, I think, nodding and smiling as they settle into their seats.

I'm still so tired from the ferry that I probably shouldn't even be cutting my own food, let alone flying an aircraft. I start the engine and focus, letting the passengers' voices blur together and listening only to the machine. Just as I thought, the takeoff from the lodge is totally fine. I go up slow, being as cautious as possible.

The Gazelle feels good a few thousand feet above sea level, but once we hit ten thousand feet, the air changes, and I can feel the machine struggling. My breath and heart get quick—not nervous, necessarily, but hyperaware. I'm waiting for the Gazelle to tell me what I need to do next. Thankfully, the passengers have no idea how much trouble we're in. I definitely don't need a chopper full of football players bouncing around. Because of the lack of power, the landing won't be graceful. Poor Gazelle will not be living up to her name today.

By the time I spot the landing area, there's almost no power. I have to approach the summit like a Boeing 747, taking a long, slow, ridiculous path that hopefully won't kill us.

"Hang on," I call back to the guys, who are only now starting to realize that things aren't going great. The rotors are turning, but there's no way to create lift. The helicopter is wheezing.

Oh no.

The Gazelle hits the ground like a dead cow falling from space.

I stay seated, trying to catch my breath while the passengers resume their conversations and begin unloading gear.

"Thank you, Fred," one of the crew members says, grabbing a medical kit and patting me on the shoulder.

For what? I think. *The bruise on your butt?*

I got the job done. Barely.

The thought forms a giant lump in my throat. It stays there for days as we bring patients to doctors and doctors to patients, as we film amazing scenes of horses swimming in the river, as the racers climb with shaking legs toward the finish.

Compared with the two weeks prior, the rest of the race is uneventful. There are periods of zero visibility and violent shifts in weather. Skating by on youth and testosterone, we manage to rescue everyone who needs rescuing, transport everything that needs transporting. We have become a team *and* had fun. Bad roads bring good people. After the final team crosses the finish, Fusil asks me to fly him back to the lodge. It sits on the edge of Bahía Drake, a protected cove in the Corcovado National Park where the rainforest seems to walk straight into the ocean. John stays back with the film crew to finish up. We did the job, we got it done. Somehow.

Fusil spends most of the ride back talking about my fantastic work, obviously not knowing how many times I nearly cost him his race, reputation, and livelihood. I feel almost guilty as he chats about his ideas for our next Raid Gauloises together. The operation was not perfect, but at least I didn't give up. I learned about my limits, developed some resilience, and got *very* creative at times. Like I promised so many years ago, I'm not a quitter; I'm a fighter. The Gazelle touches down on the helipad, and we agree to meet at the bar to celebrate . . . after showers, which we both need badly.

When it's getting dark but still legal to fly, I hear a helicopter approaching. It must be John, but if it is, he's flown past the landing zone and toward the ocean for some reason. The landing is tricky; we're in the middle of the wilderness, it's past sunset, and the only air traffic marshal around is the moon. The lodge isn't any help, either, with its low roofline and limited lighting. By design, it blends into the forest. Trying to pick out the differences between the lodge, the land, and the water with nothing to guide you is not easy, especially after the two weeks we've had. I start to worry and head out onto the deck to try and spot the A-Star. I can't see anything.

Suddenly there's a giant splash and silence. Then more silence. It hits me. *John just crashed in the water.*

Altogether, everyone in the lodge screams and starts running toward the beach.

The dark is intense now. Even in the forest, you can't see the leaves smacking you on the arms as you race by. We run for a few steps, trip over a tree root, get up. Run for a few steps, trip over a tree root, get up. Run for a few steps, trip over a tree root, get up. The stars are eventually bright enough to guide us to the beach where several inflatable canoes sit, left over from the race. Without thinking or feeling, consumed by adrenaline, I drag one into the water and start paddling like a crazy person. It's Mauritania all over again but with sharks, which I suddenly remember are plentiful in the area. More canoes burst out from the shoreline, and we all paddle madly beyond the bay and out to sea.

After about twenty minutes, my shoulders are numb and my chest is on fire. We hear voices, people calling, and one-by-one, spot the passengers. The television producer is holding onto his suitcase, bobbing like a rubber duck. A young woman is crying with one arm over a seat. John is barely keeping his head above water. The others are floating quietly nearby, eyes wide and white enough that I can see them against the black water and the even blacker sky.

We haul all six onto our tiny blow-up boats and paddle as madly back to shore as we did on our way out to find them. The A-Star sinks to the bottom of the ocean along with a suitcase full of cash for the ferry back. John can barely speak, but I make out some of what happened through his shivers. As he turned to go back to the landing zone, the helicopter started behaving strangely. All of a sudden, the engine just stopped. He dropped like a dead bird.

His voice is robotic. "It's my fault," he says.

But it isn't his fault. Not at all. The fuel was contaminated.

Is it my fault? I'm not sure.

Maybe I should have vetted our fuel provider more carefully. The guy seemed fine, but maybe I missed something?

Whether it could have been avoided or not, wondering about it ages me about a hundred years. These are *my* guys, *my* team. John is my friend, and now his helicopter is a state-of-the-art fish habitat. I feel responsible.

John, Marc, and Christophe fly back to Miami the next morning. I ferry the Gazelle back on my own, which, without the pressure of the race and the company of a copilot, is awful and lonely. It's just hundreds of miles of blue, above and below, and the echo of my father's voice.

You're a mess, Frédéric.

You're going nowhere.

You need to grow up.

I don't know what to do with you, Frédéric.

Right now, I don't know what to do with myself either. Much of my career, my life, has been fueled by good luck and adrenaline. Both are starting to run out.

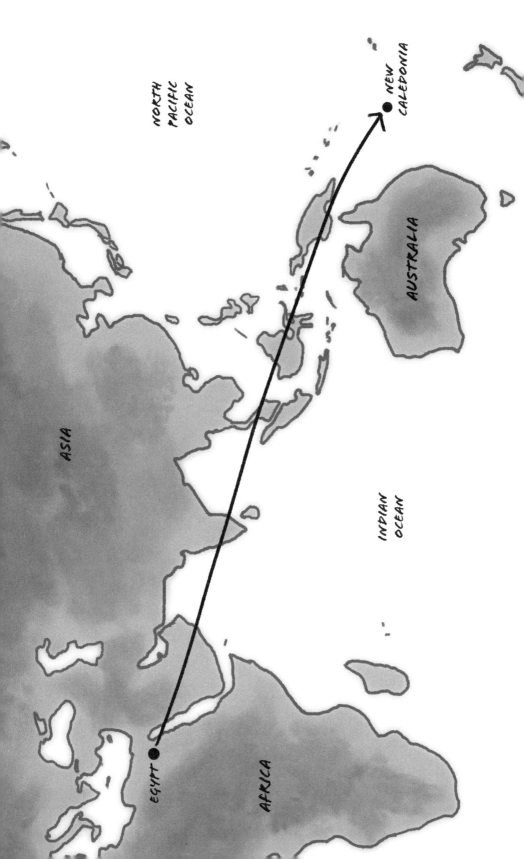

Childhood

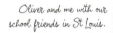

Military School "Prytanee" of
St Louis, Senegal, Africa.

Oliver, me, Catherine, and Isabelle showing off
our Christmas presents.

Oliver and me with our
school friends in St Louis.

Across the street from
our house in St Louis
lived a goat.

Vincent Regnier, camera on the shoulder, trying to get the best shots.

Dakar Rallies

Vincent Regnier, Philippe Tondeur, me, and the TV crew.

The challenges of refueling in the middle of the desert.

My forever pilot outfit: blue pilot suit, red converse, and my fanny pack.

Landing on top of a
hotel in Cairo, Egypt.

Raid
Gauloises

The Gazelle being
stripped by the DEA.

Ferrying the helicopter
from Egypt to Madagascar,
sponsored by Breitling.

The arrest in Key West Airport
on our way to Costa Rica.

World Record

Oxygen test in the chamber in Johannesburg, South Africa.

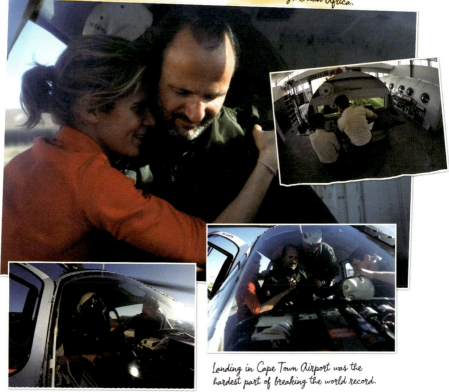

Landing in Cape Town Airport was the hardest part of breaking the world record.

Stunt double for Jason Statham hanging on the nose of the helicopter, pretending to land on a moving truck for the movie "Transporter."

Peter Allwork

Peggy posing with our Alouette II in Morocco in 2001.

Larry Blanford in Brazil

My first pilot jacket and watch.

Hovering in front of Steve Wynn, standing on top of his new hotel, Wynn Las Vegas.

New Beginnings

Flying under a bridge in downtown Los Angeles for an Alfa Romeo commercial.

Filming elephants in Gabon, Africa, for the movie "Tarzan."

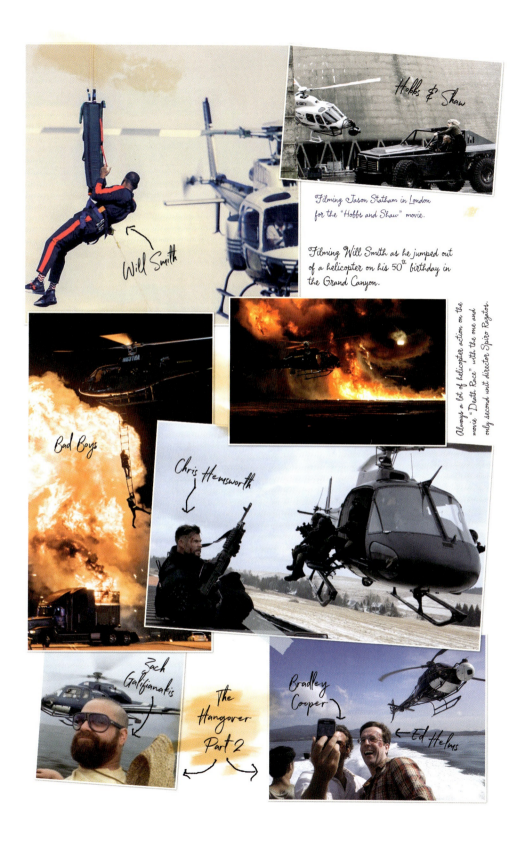

Hobbs & Shaw

Will Smith

Filming Jason Statham in London for the "Hobbs and Shaw" movie.

Filming Will Smith as he jumped out of a helicopter on his 50th birthday in the Grand Canyon.

Bad Boys

Always a lot of helicopter action on the movie "Death Race" with the one and only second unit director Spiro Razatos.

Chris Hemsworth

Zach Galifianakis

The Hangover Part 2

Bradley Cooper

Ed Helms

Family

Naomi, Tom, and Cooper, 2011.

Surfing with Tom and Cooper in Malibu, California.

Tom and Cooper on the set of "Transformers 2" in Chicago with Shia LeBeouf.

Landed on top of a glacier in Iceland when the kids came to visit me on the set of "Fast and Furious."

13

Own Your Mistakes

IT'S DECEMBER 29, 1990, and I'm about to take off for the thirteenth edition of the Paris–Dakar Rally. Gilbert Sabine is with me. He's the race director, as well as the father of Thierry Sabine, the late founder. Gilbert and I built a strong bond during last year. It's a high-stress event for anyone; even more stressful, I'm sure, when it is your son's legacy. I think my *joie de vivre* and humor help him to relax. After the trauma of Costa Rica, his kindness is certainly helping me. I'm chief pilot. It's tons of pressure, and I'm not in a great place to carry it.

The Raid Gauloises was just a few weeks ago, and I'm still pretty beat-up. I haven't had time to process what happened. My mind is spinning. *How can I prevent the next accident? What are the potential dangers?* Before, I didn't worry about a sandstorm unless I was in the middle of one, but now all I can think about are potential hazards and staying ahead of them: engine failures, pilot error, poor visibility, Gaddafi's Libya. Luckily, I have assembled the best team possible. Everyone has more than five thousand hours. Most are in their fifties and have nothing left to prove. They know how to fly safe and do their job right. Several of the pilots, guys like Bernard

Seguy, have flown Dakar enough to know exactly what to expect. Nothing else can go wrong. If it does, it will be the end of me.

Before the race I pieced together a bit of a risk assessment protocol, and I'm hoping it's enough to keep things on track. The team will be proactive, debrief every micro-incident, and learn. Our training as pilots doesn't cover any of this, but I know now that it must be part of every operation—every flight, even. You have to own your mistakes so they don't own you. Discuss them. Say them out loud so they become real. Make a pact with yourself that you will never let it happen again, ever. We will also each understand our roles. The medevac and VIP choppers will stay at five hundred feet. The two lead helicopters will follow whichever motorcycles and cars are out in front. Those machines will need to fly low and through dirty air, so they will be piloted by only the most experienced guys, like Bernard. His knowledge is priceless; he's flown all over Africa and knows everything about everything. Plus, I trust him, and he's extremely respected by the other pilots, which is important because people don't always respect me.

I am the youngest person on the team I'm leading. I might be the youngest chief pilot ever. The guys are great, but plenty of people in the French helicopter industry don't want me to succeed. People are jealous and judgmental. Part of it, I think, is because they don't understand the way I fly. They think I'm crazy, arrogant, and reckless. My connection with the helicopter doesn't make sense to them, and even though I work hard and have a perfect safety record, they still think I'm irresponsible. The other reason they don't like me is because they are haters. No matter what I do, they will have something bad to say about me.

Gilbert and I fly over Chevilly-Larue, a suburb south of the city where the race begins, to watch the cars line up. I realize as they drive into position that this is what I've dreamed of my entire career, ever since I was washing helicopters for Bastien and pissing my pants in the Enstrom with Pascal and his bad jacket. *I am the chief pilot for the Paris–Dakar Rally. Holy cow.*

I tell myself I'm ready, I'm prepared, and that the race will go perfectly. And it does. Somewhere along the way, I lose my mental virginity and grow up.

After the rally, I decide to keep going with the adult thing and settle down. I'm almost thirty years old. Everyone around me is getting serious about life, getting married, getting pregnant, getting a big job at a bank—that sort of thing. I remember my parents at thirty. Though they were also running around Africa, they were doing it in the name of education. They had kids and had each other. They had roots; I have a motorcycle. It's time to make a change. I rent a cool industrial loft in Paris near Place de la Bastille, on Rue de la Roquette. Having a semipermanent address and a place to get mail is definitely a step in the right direction.

The loft is a ground-level unit at the end of a lush courtyard. It's about twelve hundred square feet with big, tall, black metal windows and an unnecessarily large and heavy front door. A single bedroom is located up on a mezzanine level, and everything else is in the open down below. Sure, it's the perfect cliché bachelor pad, but since I'm the perfect cliché bachelor, it doesn't bother me.

I keep a small collection of pilots' helmets perched on the windowsills, and I hang my old Harley on the wall opposite the kitchenette. It looks amazing even though it is slowly leaking motor oil onto the rug. To solve the problem, I place a potted plant left behind by the previous tenant underneath it. Somehow the ficus thrives on a diet of Castrol and air. Speaking of Castrol, the finishing touch is a beautiful used Porsche 911 Carrera convertible that I park just outside in the courtyard. The aesthetic is *Secret Garden* outside, *Days of Thunder* inside, and I love it. No more *chambres de bonnes* or bivouacs (at least not for now). I have a place to land, a home. I feel proud. Whatever the next step in life is, I'm ready to take it.

I meet Camille in 1991, just after I turn thirty. Her father, Patrick, introduces us. He's the chief pilot of planes for the Paris–Dakar Rally, and I love the guy. He's friendly and passionate and sort of took me under his wing during the last race, which was nice. When I think of someone who has it all, I think of Patrick—successful pilot, married, two grown children, handsome, good hair. He likes his work, but he likes other things as well. He has a home outside the city, a charming *longère*-style house with a windmill and a little river crossing a big green backyard. When he invites me there for lunch one weekend, I accept immediately.

I show up expecting something similar to the family meals I know: quiet and orderly, a real sense of ceremony, and not enough salt. Patrick's family is different. He and his wife are warm, generous, and in love after more than twenty years. The family is close. The kids move easily around the house, joking with their parents and helping here and there with the cooking. I watch them like they're zoo animals all laughing together over braised meat, perfectly salted vegetables, and small glasses of Bordeaux. I haven't heard from anyone in my family all year.

This, I tell myself, *is what I am missing.*

I ask Patrick's daughter, Camille, to dinner that day.

Camille is kind and cute, fair-haired, and curvier than most French girls, which I like, especially after Hanna's macrobiotic diet. She doesn't smoke. She doesn't complain. She supports and encourages the work I do and even goes so far as to be interested in it. I could not design a more perfect woman. We get serious quickly, and after one month, Camille wants to move in. I can't tell whether it's sensible or impulsive, but I say OK.

The day she brings all her stuff over, I'm not home. I do ask if she needs help, but she tells me not to worry, she's got everything covered. (Like I said, the perfect woman.) I'm excited to live with her. I haven't been in a serious relationship since I was married, and I miss having someone around at the end of the day, especially someone who isn't counting calories.

Around six in the evening, the day of the big move, I shove my shoulder into the stupid giant door and call out, "Camille?"

I step inside and suddenly, my eyes sting. I start gagging. My loft smells like a retirement home. It's like every herb, spice, and flower has congregated in my sinuses. I look to the window ledge; my pilots' helmets are gone. In their place are several bowls of potpourri: crinkled carnations, giant sticks of cinnamon, shriveled berries. There's a lace cloth on the table, a few China figurines displayed on the shelf, and about seventeen floral pillows on the couch.

Merde.

"What do you think?" Camille smiles, popping down from the bedroom. *I don't even want to know what she did up there.*

My eyes are watering, mostly from the smell—but also from the reality I've gotten myself into.

"I love it," I lie, in complete shock.

She wraps her arms around my neck, and we make dinner. It all tastes a bit like rose petals.

At first it's just potpourri, but then she wants to paint the walls a deep purple color and says she can't decide between "Elegant Plum" and "Byzantium." The walls are concrete, and plums are not elegant. I manage to hold her off with a "maybe."

A few days later we're sitting on the couch, and she jogs excitedly across the room to grab a catalogue.

"Fred, I have something to show you."

I'm immediately terrified when I see how many pages she's marked. She tucks her body back in next to mine and begins pointing out bedroom furniture sets. I start to panic.

I don't want to buy a sleigh bed made from cherrywood with matching side tables and a six-drawer dresser, but all Camille wants in the whole world is a sleigh bed made from cherrywood with matching side tables and a six-drawer dresser. I'm dizzy. I don't know what to do.

"Can we talk about it another time?" I ask.

"Of course, my love." She smiles, kissing me like a little boy on top of the head, then wanders off, probably to mark more pages in her beautiful country houses magazine-thing. I go into the bathroom to splash cool water on my face and the back of my neck. When I look up, I notice a furry pink cover on my toilet seat. This just isn't going to work. I break up with her the next day. She tells me she'll never love again, which is horrible to hear, but three months later, she's engaged to somebody else and my loft still smells like a herbs and spice shop.

When Bernard Seguy calls about the Pharaoh's Rally in October, I'm ready to go and hopeful that the loft will return to its original smell by the time I return.

Flying into Cairo feels like going home, much more so than actually going home does. The race director meets us at the airport and gives both Bernard and me a big hug. He's known Bernard for years, and he loves me because I'll land wherever he tells me to.

"How have you been, boys?" he asks, slapping Bernard on the shoulder and walking us out to a waiting sedan.

"It's good to be back," I tell him, and I really mean it. As soon as I entered African airspace, I could feel my body relaxing. What I do here is simple. I don't have to manage anybody's feelings but my own. All I need to do is fly the helicopter, be responsible, and focus. No problem.

I'm in the film helicopter again—this time with Vincent Regnier, my favorite cameraman and dear friend. Everything is going amazing. Both of us want to do something different, give the audience something better, and show off the location in a way most people have never seen it.

One day we're done filming the cars and need some nice shots to show off the day's location—a strip of sand along the Nile, south of Cairo, almost to the Sudan border. The sun is setting, it's the same orange and purple Egyptian sky I remember from last time, and I'm flying toward the river at a ninety-degree angle. Vincent gets footage of the trees and small villages along the river, a postcard-perfect landscape. He's sitting behind me like always with the door open and the camera on his right shoulder.

I notice two trees a bit taller than the others, about 150 yards apart and forty feet high. It would be a perfect entry point for an epic shot. Vincent agrees.

What I don't notice are the electrical poles attached to the trees and the small power line crossing from one to the other. I fly high the first pass, and then we turn around to go again, lower. That's when I see it.

"Get inside!" I yell to Vincent, who is positioned partially outside the chopper door to get the shot.

"Vincent!" I scream again. We're headed straight for the cable, which is thin and carefully hidden against the sky. If he doesn't move now, it will slice straight into his legs.

He leaps back with a tenth of second to spare, and we brace ourselves.

The shock is massive. Vincent screams. The machine dives down forward, and when the skid catches on the wire, it flips us almost upside down. There's not a hint of sky in the windscreen. All I can see is dirt. The cable comes loose, and we're sling-shotted back up quickly. I'm reacting with so much adrenaline and intensity, all our movements are fast and jerky. The machine steadies, and miraculously, we're OK.

"Fred," Vincent says, shaking.

I look outside and see the giant converter that was attached to the pole lying on the ground. It's on fire.

Merde.

We land right away, and I get ready to radio race control. I made a big, expensive mess, and the sooner they can start cleaning it up, the better.

I open the door to get some air while we wait for race officials and, I'm guessing, the French embassy and the cops. I see two figures approaching in the distance. Most people are friendly, and I'm hoping they can help us. Before I know it, an angry Egyptian guy pulls me down from the helicopter, puts a shoe on my throat, and sticks his rifle to the middle of my forehead. He's spitting at my face and yelling in Arabic. The other guy starts spit-yelling at Vincent, who stays in the chopper with his harness buckled. A crowd gathers. For ten minutes, they all scream, and I wait to be publicly executed. They keep yelling, and we keep telling them we don't understand. We're getting nowhere, so finally they summon a translator.

A skinny teenage boy wanders over from the fringes of the crowd, looks at me, and says in broken English with a thick Arabic accent: "He wants me to translate."

The yelling guy yells again, and the boy speaks.

"You break TV."

The yelling guy points at a shack a couple hundred yards from us and yells again. The boy speaks.

"You buy a new TV, pay one million dirhams to buy new TV."

A million dirhams is roughly $10,000.

Vincent looks over at me confused, like, *Are they serious?* We were almost shot over a few episodes of *Dallas.*

"No problem, I will pay," I say, but before we can agree on a deal, a police car arrives and everyone starts yelling again.

It's 110 degrees out, dust everywhere, and I'm still in shock. Vincent is too. Before our heartbeats have a chance to return to normal, the cops load us up, drive us to the station, and throw us into a cement cell with no windows and nowhere to sit. It smells like sweat and fresh piss.

Vincent spends his time thanking God he didn't get electrocuted, and I quietly have a nervous breakdown, trying to debrief with myself everything that went wrong.

How did we not see the cable?

Why didn't we assess the shot from the ground first?

Why am I still making mistakes?

We're released the next morning after a long night with no food, no sleep, and no idea if anyone from the rally is coming to get us or even knows we're here. The race agrees to compensate the village, restore the power, and get them their precious game shows back. I don't have time to ask myself too many more existential questions. We finish the last day of filming, and three days after the Pharoah's Rally ends, I'm on my way to New Caledonia for the next Raid Gauloises.

I don't know much about New Caledonia, and as we fly what feels like an impossible distance, I keep wondering if we're *ever* going to land there. It's the farthest I've ever been from home, and I'm exhausted. My nerves are fried.

"Sir, are you OK?" the flight attendant asks. She's the only flight attendant. The plane is the size of a city bus.

I smile. "Yeah. I'm fine, thank you."

I'm definitely not fine, though. I'm more tired than I ever thought possible, and my stomach is sick from fatigue. My eyes are dry and pink. As we start to descend, my head keeps bobbing in and out of sleep.

I didn't plan any rest days. After the insanity of the last Raid Gauloises, I convinced myself that this one would be easy. Fusil sourced the helicopters locally, and my teammates are professionals—not the kind who need babysitting. I have Bernard (who I'm sure would also have appreciated a rest day or two) and a local pilot who knows the island well. My hope is he can brief us on the terrain and conditions.

From the plane, New Caledonia looks like an unfinished puzzle: one large banana-shaped island in a turquoise lagoon surrounded by several smaller land masses in irregular rocky configurations I've never seen before. We're 750 miles east of the coast of Australia, and I have no idea what season or time zone I'll be stepping into. We land in Nouméa, the capital, and Gérard Fusil is waiting for us in the airport wearing what looks like the exact same outfit I saw him in last year: an Indiana Jones hat, a blue canvas "Raid Gauloises" shirt, and cargo shorts. He has fewer walkie-talkies this time.

"*Bienvenue!*" he shouts, clasping his hands together and smiling. "Are you ready?"

I'm not. I was in Egyptian jail seventy-two hours ago and took out the power for miles south of Cairo.

"Of course!" I lie cheerfully. "Let's go."

We load our things into the choppers and fly off to a smaller island. There, the very next day, the race will begin with the crack of Fusil's pistol.

I haven't had time to scout any of the locations, and the island is more rugged than I expect—and though I wouldn't have guessed it possible, this race seems more demanding than the last. The competitors have to sail traditional Kanak boats, navigate a labyrinth of mangroves, and climb slick, bald canyon walls. We spend a lot of time just checking in on the teams, knowing that in a split second something could go wrong and we'll need to be there. Before lunch on the second day, we get ready to meet the competitors with food and medical supplies in a ravine made of black rock and ferns, dotted with fizzy white waterfalls.

Fusil rides in my helicopter, and Bernard flies the media chopper. I let him go ahead so the journalists can get a good, clear look at the terrain, and also because I'm brutally exhausted. Thankfully, we're in a remote area. There aren't a ton of buildings or natural obstacles, and we're not dealing with any crazy elevations this time around. Nobody has called for a medevac; we're just checking in. There are no emergencies. *Thank God.*

We near the mouth of the gully, and it's beautiful enough to make me sit up. I've seen rainforest, but this is new. It's totally epic, a Garden of Eden. Fusil is in heaven, and we're only about five miles from the checkpoint, where we can get out and explore.

Bernard flies right, I follow. He goes left, I follow, slightly lower but not by much. Suddenly Fusil is shouting.

"Oh merde! Oh merde!"

A big fat cable is stretching out in front of us, maybe ten feet away. It's cloud-gray and completely invisible against the overcast sky. *Jesus Christ.* By the time I spot it, there's no time to change course. We're going to hit it. In my head, I go over potential reactions the machine will have.

If the cable is strong and secured tightly, we'll flip over and drop like a rock, rotor-first. Dead meat.

If the cable is weak, we'll get tangled for a moment, but if I adjust properly, I may be able to get us out alive.

I'll be fired. I'll never fly again.

Fusil closes his eyes. I hold my breath. We brace for the impact.

Two very long seconds later, we're still flying. We missed the cable by a tenth of an inch.

"That was close," Fusil laughs. "Very close."

He is the only person on earth who would laugh about this kind of thing.

We land at the checkpoint. The place is lit up with activity, which is good because I don't want to think about the fact that I almost hit another power line when I'm still recovering from hitting the last one. I can't carry anything else right now. Bernard finds me through the crowd.

"Fred," he says, "are you OK? What on earth happened?!"

"I don't know," I reply. My voice is shaking when it comes out.

Something needs to change. *I* need to change.

Bernard and I debrief the next day and put even more protocols in place: Fly higher.

Always ground scout the locations before attempting any low-flying moves.

Check in with the locals.

Don't trust the organizers of the event because they are not pilots.

Don't jump from one event to another.

Be more involved in the preparation.

Above all, don't rely on anyone but yourself.

Thinking back, I'm the only person I have ever been able to rely on. But what if I can't trust myself anymore?

"Everything will be fine," Bernard says. "You just need to take better care of yourself."

He's right, but I don't know how to do that.

We get a day off before the race ends, and the local pilot, a Melanesian guy called David, and I decide to go swim in the lagoon. I'm thinking that a day of rest and unwinding is exactly what I need, exactly the sort of thing Bernard was getting at.

We drive to a little moon-shaped cove in David's jeep, and the beach is completely empty when we arrive. We put some music on (Jimmy Cliff, of course) and walk toward the water. The pure white sand feels like silk on my bare feet, and after days of heavy gray cloud, the sun is finally out and warming our faces.

David takes his shirt off and walks into the water up to his chest. I follow. Many people come to New Caledonia for the diving, and I can see why. The water is warm and impossibly blue. The island is protected by a barrier reef teeming with marine life: neon-colored fishes, urchins, anemones, that kind of thing. There are sharks as well, but David promises me they are nothing to worry about. The sea snakes, though, are another matter.

When we first arrived, they briefed us about the sea kraits like they were public enemy number one. Considering they also have earthquakes, tsunamis, cyclones, and bushfires here, I thought the focus on kraits was a little weird. They explained that the animals are extremely venomous, mainly because they feed in the ocean and have to kill their prey quickly so they don't lose it. One bite, and in less than three minutes, you're dead from a heart attack. Honestly, I didn't pay too much attention to the sea krait speech. I was exhausted and figured it was mostly for the competitors.

David is talking to me about the biodiversity of the reef or something when I notice a strange form floating in the water. It looks at first like a piece of wood, but as it gets closer, I notice it has stripes and it's moving like a whip. *Merde.*

David looks at me and mouths, *"Calm."*

At the briefing they told us the snake wasn't going to do anything if it felt no threat, so I focus super hard on not appearing dangerous. I close the palms of my hands, stay still, and smile—not that the snake knows about smiling.

Its long striped body moves between us, flicking the water with its paddle-shaped tail.

Jesus.

We stay still long after it passes us and turn just in time to watch it shoot up onto the beach and into the bushes.

"Are you OK?" David asks.

I'm still not OK. No matter what I try to do to keep away from danger, it always seems to find me.

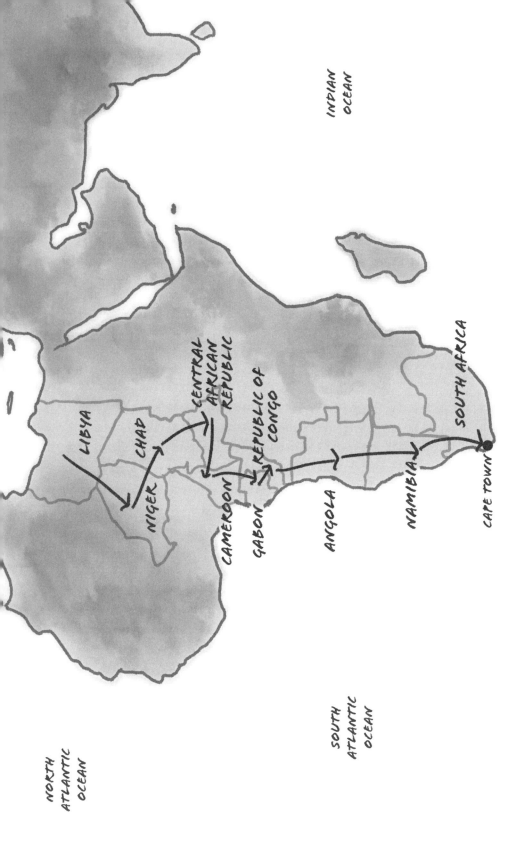

14

Read the Signs

I NEED A BREAK. I know I do.

It's late October 1992, and I have almost two months until the next Paris–Dakar. I need to go home, where there are fewer power lines, venomous sea snakes, and angry, armed Egyptians guys addicted to prime-time television. I'm exhausted. All I want to do is sleep in my own bed in my own (potpourri-free) home, prep for the next race, and recover.

But then Laurent calls.

"Fred! You're home! It's Laurent. Do you mind if I drop by?" he says.

"Yeah, sure," I reply. I'm guessing he's already on his way over, but I have no idea why.

"Great!" he shouts. "I want to introduce you to someone, a woman! Ha!"

I met Laurent during the Dakar rally. He's a gifted photographer and probably an even more gifted playboy—the kind of guy who has celebrity friends and shows up to every party with a bottle of Dom Pérignon and a string of leggy, uncomplicated blondes. I have been with plenty of girls like that—the kind who like the idea of racing drivers and pilots but get bored as soon as you start talking about race cars and helicopters. The chances of

Laurent showing up at the door with the love of my life, or even someone I can tolerate, are low. I'm not excited about it. I don't want to give myself too much credit, but I think I'm beginning to outgrow this sort of thing.

"Fred!" Laurent says again. I'd forgotten we were still on the phone. "Look, you really need to meet Stefi. She's different. She's *American*."

He says the word *American* like the word *Ferrari*. I can't resist.

Fifteen minutes later, they show up at my loft.

Stefi is beautiful, loud, and a little bit mean, a perfect mix of Cindy Crawford and Cruella de Vil. She's wearing a silly Coca-Cola-colored fur and smells like three different brands of cigarette. I like her right away. She walks around my loft like she owns the place and introduces herself while the other girls Laurent has brought trail behind him like baby ducks, too shy to even say hello. Stefi tells me she's in her mid-thirties, a real estate consultant, and the single mother of a little girl.

Wow.

She's direct.

Laurent is right; Stefi *is* different. She looks like she could be on *Melrose Place*, but here she is at mine instead. Stefi is the American Dream—big hair, big voice, big confidence.

And I like the accent too.

Sure, she's a cliché, but so am I. We make plans to go to dinner.

I pick her up in my freshly detailed Porsche on what feels like the coldest night in November. It may also be the most beautiful. Paris is always romantic, but with the holidays coming, the city is like a movie set wrapped up in warm white lights and all kinds of decorations.

Stefi is wearing her heavy fur coat again. It barely fits inside the car, and I dislike everything it represents, but I'm not going to give her a lesson on style and simplicity on the first date. Even if I do feel like I'm having a conversation with a grizzly bear. We drive along and talk, eventually settling at a tiny café near Montmartre. We stay until midnight. She tells me about her daughter and growing her business. I tell her about the rallies. She's warm and easy to talk to. I like her smile, her way of talking with her hands, and her ambitions. She likes mine too. It's the best first date I've ever been on, even if she is dressed like a bison.

On the way to her place in the 7th arrondissement, we stop at a traffic light. We're listening to music and she's trying to explain to me how she made it from Dallas to Paris. Suddenly the doors of the car in front of us fly open. Four huge guys get out and head to the first car waiting at the intersection. They pull out the driver, throw him to the ground, and start beating him senseless.

Without really thinking, I jump out of the Porsche to try and startle them, break it up, or something. They just keep going, kicking him in the ribs and stepping on his face. At first I think it's a carjacking, but then I notice the guy is Black and start to worry it's some kind of racist thing.

"Hey!" I yell at the guys as loud as I can.

They stop long enough for the victim to get up and take off down a side street.

The thugs aren't too happy with me. Before I even understand what's happening, I'm on the ground and they're kicking me like I'm a dog. I try to cover my face with my hands, but it's useless.

I figure Stefi will start screaming, honk the horn, or something. She doesn't.

Out of the corner of my eye, which is beginning to swell, I see her in the front seat. She is sitting still with no emotion on her face, petting at her fur. *What the heck?*

The guys kick me around for a few minutes but eventually decide I'm bruised enough. They get back into their crappy little Nissan and take off. I lay on the road, slowly rolling my head from side to side in a small, warm puddle of blood.

I make a sound.

My eyes are puffed up, my ribs are broken, and judging by how many sets of traffic lights I see above me, I have a concussion. Then I hear a voice and realize the driver who was attacked has returned.

"Are you OK, man? I . . . I should have stayed. I was scared."

"I think so," I tell him, but I would have been more OK if he'd stuck around and given me a hand with the others. He walks me over to the car. Stefi seems totally unaffected. She reaches over and unlocks the driver's side door, picking at her nails while I buckle in. I take her home.

"I hope you feel better." She smiles.

She's acting like I have a stomachache. I have two black eyes and a possible brain injury.

It's rude. And bizarre.

Even more bizarre is the fact that I want to see her again. I like her. I might be crazy about her. Or maybe I'm just crazy.

Stefi and I go out a few more times before I leave for the Paris–Dakar Rally. I'm still crazy about her, but thankfully I haven't been caught up in any more random street fights. My injuries heal quickly, and I have time to finish prep, which is good because this Dakar is a big deal. The race is going all the way to Cape Town.

I'm managing a team of eight helicopters: eight pilots and four engineers. We have to cross Africa from north to south, and this time, Gaddafi's Libya will be the easy part. It's a complex route through even more complex territory. We'll cross Niger, Chad, Central African Republic, Cameroon, Gabon, Republic of Congo, Angola, and Namibia. We're hoping to bypass the region of Zaire completely because it's too unstable. Even though I'm chief pilot, I'm flying the camera helicopter, filming the leading cars, and working with Vincent again. More and more, I'm drawn to this kind of work; chasing a great shot of the cars is more exciting to me than chasing the cars themselves. But maybe more excitement is not the answer.

At the end of the first week, we're at the border between Niger and Chad. We've been flying above the Sahara for days and are happy to see grass and trees again.

Typically, when you cross a border, you have to clear customs. Because of the race, we're exempt from those formalities. The Paris–Dakar officials have arranged for us to cross from country to country easily, the same way the cars are doing it. No one stops for long. If they did, it wouldn't be much of a race. Each country has a simplified customs procedure for us that hardly takes any time.

We head from Niger to Chad a little bit before the leading car, waiting for him in what feels like the middle of nowhere. Vincent wants to film the Peugeot car crossing over—nothing special, just a shot to tell the story of the day—but the car is taking forever. There are a few dry-looking bushes, some baobabs, dust, and not much else around us, but I do notice a little military post not far off. The tower is maybe twenty feet tall with a big rifle on top and a little shack sitting beside. A couple of soldiers are hanging around and talking. It's the kind of thing you see at every border in Africa, and we have no reason to think anything of it. We were told there were some tensions between the two countries, but nothing we should be overly worried about. The drivers were still going through just fine.

"Come on," Vincent says. He's not complaining. He's just ready to get the shot and move on.

We're hovering, crabbing slowly sideways about two hundred feet up, just waiting for the car to arrive. Vincent is smoking a cigarette and has his handheld camera ready.

Suddenly we hear the sound of heavy weaponry—slow-motion firing in a very consistent rhythm, *bah-bah-bah.*

It seems pretty far away, and guns aren't uncommon here, so we aren't freaking out.

Then a round of bullets passes about fifteen feet in front of us. They're a few inches long and have red trackers on them, added so the shooter can adjust the aim and orient himself to the target.

We don't say anything. Vincent's face goes white. I'm sure mine does too. Both of us realize at the same time that *we're* the target. The engine is drowning out the sound of the guns, but the bullets are certainly coming for us.

Bah-bah-bah!

I dive down from about fifty feet. Unfortunately, the terrain is flat and barren, so there's no place to hide. We're toast. I'm only about five feet off the ground, but I fly like a maniac, as fast as I can away from the tower. They keep shooting at us. The bullets come closer now, and I see they're about the size of my finger. Any contact, and we'll be done. Every single muscle in my body is tense. I just keep flying as fast as I can until we're finally out of range.

About ten minutes later we land, covered in sweat, and check over the machine. Somehow it didn't sustain any damage, and we're able to fly safely to the next race stop and report the incident. That night, the journalists covering the race in N'Djamena wake up to dead bodies just outside their hotel doors.

Our stay in Chad is short. Locals had warned race officials about potential rebellions, but nothing was going to stop the race. We try our best to stay safe, to keep on top of the issues inside and outside the helicopter, but the political climate—like the weather—changes from mile to mile. By the time we enter the Central African Republic, refugees have begun fleeing Chad to Niger. A strong wind eats up our fuel supply and we *have to* fly over openly mutinous Zaire, which we do with our butt cheeks clenched. Despite all the preparation in the world, we can't predict the future. We don't always know what we're flying into, and there is no promise that we'll be flying out.

When the race ends in Cape Town, I'm just happy to be in one piece. All I want to do is relax and forget about things like risk assessments. But I can't forget about it too much because Stefi is coming to see me.

Things are moving quickly between us, but really, we don't know each other well. I can tell Stefi likes adventure; so do I. And I can tell she likes the finer things in life—no crime there. We need to spend some real time together to see if this can be something. She decides that a little vacation at a lodge by the Orange River near Augrabies Falls is the perfect opportunity. I fly us there in the A-Star, which, as I'd hoped, impresses her. Bernard and the rest of the team are staying at the hotel too.

The lodge is located on top of a steep cliff overlooking a crazy-powerful, diamond-white waterfall that shoots down into a canyon. The whole place is stunning. Our guide, an incredibly tall, incredibly friendly Afrikaner named Johan, shows us around the property pointing out the restaurant, the pool, and the hiking trails. We turn a corner that opens up to a ridge.

"My friends!" he says with a more serious voice. "Do not ignore the signs."

I look around.

DO NOT CROSS

DANGER AREA

NO TRESPASSING

KEEP OUT

WARNING

DO NOT ENTER

The guy has every kind of danger sign they print, and he's posted them everywhere.

"Since the sixties," he goes on, "nearly *twenty* people have been swept over the falls and died."

He says the number twenty like it's about forty thousand, just to be sure it sinks in.

Sadly, the statistic doesn't surprise me at all. People are reckless. They don't have any respect for nature or each other.

I look over at Stefi and she's nodding along, taking all of it in.

The next morning I have some prep work to do for a springtime race in Morocco, and Stefi tells me she's going for a hike. She's wearing tennis shoes and a pair of tight denim shorts that go all the way up her butt. I don't think she'll make it very far in those.

"Have fun," I tell her. "Be safe."

She kisses me and rolls her eyes, flirting with me.

"I'll see you at lunch." She smiles and walks off.

Around noon, I head to lunch with the rest of the team as planned. Stefi doesn't show up.

"Well, it didn't take her long to figure out you're a loser!" Bernard jokes. We all laugh, but I have a bad feeling. A couple of hours later, we all do. Stefi is gone.

We search the property, checking the typical places: the pool, the gym, the bar, and all the hiking trails. We ask the other guests. There's no sign of her. When she's gone five hours, I start to really worry. It's a hundred degrees out, she doesn't have any water, and she's definitely wearing the wrong shorts. She could be in real trouble. Since we're making no progress, Bernard and I decide to get in the A-Star and fly over the area. Johan comes too. He's panicking worse than both of us, going on again about the signs.

We fly for forty-five minutes. Nothing.

"Check the river," Johan tells us.

"No, no . . . she wouldn't do that," I tell him.

I start to turn back to the lodge. I'm low on fuel because I didn't plan for a missing persons search on my vacation.

"Just check the river," Johan says again.

As soon as we make our turn toward the falls, I see Stefi. She's kneeling on a flat rock, sunburned like a burst tomato. The rock is maybe fifteen-by-fifteen feet, right at the edge of the humongous waterfall. One wrong move and she's gone. I have no idea how she got there, and there's no clear way to get her up.

The falls create a strong, unpredictable wind. I'm not sure if we can get close enough in the helicopter to rescue her. Every second she's stuck there, she's at risk. The rock is right up next the canyon wall, and the only option would be for her to come as close as possible to the edge and grab onto Johan's hand while I hover. I'd have to fly her all the way to the top, hanging from the side. It's beyond crazy.

We get close, but the force of the waterfall is shocking. It jostles us around and covers everything, including Johan's arm and Stefi's rock, in mist.

I hover a tiny bit closer.

Miraculously, she grabs Johan's arm and manages to hang on as we fly her to the top of the canyon. I don't look down at her. I can't. She has no respect for life or death. She has no respect for me. Stefi is dangerous.

I can't stand to be in the same room as her, but I can't let her go either.

We go back to Paris, and I stay busy. I know I need to sort out my feelings. Stefi is fun and exciting. She does what she wants, when she wants, and I never know what's coming next. But Stefi is also terrifying. She's impulsive and dramatic, she never apologized after the waterfall incident, and when I really think about it, I don't know if I've ever heard her apologize for anything. One minute she's the girl of my dreams, the one I want to build a life with—the next, she's a total nightmare. I have no idea what to do about it, but since flying over St. Petersburg feels safer than sleeping next to her, I leave for the Paris-Moscow-Beijing Rally.

The Paris-Moscow-Beijing is a 9,600-mile cross-continental trek that spans eastern desert, mountains, and eleven countries. Since much of the territory was totally forbidden to us during the Cold War, I never thought a race like this would happen. It was dreamed up by one of the Dakar racers, René Metje. For ages, the poor guy would tell me, "Fred! This is going to be the year! This is going to be the year!"

Gorbachev had other ideas. But finally, in 1992, it's going to happen.

This race is different from anything else I've ever done before or even imagined. Each leg of the race is punishing, and the whole thing will take a month from start to finish. Many of the areas we'll be traveling through are places none of us has even heard of. The world suddenly feels as though it's doubled in size, and it's good a thing. Space is exactly what I need right now.

Before I leave Stefi, she tells me she loves me. I say I love her back, but I have no idea if I mean it.

I'll be flying the lead helicopter, filming cars for French television with Vincent as well as a famous sports announcer called Bernard Père who signed onto the project as a producer. I remember him from sportscasts in the eighties—brown hair, tall, kind of a serious guy who isn't going to crack jokes or miss any details. He covered the French soccer team when they were at the top of their league, so everyone likes him—but before we take off, the team warns Vincent and me that Bernard, though extremely professional, has a temper.

"He's a bit of a character," one of the assistant directors says. "You probably don't want to mess with him."

I get the message: *For the love of God, behave yourselves.* Vincent and I are known for capturing incredible footage but also for having a certain amount of fun while we do it. Not this time, I guess.

We leave Paris when it's still dark and everything is quiet. Instead of stretching out in the back like everyone else, Bernard Père sits up front with us in the middle, all six feet three of him.

"So, tell me about yourselves," he says.

I'm surprised. Most of the other television guys I've met are just a bunch of amateurs looking for free helicopter rides.

"What do you want to know?" Vincent asks. Both of us are curious now.

"I don't know." He laughs. "How long have you guys been working together?"

"Too long," Vincent jokes.

We don't expect to like Bernard much, but he fits in perfectly. Suddenly we are the Three Musketeers.

Bernard is a good listener and incredibly kind. He may not be totally cut out for adventure races (he packed a lot of ties, and he doesn't like washing in the river), but he's done his homework. He's studied all the competitors, the teams, and the backgrounds of the drivers. Like us, he understands that his work matters. The stories he tells can transport people—move them—connecting them to their world and to this corner of the world, which nobody really knows about.

The route is a human mosaic. There are complex cultures we never knew existed, languages we've never heard spoken, and places we've never read about in books because nobody has written of them. We just keep going east, then farther east: France, Belgium, Germany, Poland, Belarus, Russia,

Kazakhstan, Turkmenistan, Afghanistan, Pakistan, Nepal, and China. The poverty of the people in many of the countries is real, and so is the wealth. In provincial Russia, you can feel the weight of the war on the locals. Outside Moscow, in the small agricultural communities, people look at us with fear and suspicion. In Mongolia, they invite us into their yurts and share their meals even though they have hardly anything to spare. In Kazakhstan, a skinny guy on an even skinnier horse helps one of the competitors fix his car despite no common language but mechanics, no motivation but human connection. It's new to all three of us and very moving. We soon become a little family flying over the Great Steppe, the Gobi, and so many places in between.

At the end of each day, Bernard always wants to find a special location to present his show. It's only a two-minute segment, but it's important to him. He talks about the winners (and losers) of the day and what happened on each of the twenty-four legs of the race. Most other guys would just phone it in, but he wants to make an impact. He's committed to showing people something new. I don't know if I've ever had so much admiration before for someone who didn't fly a helicopter or drive a race car. Vincent and I are in the business of blowing people's minds. Bernard Père opens people's eyes.

Just as the sun is setting one day on the western edge of Mongolia, we pass a giant finger-shaped rock that rises almost straight up from the desert about a thousand feet high. Vincent and I give each other a look. It would be the epic location to shoot Bernard. We pitch him the idea and, not surprisingly, he isn't comfortable—especially after I tell him how I'd get him there: landing on only one skid, then having him get out and lie on his belly so the downwash won't push him over the edge. Dangerous stuff. Once I move away, though, he could stand up and pretend to talk on his microphone while we fly a full 360 around him. The shot would reveal the desert and the beautiful, rare landscape around us, a part of the world hardly anyone has seen.

"OK," he says finally. "Let's do it."

Honestly, I don't even know if *I* would go through with it.

It takes us a bit of time to set up, but when he rolls out onto the rock, stands up, and looks around, it's totally worth it. It's the closest cinematic shot we've ever done. He looks like a hero.

We go back to the bivouac that evening and watch the footage over and over. It's perfect—the kind of shot that changes the way people see the world, that changes the way *I* see it.

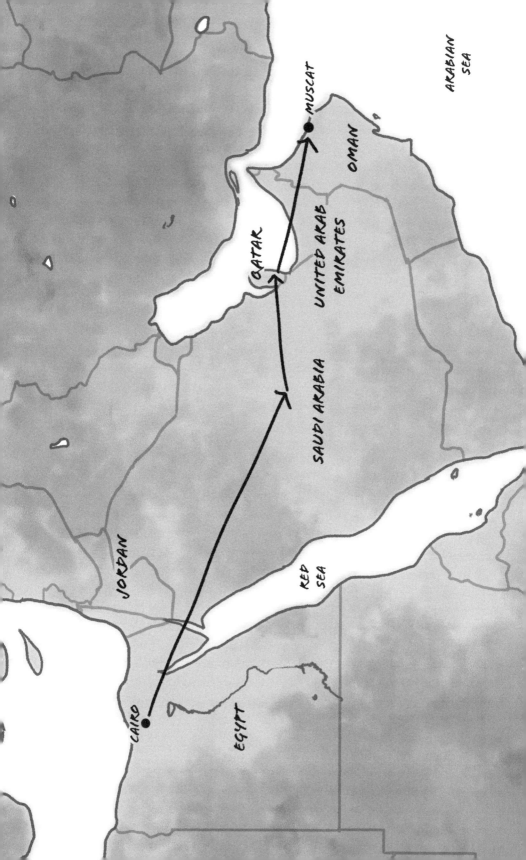

15

Do Something Different, Somewhere Different

"OPEN EVERYTHING UP."

I'm standing in a hangar in Cairo, sweating my balls off and talking to the engineers on my team. It's October. We just flew the 1993 Pharaoh's Rally and spent a lot of it pushing the machines, flying sideways to film the competitors, and chasing the lead cars through desert. I want to make sure everything is in perfect working order. We're supposed to begin a ferry to the sultanate of Oman for the Raid Gauloises in the morning. To spice things up, Gérard Fusil has decided that this year's race will take place in the middle of one of the most politically unstable regions on earth, as well as the most physically demanding for his competitors. There's practically a civil war in Yemen, and after the Gulf War, not everybody in the area will be excited to see a bunch of white guys in helicopters. Fusil has a way of making operations like this sound totally epic, though, so I'm not only on board but excited. The ferry will take us from Egypt over the Sinai Peninsula, across the Red Sea, then over Jordan, Saudi Arabia, Qatar, and the United Arab Emirates. It's a long trip, and I can't shake the feeling that something is wrong.

"Inspect the whole beam, all the bearings, everything," I say firmly, knowing the engineers are tired and will be pissed. We have to inspect the machines every hundred hours and it's only been about forty, but I need to be absolutely sure the machines are in good condition.

"I don't want anything to be left unchecked. We must do it. Period," I insist.

"What? Why?!" Denis yells.

Denis is one of the mechanics.

"We don't even have time, Fred."

I shrug. "We have to make time."

They get their tools out and start to work. I feel bad. The hangar is blazing hot, and for some reason, everyone is wearing jeans. I know it's the right thing.

A call comes through in the morning.

"Fred, you are one lucky bastard!"

It's Denis. And he's going nuts.

"I don't know how you do it, man, but remind me to never question you again. How did you know?"

One of the five brackets holding the beam going down to the tail rotor on my helicopter is cracked. If even one is gone, it means you have six feet of beam and a tail rotor about to come loose. You crash and probably don't walk away. Denis says they have to fly a new part in from France, so our departure will be delayed by two days.

The authorities had wanted us to go from Egypt to Saudi Arabia to Oman, the safest route over a not-so-safe area, but we'll have to fly directly over Qatar and the UAE to make it on time. We file our flight plans in Egypt with civil aviation, claiming it will be a seven-hour flight going around the restricted airspaces as instructed, but we leave with four hours of fuel. The only way to get there in time is to go straight. We agree to fly five miles apart to avoid being seen as a convoy and to have absolutely no radio contact. Thankfully, nobody tries to shoot us down.

We arrive in Muscat to a pissed off, heavily armed welcoming committee.

We didn't fly where we were supposed to!

We went over Qatar!

We didn't contact this tower and that one!

I tell them we tried to call everyone, but nobody responded. Thanks to Stefi, whom I still haven't been able to break up with, I'm now an expert at being yelled at. I just yell back, and I don't know why, but they buy it. A few hours later, we're checked into a crazy hotel not far from the corniche with a huge pool, domed ceilings, and four-poster featherbeds. Compared to the usual in the desert, it's like the "Eight Seasons."

Oman is small but breathtaking, like an entirely different planet filled with dry heat and strange rock formations. It's on the southeastern coast of the Arabian Peninsula overlooking the sea. Oman is an absolute monarchy, but Sultan Qaboos seems like a pretty modern guy. He takes good care of the people, invests in health care and education, and delivers food and supplies to communities in remote regions by military helicopter every week. Whatever they're doing here, it's working. Everyone (except the airport guys) is friendly. The only thing I don't like about this place is the scorching air temperature, and the choppers don't like it much either. We have an AS350BA and an AS350B1, better known as *Squirrels*, a word that is awkward and nearly impossible to pronounce with a French accent.

The heat sucks the life out of everyone and everything in a way I've never seen before. By the end of the first day, the competitors are suffering from serious dehydration, as are the horses. The poor horses. They seem to be a bigger part of the race this year, and they're also a bigger problem. Some of them get so sick I have to medevac them to the shade by longline. They're drugged, of course, but I'm not thrilled to be dangling a drunken Arabian pony above the desert. The camels do much better. Fusil has added camels to the race this year, as well as a lot of crawling through dark caves. His imagination is wild and I'm honestly terrified of what he'll think of next.

After the first week, we're all exhausted, and it feels like a miracle that nobody has died. Everyone is pushing themselves beyond the limit.

It's noon and the sun is burning. I've just refueled the helicopter at the race stop on possibly the hottest day of the entire competition, maybe of my entire life.

"Fred!"

Fusil is running up to me with a doctor and a nurse. He's gotten rid of his mustache this year but thankfully has kept the rest of his uniform: a blue shirt and safari hat.

"We've got a girl in the canyon with her team. She's unable to walk and they're out of water. The situation is critical. We have to get to her."

Great.

Having a full tank is normally a good thing, but with the heat and the combined weight of the equipment, the medical team, the fuel, and Fusil, I won't have the power to hover inside a canyon.

"I'm sorry, but it's too dangerous right now. I just refueled. We'll send someone else."

Fusil insists.

"If we don't leave now, she'll die."

I don't have any idea if it's true or not, but what if it is? I have no choice but to try. We load up and take off.

The canyon is narrow, a deep split in the earth made of bluish rock with a barely visible river at the base. The wind is blowing my tail, and we're carrying too much weight—the worst possible conditions for the situation. I'm coming into the location too flat. I should have chosen a steep angle. I might have landed hard that way, but at least I'd have ended up in the right place had I lost power. Now I *am* going to lose power. It's inevitable.

I see the girl and her team as we sink a hundred feet into the canyon. She looks like terrible, and she'll be difficult to get to, laid out in a little nook on the canyon wall surrounded by rocky outcrops. The canyon is so narrow the blades are almost touching the sides of the rock as I approach. The Squirrel is not happy, and I'm losing my RPM. I don't know how to fix this.

Fusil is looking at me trying to understand what's going on. He's been in a helicopter with me enough times to know when something's off. The doctor and the nurse have no idea, which is good. They're in the back talking on a radio to one of the team members. They don't need to know we're in a "maybe we'll see tomorrow but maybe not" kind of situation. The sweat is pouring out of me, as much from the focus as the heat. There is no protocol. All I can do is respond to the machine and try my best.

I lower my collective, something I would never normally do. Instead of trying to get more power that I know I don't have, I pull down my control to give the engine a breather. Then I pull back up about four feet and get right next to the niche. There isn't a ton of room, so I land on one skid only a few feet from the girl's face. Her skin is papery and pale, but all I can focus on is the helicopter's performance.

I'm about to talk to Fusil about the transport plan and tell him to wait in the canyon while we get the girl to base, but he's thrown his headset off and is already out the door of the chopper. Full-on French Indiana Jones. The good news is that we're burning fuel. The nurse unloads a case of water for the team. We're getting lighter by the second, and my Squirrel is perking up.

"We need to get her back quickly," the doctor says, looking serious.

They lift her on board, wrapped in a reflective blanket. Her body is limp.

Because I don't really have the power to take off, the only option is to let the helicopter free-fall off the side of the ledge to gain speed. We plunge through the air holding our breath, and I raise the collective at the exact right second.

We land safely at the base. We finish the course. The girl recovers, but I'm not sure I do. She almost died for a *race*. I don't understand how anyone could willingly put themselves in that kind of danger.

I wonder how many people have said the same thing about me.

I head back to Paris after the race, totally drained, determined again to be in love with Stefi. I want some stability in my life, and a relationship is the closest thing I have to it. But Stefi? Pure chaos. Her life is a mess. Any career she had she's thrown away. She's unhappy, and all she wants to do is dance, shop, drink, have sex, and argue. She's there, but she's not there for me. I want it to work. I want her to take care of herself, her life, her kid, but I can't seem to get through to her. She blames me for being away. Then I feel bad for being away. We fight. I tell her it isn't working. She promises to do better, saying that maybe we just need to spend more time together. I wonder if she's right. Reluctantly, I agree to bring her along while I location scout for Gérard's next race in Madagascar, but I don't love her any more in Madagascar than I do in France.

"Mada" is an island nation located in the Indian Ocean off the coast of Mozambique in East Africa. It's the second-largest island country in the world. Gérard Fusil is always looking for unknown territories, and he and Madagascar are made for each other. It's full of impassable roads, creatures that exist nowhere else, and some of the most beautiful landscapes on earth. It's isolated and has the feeling of being undiscovered, a little bit like Jurassic Park but with lemurs instead of velociraptors.

We're flying out of Antananarivo, the capital city, to check out a river path on our first day of scouting, but the Alouette II Fusil sourced is too heavy. We can't take off. Tana is located at over four thousand feet, and the machine is struggling. It's me, Fusil, Stefi, and a local guide named Thierry Ranarivelo, who strikes me right away as a know-it-all. I know we're too heavy. There's no point even trying to take off; we just don't have the power. Thierry looks at me. Then at Stefi.

"You need to lose the dead weight," he says. "Your blonde."

It's true. Stefi doesn't need to be here, but I don't like the way he's talking—as if he's trying to piss me off. I know it's just about getting a helicopter off the ground, but it feels more personal than that.

"What a wart," I mutter at him.

Thierry and I argue back and forth. Stefi starts complaining. Then Fusil starts complaining. It's not good.

"Look, Fred," Thierry says, "I'll arrange fuel for our first stop, and then you can lose some here and lighten things up. Would that work for you?"

It would work great, actually.

I just called this guy a wart and he's saving the day.

"Yeah, that sounds good. Thank you," I say back.

Quickly, we dump some fuel for what is a truly elegant takeoff. Maybe this Thierry guy isn't such a jerk after all?

We fly from the high plateau and over the magnificent island, through green jungle, over small villages, and along the coastline. Thierry knows the island by heart. He's a problem solver and has a cool head in stressful situations. I like working with him. By the end of the day, we're friends. By the end of the race, which takes place a few months later, we are brothers.

The biggest setback of the whole operation is Gérard Fusil coming down with *la tourista,* a case of diarrhea so epic that we're forced to land so he can take the most expensive dump in the world. Madagascar is the closest I've felt to home since Saint-Louis, and when it's time to leave, I'm not ready to go. But Stefi and the 1994 Paris–Dakar Rally are waiting.

There are no surprises in the rally besides the ones we know to expect: fueling issues, getting lost, sandstorms, heat. The race is under new ownership, but you wouldn't know it. Everything from the prep to the teams to the food at the bivouac is the same. We leave in January, and though the route is slightly different—France, Spain, Morocco, Mauritania, Senegal, and then *back*—none of it is new territory. We get great footage, a cool French guy in a Citroën wins, and everyone is happy. At least it seems that way.

A couple of months after the race, I'm sitting in the boardroom of a giant sports organization that now owns Dakar, along with everything else: the Tour de France, marathons, some sailing, and a bunch of ladies' golf. I don't know why they called me in. A blond guy about my age wearing a polo shirt with an extremely deep side part comes in and shakes my hand, and a woman ten years younger brings me a coffee that I don't drink.

"Frédéric," the guy starts in, "you've been with Dakar for a long time. We appreciate the work you've done but. . . ."

Merde. I know exactly what is happening.

"We'd like to go in a different direction."

Basically, they want to do it cheaper, which I wish he had the balls to say. They want to go straight to the source and hire machines from established companies. They don't need a "middleman" like me.

I disagree completely. You can't just pick a pilot doing sightseeing tours of Versailles, throw him into the Sahara, and expect him to do the job. You can't just put a cameraman on board and expect to get great footage. It doesn't work like that.

The guy is still talking about efficiency, the bottom line, and how the sport is changing, but I don't care about those things. I get up.

"You're making a mistake," I tell him.

And I leave, totally crushed by their decision. These races have become a part of me. It isn't just a skill, but an identity.

Not knowing what to do next, I fly to Madagascar to visit Thierry. For two weeks, the program is simple: fly helicopters, watch crocodiles in the river, water-ski, repeat. We fly barefoot from Tana in the morning and don't come back until sunset. Again, when it's time, I don't want to leave, so Thierry and I make plans to start Madagascar's first helicopter company. I'll teach him to fly, and we'll build a helipad in Tana. I'm ready to put down some roots, and I know in my heart I won't be putting them down with Stefi. I want to do something different, somewhere different. It's finally time to end it.

Stefi spends most of late summer on rich people's yachts and planes, ping-ponging between the French and Italian Rivieras. I hardly see her, which really seems to be fine by both of us. I focus on prep for the next Raid

Gauloises and try to sort out whether there is any hope for my relationship. Stefi is beautiful and funny, and she can be kind (when she isn't being ruthless), but wanting it to work is really the only thing we have in common. It isn't enough. Most days are filled with drama, yelling, and tears. I can't go on like this, and whether she knows it or not, neither can she.

One afternoon, after just getting back from a weekend on the beach with her celebrity friends in Saint-Tropez, Stefi walks into the kitchen.

"I'm three months pregnant," she says.

I'm frozen. Totally in shock.

I don't handle it well.

"What do you mean you're pregnant?!" I ask.

I hear what she's saying, but I can't process the information.

"But *how*?!"

I'm shouting. I don't mean to, but I can't help myself. Stefi stopped taking her birth control pills without talking to me. I don't even know if I want children. I'm gone ten months per year.

Then there's the thought of having a kid like her. . . . I picture it coming out bleached blonde and pissed off at me right out of the gate. It's going to be a disaster.

"This is not the kind of decision you make on your own. I can't believe you would do that."

Her eyes are filled with tears and she's pouting, but I'm done being manipulated. She looks at me dead in the eye and says calmly, "Well, if you're not happy, you can just go away."

"Fine," I tell her. "I'm leaving. We're done."

Now it's her turn to be shocked.

I grab my toothbrush and duffle bag.

"But who's going to pay for this?" She points at her belly, which is not a belly yet.

"That's something you should have thought about before making a decision like this alone. Have a nice day," I yell, slamming the door behind me.

For the next month, I don't pick up when she calls. I focus on my work, on any work, so I don't have to think about being a father.

The next Raid Gauloises is in Borneo, an enormous island east of Singapore and southwest of the Philippines. It's covered in ancient rainforests, complex river systems, and of course, Fusil's favorite: impassable terrain. Every year he seems to pick a destination more difficult for me to get to than the last, but I don't see how he's going to top this one. We had hoped to ship our five helicopters disassembled on a cargo plane from Paris, but the runway in Borneo isn't large enough to accommodate it. We're instead forced to land in Kuala Lumpur, assemble the helicopters, fly the choppers to Singapore, and then fly across the Java Sea to Borneo.

Getting to Singapore is fine, minus the fact that the mechanics have only forty-eight hours to put the helicopters back together and get them in perfect working condition. Crossing to Borneo will be brutal. We'll have to fly five hours over open water with no possibility of landing to refuel. The weather conditions are reliably hazy, and we won't be able to see the coastline until less than five minutes before landing. Our fuel will be at less than ten percent when we arrive—*if* it all goes well. If it doesn't, we'll have to do an emergency landing in the water.

I spend my time in Singapore checking everything ten times, going over each detail of the flight plan, making sure the auxiliary fuel tanks that will allow us the two extra hours to cross are functioning properly, and discussing everything with the pilots on my team. Occasionally I stop, panic, and think about the baby, but I quickly push those worries aside. Only two other pilots on my team of five agree to the last leg of the ferry, so two of us will take a plane back and do the whole thing again. I don't hold anything against the guys who aren't willing to do it. It *is* dangerous, and right now I'm the last person who is going to force a big life decision on someone.

The morning of the first ferry, there's a thick haze over the water. We take off knowing that we'll have only one mile of visibility at best, probably for the whole trip. In minutes, the land disappears and I'm flying fifteen feet above the water and into hundreds of miles of dense cloud, hundreds of miles of deep focus. There is no one but me and nothing to do but concentrate. So that's what I do. For five hours, the world is as big as the helicopter.

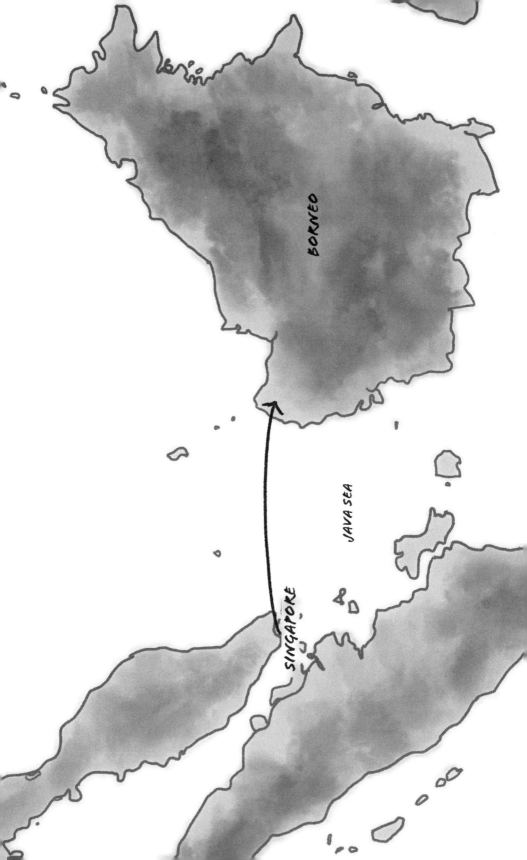

The fog is so thick, it begins to curl underneath the helicopter, collecting right on the surface of the water. I just keep focusing, communicating with the machine. It feels more comforting than maybe it should.

When I see the coastline up ahead and check in with Henri, the other pilot, I know we're going to make it. The haze begins to lift, and I prepare to land.

As the skids touch down and the first ferry is done, it really hits me: I'm going to have a baby. With Stefi. Crossing the Java Sea doesn't scare me, but that does. I know what I have to do.

When the race is over, the ferries are complete, and the helicopters are disassembled and put on the plane, I go back to Paris to try and work things out with the mother of my child. I want to be there for my kid. I have no more love for Stefi, but we're family now whether I like it or not. I'm going to be a father. For the first time I can remember in my adult life, my parents are genuinely happy for me.

I am *not* happy. I'm still trying to work out how it happened, what went wrong, and why I put myself in such a messed-up position.

Part III

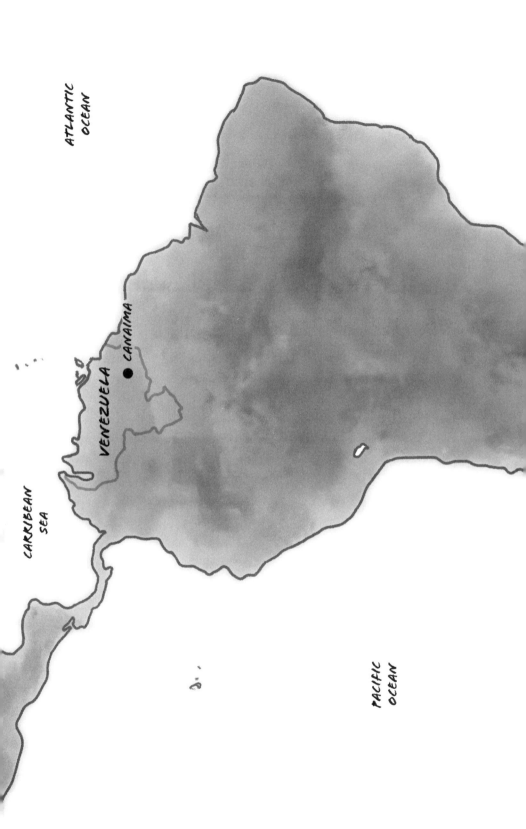

16

Dream Bigger

THE DAKAR RALLY will be starting in Granada, Spain, this year. It's September 1994. Normally I would be busy making preparations, sourcing machines, getting the customs documents together, and assembling my team. Instead I'm flying wealthy people home from the airport, working for the Formula 1 circuit director, Philippe Gurdjian, and occasionally training rich guys to be pilots. I'm no longer the extremely busy chief pilot for the world-famous Paris–Dakar Rally; I'm a regular guy named Fred who wanted to break up with his girlfriend but got her pregnant instead.

Merde.

I lived my dream, but now the dream is over. I need to find a new one.

I'm securing the blades of the helicopter for the night after a long day of flying. It's a tedious routine: I lift my arms high, catch the blade, slip a rope through the socket, then tie it tight to the skid—again and again for each of the three blades. Each time I do it, my aviator jacket slips up to my ribs. It happens to all of us, and it's super annoying. This time of day, the hangar is a horrible peep show, just a bunch of middle-aged guys showing off the amount of hair they have on their bellies. I finish up a blade, pull down my jacket, reach up to the next, then pull down my jacket. I finish up and watch the rest of the guys doing the same. It's not an inspiring scene, but it gives me an idea. I spent my formative years in the Avirex store. I've seen *Top Gun* a hundred times. I lived in New York City. *Of course* I could create the perfect pilot jacket. "Fashion designer" will be my new identity.

One week later, I bring my plans to businessman and private pilot François Michaud.

"Yes, Fred!" he cries. "I love it."

By the end of the month, I'm staring at our first prototype: a GORE-TEX bomber that does not turn into a bikini when you lift your arms. It's lined with emergency blanket material so you could turn it inside out in case of trouble. There's a little pocket on one of the sleeves with a "survival mirror," and on the back it has a giant North Helicopter logo. We decide our company, North-by-North, will produce five hundred pieces in blue, yellow, orange, and red and see how people like them. They sell out. Our next project, the North-by-North watch, also sells out, but I'm frustrated and restless.

The design process is exciting, and Francois is a great partner—a much better partner than Stefi, who is getting rounder, more irritable, and more expensive every day. I look in the mirror every morning hoping to see a new man, but all I can see is a helicopter pilot. I hand the company over to Francois just in time to meet my daughter.

On April 28, 1995, Naomi is born purple-blue with the umbilical cord wrapped around her neck. Stefi went into labor and screamed our daughter into the world, just like it happens in the movies. It is not an easy delivery. To be honest, the entire thing is more terrifying and intense than anything that has ever happened to me in a helicopter.

Naomi spends three tense days in the hospital for monitoring but recovers quickly. Within weeks she develops into a fat, happy baby, laughing all the time, grabbing onto my index finger, and shoving it in her mouth. She grows a small amount of blond hair on her head. I'm glad there is someone in the house balder than I am.

I'm not sure what to feel or do as a father, but I'm ready to assume responsibility. I want to be the best man I can be for her. I can't let her grow up with a father who is missing a piece of himself. I need to figure out what I want to do with my life, with our lives.

During Naomi's first six months, I try one thing after the other, aiming to strike the perfect balance between what puts joy in my heart and what puts food on the table. During this time, Stefi makes it clear that she would like me to put Christian Louboutin shoes on her feet as well. After you see a woman having a baby, it is impossible not to want to give her everything she wants. Even if you don't like her.

First, I'm given an opportunity to do business in Gabon on the west coast of Africa near Cameroon. I'll be trading engines for the local airline company. On paper the job is perfect, but once I begin, I discover that the business practices are unconventional. I know better than to ask a lot of questions, but something is off. Instead of paying my commission, they try to compensate me with a house on the beach in the capital city of Libreville. The beach is bright-white there, elephants swim in the ocean, and it seems like a pretty good deal . . . until they "forget" to put my name on the title. After that, I return to Paris to do private transport. It's boring. It feels like an office job.

No matter what I do, nothing works and nothing fits (except the North-by-North jacket). I feel alone.

Naomi begins crawling and babbling, pointing at every dog, tree, and cloud, saying "papa." Stefi returns to her old ways, going to the clubs and partying. Then we get back to *our* old ways, fighting a lot and resenting each other. None of us knows where we belong in the world.

An aerial cameraman named Charlet Record approaches me one day in winter, just as the helipad is quieting down for the night. I don't know much about him, other than that he films a lot of French documentaries and movies—but nothing overseas because his English is nonexistent. Not bad, totally nonexistent.

"Fred." He holds out his hand. "I was wondering if you'd be interested in taking on some work as a film pilot."

At this point, I'm interested in anything that doesn't try to pay me in houses five thousand miles away from my family.

"Sure!" I tell him. He describes what he does and how it works, and it all sounds pretty basic.

I thought after the rallies that I was a film pilot, but really, I was just a pilot *for* filming. Vincent and I were creative when we worked together, but we only delivered whatever the network needed: first car, third motorcycle, host hotel, whatever. We could be aggressive, dynamic, and experimental, but only within the boundaries set by La Cinq, the television network. With Charlet, the boundaries don't exist. Suddenly it isn't about capturing the story; it is about telling it.

Charlet doesn't make a big deal of his talents, but he's casually revolutionized aerial photography in France (something he doesn't mention when we first meet). He's designed and built his own gyrostabilized head for helicopter filming. It looks like a giant globe on a beam with a lens at the end. Honestly, it looks like it could fall apart at any second, but Charlet is the only one offering this kind of equipment in France. The freedom it gives him as a cameraman and me as a pilot feels infinite. I can create the movement, the tempo, the timing of the shot. The helicopter is like a dolly in the sky.

The first scene we shoot is a car driving down the street, familiar territory for me. This isn't a rally car though. It's a Fiat Panda—small, box-shaped, ugly, and as powerful as a tricycle. We're not in Mali surrounded by sand dunes; we're in a suburb called Sèvres near a porcelain factory and a playground. I am happy to have the job and all, but I'm not expecting emotional fireworks. It's a cloudy day, the crew is small and unenthusiastic, and it's a Panda car. The director calls action and we go.

The world looks entirely new. Every move we make is intentional and impactful, designed to produce a certain amount of energy or emotion. We are not just out there to show what's happening but to convey meaning. Charlet and I try several approaches, and I'm shocked to see in the playback the different feeling each produces. Some shots are tense moment-to-moment, and others are meant to give the viewer a sense of what's coming next. I didn't know flying could do that. All day my brain is spinning, and when the skids touch down at the end, I'm numb with excitement. Charlet thanks me and says goodnight. I say it back. As I secure the helicopter for the night, tying down each blade to the skid, I know I am going to be a film pilot.

For the next month, when I'm not working with Charlet or at home with Naomi, I am at the movie theater on the Champs-Élysées watching *GoldenEye, Mission: Impossible*, anything and everything that Tony and Ridley Scott have touched. I pay attention to every angle and aerial shot, and I especially pay attention to the credits. The circle of the aerial filming is very tight, and according to Charlet, no one is willing to open the door. I will have to force it open and shine with what I have: my experience, convictions, and passion.

Peter Allwork was the aerial cinematographer on *Superman, Never Say Never Again, Indiana Jones and the Last Crusade, Highlander*, and *Good Morning, Vietnam*. I show up on the doorstep of Aerial Camera Systems (ACS) at Shepperton Studios outside London like an alley cat looking for scraps. Showing up uninvited is a bold approach, and I'm nervous, especially after what Charlet said.

I knock on the door, and Peter Allwork himself answers. He's in his early seventies with pink cheeks, a big smile, light hair, and a wool sweater. If somebody were asked to produce a quick sketch of a British gentleman, it would look exactly like Peter. His daughter-in-law, Suzie, and son, Matthew, are there too. They're also very proper and British-looking. I start right in and tell him I want to work together. He's a little confused but invites me in for tea. Naturally.

I tell him about my experience covering the rallies and shooting with Charlet, then share that I want to be a great film pilot and work on Hollywood action movies.

He smiles. "Fantastic."

I'm always surprised when a man my father's age is excited about something I've said. My dad accepts what I do now, but he doesn't understand or support it.

Peter tells me about ACS, when he started it, and why.

"ACS is a family business," Peter says proudly to me. "Like you, we love what we do here."

And after that day, I am a part of the family.

For several months, Peter and I work on small projects together—mostly commercials and television series. Then one day he calls and offers me something totally different.

"Fred, have you ever been to Venezuela?" he asks. "Francis Veber is shooting a movie called *The Jaguar*. They need aerials, and I'm just too old for that kind of thing. Would you be interested?"

Interested is an understatement. This is a feature film, my big break, and I only have one question.

"Who will be the cameraman if you are not coming?" I ask.

"Oh! A lovely chap called Larry Blanford," Peter says. "He's American, lives in Los Angeles and everything. His first movie was *Top Gun*."

I almost drop the phone. Naomi looks up at me, worried. She has lots of hair now and several teeth. I pat her back and tell her everything is OK. It's better than OK.

"No problem, Peter. I'll do it," I say.

Stefi, it turns out, is not the American Dream. Larry Blanford is. The Midwestern accent, the long hair, the way he walks like he's just gotten off a horse—I love all of it. The guy is cool. I don't just want to work with Larry; I want to *be* him.

Canaima, the small village south of Venezuela where we're filming, is situated in a national park close to the Brazilian border in gold-mining country. The jungle is dense, as if Borneo, Madagascar, and Costa Rica were stacked on top of each other. Half the park is covered in tabletop mountains or *tepui*, giant flat formations, many of which have wide white waterfalls spilling down from them into the Amazon. The air, unsurprisingly, is humid and filled with bugs. I can see why they would film something called *The Jaguar* here. Every time a twig snaps, we all brace ourselves to be pounced on and eaten by something.

I'm intimidated to work with Larry, but he doesn't seem to notice and does a good job putting everyone at ease. He tells stories about growing up in Indiana, serving in the military, and shooting *Top Gun*. Whenever we land, he takes his shirt off and works on his tan, using whatever reflective surface he can find to get darker faster. Sometimes it's just aluminum foil or a piece of scrap metal. He reminds me of the surfer guy in *Apocalypse Now*. Larry is laid-back and not picky outside the helicopter, but when we're in the machine, he wants the best footage possible. So do I.

The shots we need are important ones; they will open and close the movie. They must feel giant, impossible, and totally epic. *The Jaguar* is a comedy—the story of a sleazy French guy, a scientist, and a shaman trying to save each other's souls. It's not about jaguars at all. It sounds silly to me, and though I have no idea whether the movie will be any good, the aerial filming will be.

Larry and I go up to shoot in an AS350B, another Squirrel, taking a long approach over the Amazon basin and following a small white plane flying low on the river, close to the local mountains. The scene is stunning, vast, and has the feeling of something unexplored. The sense of vastness and wonder is exactly what we must convey. I fly carefully, considering everything around me—the sun, the wind speed, the reflection of the water.

Working together is natural. Larry's attention to the lighting, angle, and setup for every shot is meticulous and creative. I'm able to be precise with the speed of the shot and put the helicopter exactly where it needs to be to produce the right feeling. The light is soft and pale orange, the sky is hazy, and the wings of the little plane glint every so often, reflecting the sun like Larry's aluminum foil. After a few passes, we have what we need.

Larry turns to me after he stops filming, pulls his aviators to the end of his nose, and says, "Fred, you're not just a helicopter pilot. You understand the camera and the process of filmmaking: the light, the edit, and what we're trying to do. *You* are a natural born filmmaker."

And I believe him.

When the shoot is over, Larry flies back to Los Angeles. Then I have to ferry the helicopter back with my crew—Jim, who is responsible for taking care of the camera equipment, and Yannick, a mechanic from Paris.

Jim is great, but Yannick is a punk. He's stubborn, grumpy, and arrogant. He wasn't respectful to me or the locals during the shoot, and I'm not looking forward to the 750-mile trip together back to Guadalupe, the tiny butterfly-shaped island in the Southern Caribbean where we sourced the machine. Eighty percent of the ferry is over crazy-dense jungle we call "broccoli," where there's no place at all to land in an emergency.

The first day of a ferry always feels like the longest. I'm normally tired from finishing the job and not wanting to talk much. Luckily, Yannick doesn't want to talk either. We hardly say a word between Canaima and our first fueling stop, a small airfield made of dirt on our way to Guyana City, which is still in Venezuela and not far from the gold mines.

The drums are cherry-red and easy to spot as we approach, sticking out against the jungle and small clay houses that line the airstrip. I land right next to the drums, shut down the engine, and get to work fueling while Jim and Yannick hop out of the helicopter to stretch their legs and piss.

"Aye!"

Four guys are walking quickly toward us, and they all have machetes.

The jaguars don't seem so bad anymore.

Within seconds they're in my face, talking in fast, aggressive Spanish, too fast for me to understand. If I had to guess I'd say they were somewhere between forty and fifty years old, all with dark hair, bad teeth, frizzy black beards, and pissed off, scrunched-up eyebrows. Their clothes are dirty (mine are, too, to be honest), but their machetes are freakishly well maintained, along with their guns. *Merde.*

We have done something wrong, and I don't know what, it is, so I try to reason with them using my hands and basic words like *helicopter, fuel,* and *movie.* I hope they will understand that we're not here for any trouble and have no interest in their gold mines, lumber, drugs, or anything else. I try to make eye contact with Jim and Yannick. It is important for us to stay calm because these guys are *not* calm.

One of the men gets about an inch from Jim's face and Yannick loses control, shoving him away. The man screams, pulls back his machete, and draws it quick across Yannick's throat. Jim and I freeze as a wave of blood pours out of Yannick's neck, and a helpless expression falls over his face. He drops to his knees.

The four of them start to argue and yell at each other. I'm guessing murder wasn't something they discussed when making plans for the day. If we're going to get out, this is our window.

"We need to get him into the chopper," I tell Jim. "Take off his shirt and put pressure on his neck."

Jim nods and we lift Yannick into the back. His shirt and shorts are soaked and deep red. His skin is looking blue.

The guys disappear into the jungle, and an old man runs up to us from one of the little houses. He points out the nearest clinic on my map. I only have thirty-five percent fuel left, but it's enough to get Yannick there. The flight is a blur.

We arrive, and before the blades even stop turning, Jim is running into the little white building carrying Yannick like a baby. The doctors stop the bleeding and stitch him up, but a couple more millimeters closer to his carotid, and he would have died in less than a minute. We fly him back to

Canaima, and from there he's transferred by plane to Caracas. Jim and I begin the ferry all over again—still in shock, distracted, and not able to focus. Then the low oil pressure light comes on. *Merde.*

We're forced to land on a fifty-by-fifty rock in the middle of the sea because I forgot to close the cap on the engine oil tank after our fueling stop. The problem is easy to fix, but running out of oil over the open ocean is not great. I'm pretty sure that, after this, poor Jim will never speak to me again.

After *The Jaguar*, Larry Blanford calls me for every single project he books outside the US, including lots of stuff in Central and South America. When we aren't working together, we talk often on the phone. He knows that I'm ambitious, that I want to be the best at what I do, and he gives me sort of a crash course in Hollywood. I feel like I'm living the dream, but Larry convinces me it's time to dream bigger.

When I tell him how much I charge for work in Paris, he starts laughing. He says I need to charge more, at least $1,000 a day, for anyone to take me seriously in Los Angeles.

"Fred, people want the best," Larry says. "And the best has a price. Yours is a thousand per day."

The number seems crazy. Right now I don't charge a fee for my talent; I just make commission off the ACS rentals.

"One thousand per day," Larry says, making sure it sinks in.

We talk about film pilots in America, and he explains that breaking into Hollywood, my ultimate goal, will not be easy. The helicopter film pilots there are like gods. They do stunts, shoot, coordinate—all kinds of things. I'm not ready yet.

"There are only a couple of guys," he says. "They're famous. The circle is closed, my friend. Untouchable."

I might be a nobody in America, but there's nothing to prevent me from being the best film pilot in Europe—so I decide that's exactly what I'm going to do.

In December 1996, with Peter Allwork's blessing, his son, Matthew, and I start Aerial Camera Systems France. If the circle in Hollywood is closed, we'll make our own. We put our heads down and work, sourcing equipment, putting together a business plan, and getting an office up and running.

One day when we're assembling desks, Peter calls. He has a job for us, our first: a film shooting in Austria called *Seven Years in Tibet*.

17

Some Things Are Worth Waiting For

I'M AT MY BIG WOODEN DESK looking out at the runway. It's early July 1999, raining, and hot. Joyce, my assistant, has dropped the gigantic leather folder off already. Inside it are my schedule for the day and a stack of prefilled checks I have to sign. "Only twenty-six this time," she's written on a yellow Post-it with a smiley face. Joyce puts smiley faces on everything.

In the three years since we started ACS France, I've worked on about ten feature films and shot more commercials than I can count. Business is booming. I'm the head of a company with dozens of employees, and we cover some of the biggest events on French television. We have the best camera systems, offer the most innovative shot options, and are widely considered to be leaders in our field. When I was screaming in the Alouette II and deciding to be a pilot at eight years old, I wasn't expecting this part.

"Hi, Fred." Matthew waves as he heads into his office. He's still living in England mostly but comes to Paris every month for meetings.

I wave back at him.

ACS outgrew the tiny office in my apartment quickly, and M. Bastien from HeliFrance, whom I now call Joel, leased us a fifteen-thousand-square-foot hangar. The space didn't need much work. We had to make offices for management, marketing, production, and technical employees, set up storage for all the camera equipment, and of course, save parking spots for my two helicopters, but my approach to decorating is "go big or go home," so we went big. Everything is sleek and high-tech. I had a special company make a huge ACS logo in shiny silver chrome that we rigged outside the entrance of the building. Inside we have lots of metal and automatic doors with electronic keypads. There's some fun stuff too: framed movie posters of all our projects and a broken JetRanger my mechanic turned into a bar. ACS is like a mix between the starship *Enterprise* and the Batcave. I love it. My personal office is slightly simpler, with wooden panels on the walls, sisal carpet, a red sofa from a fancy Italian brand, and tons of photos of Naomi. She is four now.

I open the envelope and pull out my schedule, which should be clear. I'm supposed to be scouting locations for a commercial all day, but I notice that our marketing guy, David, has scheduled a last-minute meeting at noon.

"Interview: Peggy."

David is always pulling stuff like this.

We're having trouble finding a production coordinator to handle television and film projects, and everyone he's brought in so far has been a total disaster. I wouldn't trust most of the candidates to coordinate a sandwich, and I doubt "Peggy" will be different from the rest. I have no interest in wasting my time with yet another unqualified job candidate who isn't ready to work hard. I don't know why he thinks Peggy will be any better than Hubert, Simone, or Benoît, and honestly, I don't care. I have five quaint country villages to evaluate before lunchtime. If I'm going to make it back in time for the interview, I should have left ten minutes ago. I grab my sunglasses and a bottle of water from the JetRanger bar and leave.

It turns out all quaint country villages within an hour of Paris are the exact same.

I'm not in a good mood when I come back to the office a few hours later. This is the time of day I normally sign checks for Joyce and envision the company's bank account getting smaller and smaller. We're doing well, but I can't imagine a more expensive business on earth to run. Our basic equipment is helicopters and specialized cameras, and that's not even the fancy stuff. I'm not looking forward to the afternoon, so I walk to my office with my head down, not wanting to make small talk with anyone.

I'm about to walk through the door when I notice that it's occupied.

I forgot about Peggy.

A young woman is seated on my red sofa with her back toward me. David is seated across from her with a big grin on his face, focused like he's in deep conversation. He's normally a bit of a flirt, but he looks genuinely excited this time. I glance quickly at the girl. She's just a kid. I'm not in the mood for this.

"Hey, Fred." David smiles. "Let me introduce you to Peggy Père. She's interviewing for the production coordinator position."

I barely let him finish his sentence.

"Does she have any field experience?" I ask, not even looking at her. "Because otherwise, I am not interested."

I'm acting like a big shot, being super rude to this poor girl who has probably never held a full-time job in her life. Really, though, I just want my office back.

Peggy stands up. "Yes, as a matter of fact. She has years of field experience *and* is super qualified. She is probably too qualified for the job. Nice to meet you too."

Without ever saying it, she manages to finish her sentence with "asshole."

I feel like I've been slapped. The room goes quiet.

I'm about to apologize, but when she turns to glare at me, I realize she's beautiful. Her eyes are a shade of blue I've never seen before—which, considering my line of work, is impressive. She's also confident enough to do the job, unlike Hubert, Simone, or Benoît.

Before I can say another thing, she decides the meeting is done and says goodbye to David, not me.

"It was nice to meet you, David. I'll think about your offer and let you know when I come back from New York."

She looks at me with her right eyebrow raised and walks out the door. I'm speechless. David isn't; he's mad.

"Seriously, Fred? She's the first qualified person we've met in weeks, and you pull this crap?!"

He's shaking his head at me, the way my parents used to.

"And on top of it, her mother is one of the most respected directors in French television. What do you think she's going to tell her about us? That ACS is run by a bunch of arrogant idiots—that's what!"

I blew it, but I'm not ready to concede. I try to calm him down.

"David, we'll find someone else. You'll forget about her by tomorrow."

"We need her, Fred," he says flatly. "She's the one."

David doesn't forget about her, and neither do I.

The whole summer passes. Then one day in September, Peggy shows up for her first day of work wearing sunglasses and a vintage blazer. The whole energy in the office shifts. Every one of us sits up and pays attention, not just because she's pretty but because she's commanding and totally un-afraid. She has so much presence. I watch her from my office talking to everybody, asking millions of questions, and wanting to understand who is doing what and why. She's too qualified for this job and knows it. She also thinks I'm a jerk, though she never lets it interfere with her work. She never lets anything interfere with her work.

During her first week, Peggy asserts herself not as the heart of ACS but the balls. She doesn't wait to be invited to my office like the rest of the staff; she shows up, waits respectfully if I'm in the middle of something, then gets whatever she needs to move forward with her work and nothing else. There's no small talk, no, "How is your morning going?" I'm curious about her, but mostly I just try not to get in her way. She's twenty-three years old and running her own department. Flawlessly. It's intimidating.

"David isn't making any money," Peggy says, walking into my office at the end of the day and shutting the door behind her. This is her second week, and I've gotten used to her coming and going as she pleases.

"He's rude to the staff and pushes it to the limit with your clients too. It's unprofessional."

David is the one who insisted on hiring her, who went out on a limb for her. If it was anyone else other than Peggy saying this stuff, I'd have questions about their loyalty. I'd partnered with David because he had a lot of connections in television, and I thought he could open some doors. But now that I think about it, he hasn't really.

She sits down on my sofa, and I smell her perfume, spice and cedarwood, not like the typical stuff girls wear. Not a hint of potpourri. I get up from my desk and sit across from her, and she breaks down David's department for me—what's working and what's clearly not. When she's finished explaining, she doesn't sugarcoat anything.

"Look, Fred," she says, "I have nothing against him, but I disagree with the way he's running things and thought you should know."

She stands up and walks out of my office. I try not to watch her as she slips through the door, and I fail miserably. I go over the numbers and she's right. We let David go the next week.

At the end of summer, I promote Peggy to my team to oversee all the movie and commercial productions with helicopters, expecting that she'll be excited. She isn't.

"How do you expect me to do a good job when I don't know anything about helicopters?!" she asks, looking at me like I've put her in a terrible position even though she'll be making nearly twice what she is now. We're in my office. I seriously thought she'd be celebrating, but she's pacing back and forth across the length of my office and again, I'm trying not to watch her.

An idea stops her suddenly.

"OK, I'll do it. I just need to learn to fly. That way, I'll know exactly what you need for each project. Then I'll be properly qualified."

She's nodding, and her eyes—a color that after months I still can't name—are shining. She walks out of my office and I hear her pick up the phone to book her first flying lesson.

"Yes, hello," she says into the receiver, "I need to get my private helicopter license. I'd like to start as quickly as possible."

I'm smiling.

Merde.

I'm falling completely in love with her. She's fifteen years younger than me. I have a kid. I'm her boss *and* I'm still (sort of) with Stefi, though she's been cheating on me with some tennis player for at least the past six months. I can't deny my feelings for Peggy, but I also can't act on them. I refuse to—not in the traditional sense anyway.

By the end of September, Peggy mentions that she's having a hard time getting to work. She's living in Saint Germain in a one-bedroom Parisian apartment not far from Café de Flore, an expensive old coffeehouse where Simone de Beauvoir and Jean-Paul Sartre used to hang out. Today it's a hip area for young artistic types, but in order for her to get from Saint Germain to Toussus-le-Noble, she has to take two subways, one train, and the bus. David had agreed to give her a company car to help with the commute, so I hand over the keys to a crappy old Citroën BX. The gas mileage is terrible, and it looks like a spaceship. I know there's zero chance Peggy will drive it, and sure enough, after one round trip, she walks into my office and drops the keys on my desk.

"Yeah, no thank you." She wrinkles her nose. "Fred, I love the job. But if we don't find a better way for me to get to work, I won't be able to stay."

My heart sinks, and I hope she can't see it. I can't imagine the company without her, and honestly, I can't imagine my life without her. She's the best part of my day.

Then I smile. "No problem. I can drive you. We'll meet halfway between our apartments in Paris. What do you think?"

She raises her right eyebrow like she always does and thinks about it. I can tell she's unsure, but Peggy can't resist a practical, efficient solution.

She shrugs. "Sure. I'll see you tomorrow morning."

She walks out of the room before I can mention that I drive a huge BMW K1200LT motorcycle with custom speakers.

Peggy is standing just outside the Châtelet station wearing a summer dress and jacket. The sky is charcoal-gray, and there's a light rain. I'm driving with the music blaring. Today, it's Jimmy Cliff. I pull into an alleyway close by, park, and wave her over.

"Good morning!" I say, handing her a lemon-yellow helmet and a full-on rain suit. "These are for you."

Her eyes go wide.

"You're kidding me. Are you insane?"

I don't answer.

Shaking her head, she steps into the suit, straps on the helmet, and hops on the bike behind me, wrapping her arms around my waist. Nothing has ever felt so natural to me. It feels less natural to Peggy. She's never been on a motorcycle before and hangs on for dear life as I weave in and out of traffic at one hundred miles per hour.

For days she complains about her arms being sore, but I've never been happier to have someone hold on tightly. I wake up every morning with a smile on my face, excited to see her on that corner.

At first I try not to acknowledge how I feel about Peggy, but we grow closer as we go on missions and scout locations together. I tell her about things with Stefi and Naomi—things about my family I've never told anyone or even said out loud before. Home is getting worse and worse. Stefi is unhappy and so am I, something we don't bother to hide anymore and couldn't if we tried. She deals with her problems by drinking too much; I deal with mine by working too much. If we didn't have Naomi, the relationship would have been over years ago. Neither of us has the courage to leave, but we both have the desire. Peggy listens to all of it neutrally, offering no judgment or advice. If she's interested in me at all, I don't know it, but my feelings are growing stronger every day.

I have a job in Normandy on a Sunday morning in October, and Peggy asks if she can come along to get some of her flight hours and learn the navigation. We've spent a lot of time together, but this will be a twelve-hour day, just the two of us. It feels different. We take off early in the morning headed toward a village, Saint-Something-or-Other-sur-Mer, where we're supposed to meet with a French director named Xavier Beauvois. The flight there is smooth and only about an hour, most of which I spend trying not to say anything stupid and hoping that I smell good. When we get to Saint-Something-or-Other-sur-Mer, I don't see a film crew, so I pull out my map.

The ocean is on our right side and should be on our left. There are two villages with the exact same name in different counties. I feel like an idiot, but Peggy laughs the entire thing off while I fly low next to the road so I can read the signs and figure out where we are.

Eventually we arrive in the right village and shoot the commercial, which goes great. On the way back, we decide to stop for tea at a friend's estate in the area. I know there's a chance we'll run short on fuel before we get home, but with a little luck and tailwind, we should be fine. Unfortunately, by the time we leave, there's neither luck nor tailwind to be found—*and* it's pitch-black. I can see the airport lights in the distance, less than one mile away, but then the low fuel warning light comes on. In a Hughes 500 helicopter, you don't mess around with stuff like that. We land in a muddy potato field.

"What are you waiting for?" Peggy asks, hopping out of the chopper and landing up to her knees in muck "Let's go."

Hand in hand (just for balance, I'm afraid), we walk through the field to a little gravel road—slipping, sliding, and laughing. It is the worst best night of my life.

After hitchhiking to the airport, getting gas cans, hitchhiking back, and refueling, we take off again and finally land at the airport around eleven p.m.

"I had fun today." She smiles.

"You mean tonight?" I joke.

"Even tonight," she assures me, giving my hand a squeeze.

Right then, I know it isn't just me. There's something between us.

We sit next to each other while the blades stop turning. I look over at her, mud on her pants, messy hair. There's nowhere on earth or in the sky I'd rather be. I want to kiss her, but I don't. Some things are worth waiting for. I just sit there processing the fact that the greatest rush of my life didn't happen at eighteen thousand feet; it happened in a potato field.

A few weeks and all of my courage later, I finally kiss her. It feels like coming home for both of us. She is instantly my family and I move straight into her tiny apartment in Saint Germain.

Stefi is pissed and I don't blame her. My parents are pissed, too, but really, like so many other things I've done in my life, they just don't understand. Around February 2000, we begin a brutal legal battle to get full custody of Naomi that the lawyers predict will take years. In the meantime, Naomi moves in with Peggy and me, into the top floor of a charming old building on Île de la Cité where she'll have her own room and a breathtaking view of Paris. Life finally begins for me.

There is not much to unpack from my old apartment. I left everything to Stefi except for Naomi's things and a couple of boxes filled with photographs from my rally days. Of course, Peggy is eager to look through them. Even though we feel like we've known each other forever, we've been a couple for less than three months. On a snowy afternoon, she tears into the boxes while Naomi and I are in the living room listening to music. Naomi likes reggae too.

Every five minutes, Peggy is either laughing loudly, asking a question, or telling me we need to get something framed.

"These are amazing!" she calls out.

I smile. I've never been with someone so excited about my life before, somebody so in love with all of me. Suddenly, her tone changes.

"Fred, what were you doing naked with these two men in this river?"

Oh.

It's a fair question, especially in a new relationship. Before I can answer her, she starts to get frantic.

"Where was this?

"When was it?

"Fred, please, you have to tell me."

She runs into the living room looking pale and almost in tears. I put my arms around her. I have no idea what's happening. I take the photo from her hand and explain.

"It was during the Paris-Moscow-Beijing Rally in 1992, I think. We had only rivers to rinse ourselves, you know. It's nothing to be embarrassed about, definitely nothing for you to worry about. What's the matter?"

We stand there for a moment. I can feel her tears on my chest.

She steps back, takes a shaky breath, and points at one of the men in the photo.

"That's my father."

I look at her speechless. It takes me a full minute to find any words.

"Bernard? Bernard Père is your dad? Why didn't you tell me?!"

I'd flown hours with him. I liked him. He meant something to me. I remember him talking about his teenage daughters. Peggy is one of them.

She starts to cry harder. Not louder, but deeply.

"He died last April, out of nowhere. I don't talk about it much. He was in Belgium, passed out in his hotel, and died three days after. He'd just come back from a trip in Brazil with his best friends. He was happy. I was happy for him."

She pauses a second to wipe her eyes and nose. I'm shaking now too.

"The last postcard he sent me said, 'If laughter brings you youth, then I think I am back to childhood.' I can't believe you knew him. I forgot he had covered a couple of rallies. I was just a kid."

I take her over to the couch and we sit down, in total disbelief. Naomi comes to curl up with us.

"The sunset shot of him in Mongolia, on that crazy rock in the desert—that was you?" she asks.

"Yes." I smile. "That was me."

She leans in close and I tell her about the rally, my friendship with her father, the shot in the desert, and how we made it happen. We had to convince Bernard that it would be a totally epic moment, kind of like this one.

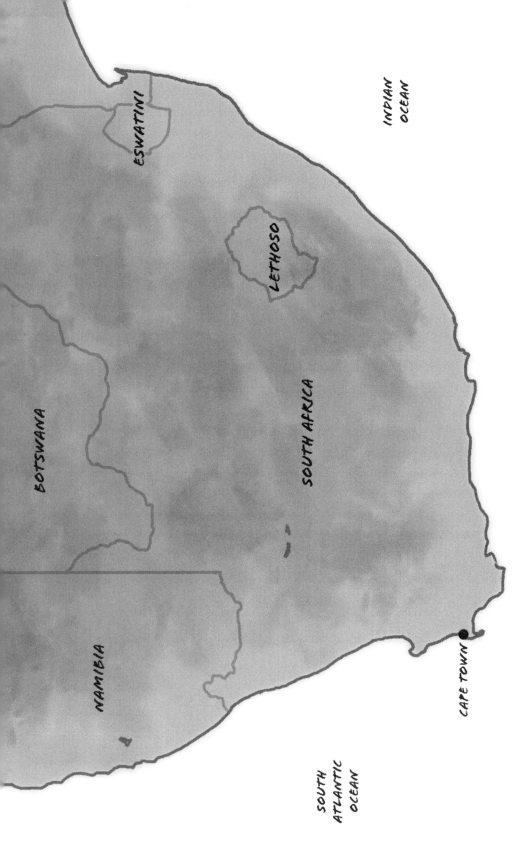

18

The Landing Is the Hardest Part

TWO THINGS I HAD ASSUMED my entire life to be myths turn out to be true.

One: A man reaches age forty and begins to question whether his life has been fully lived.

Two: Love makes you do crazy things.

Life is good. Peggy and I are in love. Naomi is happy. ACS France is thriving. I have over twenty major film credits to my name. Really, there is nothing more I could want.

In spring 2000, the young new king of Morocco, Mohammed VI, opens the country's sky to civil helicopters—something his father, King Hassan II, had forbidden. Morocco is a popular destination for American and European film productions, so we jump at the opportunity to open Dunes Helicopter, the first helicopter company for making movies in the country. Peggy sets up an office in Casablanca and we build a hangar in Ouarzazate, a small town south of the High Atlas Mountains right at the edge of the desert. It's known as the gateway to the Sahara, and everything from *Lawrence of*

Arabia to *The Mummy* has been shot in there. For months the two of us go back and forth from Paris to Morocco getting the operation going and eventually extending our services to VIP transport, aerial work for local construction, and medevac for rally cars. Basically, every kind of flying you can do with a helicopter except military missions and reporting the weather.

I love being in Africa. I especially love being there with Peggy, but lately, my mind is preoccupied with other things.

The burden of running the company in France is heavy. I'm proud of what we've accomplished, but I feel like I'm in school again—sitting at a desk, signing checks, getting older, watching my time pass by. I spend most days dealing with paperwork, taxes, lawsuits, and employee drama. It doesn't interest me. I want to do something different. I think it's just a midlife crisis at first, but I don't want to buy a sports car, pierce my ears, or dye what's left of my hair. I want to make history.

My initial plan is to land on top of Mount Everest, to be the first helicopter pilot ever to do it. Nothing is more epic than Everest; it's twenty-nine thousand feet of crazy weather, glaciers, yetis, and ice fields. After looking into it, I discover that the only thing more epic than Everest is the pile of paperwork required to land on the top of it. The summit is shared by two countries with two different languages and two different alphabets. That means filling out two different sets of forms I don't understand. No thanks, I'm doing enough paperwork at ACS as it is.

Besides, something about it doesn't feel quite right. I want to go higher than twenty-nine thousand feet, and I know I can. I want to go higher than anyone else has ever gone before. I'm going to break the world record for altitude in a helicopter.

Maybe it's about getting older. Maybe it's about my father. Or maybe it's something bigger. Suddenly it's all I can think about.

At home on a Thursday afternoon, I tell Peggy about my plan to break the record. She's just gotten back from Orly after working in Casablanca for the week. Her hair is up, and her face is tan, even though it's just early spring. She manages to look a little younger than me every day.

Peggy is fun and she believes in me, but she's also a businesswoman.

She's smart, rational, and not the kind of person who's going to tell her CEO (who also happens to be the man she loves and the father of a young kid) to spend the year trying to do stunts. I'm expecting she'll laugh at me and tell me to go pierce my ears, but after I tell her my idea, she sits me down, pulls out her computer, and says,

"OK. What do we need to do to make it happen?"

We spend the next few days researching and find that the current world record holder, Jean Boulet, lives just outside Paris. In 1972 he was able to reach 40,820 feet (12,442 meters) with a Lama helicopter. No one has been able to beat it.

When I call, totally out of the blue, Jean Boulet is surprisingly happy to hear from me. Maybe that's because after thirty years, his record is still standing. I'm sure he's used to pilots trying to break it and failing, so he's enthusiastic and ready to help when I tell him I want to try for forty-five thousand feet.

Back when Boulet achieved the record, he was a test pilot for Aerospatiale (now Airbus Helicopter) and constantly pushing the limit of the machines. No one else on earth can give me the advice he can, and he's a cool enough guy that he doesn't pretend the record was easy to achieve. It wasn't. His engine flamed out on the way down, forcing him to land with no power. He says the only good news there was that he also achieved a record for longest autorotation.

He patiently answers question after question about equipment, technical problems, and prep. Basically, he gives me a road map to forty thousand feet.

"Fred," he says seriously, just before I'm about to thank him and say goodbye, "focus on the mental preparation. You're going to encounter challenges on the way up, and if you don't have the mental stamina, you will find a thousand reasons to go back down."

I hadn't even thought about any kind of psychological training.

"Good luck," he says. "I'm looking forward to hearing all about it."

I'm feeling confident, but not everyone is quite as excited as Boulet is.

It never occurs to me that I won't be able to go for the record in my home country. France has a rich aviation history, and French pilots (including

Jean) hold several world records. I don't need the French Civil Aviation Authority to throw me a parade or anything; I'm just looking for a permit. They turn me down almost immediately. Eurocopter, the manufacturer of the A-Star AS350B2, the only helicopter I want to be in at forty thousand feet, also makes it clear that they are not at all interested in partnering with me. Even buying the proper safety essentials is a problem. Nobody in Europe wants to sell me a counterpressure jacket or oxygen system because neither is civilian-tested. I need both to counteract the lack of oxygen at such a high altitude. The jacket will gradually inflate as I ascend, putting pressure on my lungs to make sure they don't expand too quickly and begin to bleed. The oxygen system will serve as a supplement and hopefully ensure that I don't suffer from cerebral hypoxia (a low level of oxygen in the brain) and pass out . . . or worse.

With no helicopter, airspace, or safety gear, I need to get creative. A retired military fighter pilot from Russia I'd met during the Paris-Moscow-Beijing Rally sets me up with a manufacturer for the equipment. Russia, as it turns out, has no problem taking my money. Then I contact Turbomeca, the engine manufacturer of the A-Star helicopter. They can't lend me a machine or anything, but they can share data from tests in the pressure chamber to give me an idea of how the engine could behave at high altitudes. They're more than happy to show me the findings:

The engine quit at forty-five thousand feet.

If I lower the power too fast above thirty thousand feet, the engine will flame out due to lack of oxygen.

If the engine *does* flame out, I can restart it beginning at fourteen thousand feet but *not* before.

Merde.

The numbers aren't encouraging. I know the record is possible, but it won't be easy.

By summer, I have almost everything I need to begin training. My twin sister, Catherine, who now runs a successful PR company in Paris, even finds me sponsors: FORTIS, a Swiss watch company, and Columbia Sportswear, who will provide me with a pilot suit and shoes to keep me warm during the flight. The temperature at forty thousand feet is expected to be about minus sixty-nine degrees Fahrenheit. All I'm missing is a helicopter and airspace. They are both hand-delivered to me by a South African angel named Dave Mouton.

I spend a lot of 2001 in South Africa. Producers and directors like making movies there because the sky is reliably blue, the people are reliably friendly, and it's cheap—much cheaper than filming in Europe or the United States. The dynamic landscapes, out-of-control wildlife, and great weather don't hurt either. Not many places can give you snowcapped mountains, zebras, penguins, beaches, diamonds, deserts, forests, and huge, modern cities in the same day.

I'm in Cape Town shooting a car commercial and talking to my friend Dave about my struggle to find a location for the record. Dave Mouton is a sweet guy and the best kind of aviator—not competitive or jealous and completely devoted to making the field as good as it can be. His company does a lot of aerial work in Western Cape, and I use his machines whenever I'm in the country. I've just finished telling him how France broke my heart when he stops me with a crazy look on his face.

"Fred," he says, "why don't you do it *here*?"

Honestly, I can't think of reason why I shouldn't.

Dave has a position with the South African Civil Aviation Authority and can help with the permitting process. He also has military contacts that can offer training in a pressure chamber. When he offers to let me use his brand-new A-Star AS350B2, I can't even believe it. People don't just lend other people their helicopters. I'm not sure I'm hearing him properly, so I ask if he's sure.

"Of course!" Dave says. "Let's make history!"

After hearing so many people say no, his belief and excitement are everything.

By the end of the week the entire thing is set up, and we have a date on the calendar: March 23, 2002, only about two months away.

Everything gets real. Overnight, my training goes from "You Can Get It If You Really Want" by Jimmy Cliff to "Eye of the Tiger" by Survivor. Per Jean Boulet's recommendation, I bring the oxygen equipment back to our apartment and wear it every night for as long as I can stand. The mask smells like new rubber boots and makes me claustrophobic. The helmet weighs as much as a bowling ball. The first time Peggy sees me fully dressed up with my helmet and mask, lying in our bed, she laughs so hard she almost falls over. The spare bedroom becomes a home gym with a weight bench, a NordicTrack treadmill, and of course, a stereo. I use every single opportunity I have to get better, whether I'm doing push-ups while Naomi plays, or climbing to eighteen thousand feet on a ferry and trying to memorize the changes in the machine's behavior. After a month of training, I'm stronger, mentally disciplined, ready.

My mom and dad still live near Le Mans in their *manoir* full of bookcases, art, heavy wooden furniture, and other things I don't relate to. They're not entirely thrilled that I left Stefi and still don't have any real understanding or interest in what I do. They are my parents, though, and I love them. I decide to call my mother in mid-February to tell her about the record.

"Frédéric!" my mom cries when she picks up the phone.

She's surprised to hear from me, and happy, I think. We don't have a lot to talk about, so as an unwritten rule, we don't talk often.

To avoid any awkward small talk, I jump right into explaining to her at length what I'm going to do, when I'm going to do it, and why. She does *not* take the news as well as Dave Mouton, but she tries. She always has.

"Do you promise me you'll wear a parachute?" she asks, taking a long breath.

"Yes, Mom, I promise."

That week I find a parachute, the nice kind that will open by itself in midair if I fall unconscious and can't trigger it. It will be totally useless, of course, but a promise is a promise. My mom doesn't need to know that if I jump out of my helicopter, I'm headed straight into the blades.

By the end of the month, with only a few weeks left of training, I realize I'm missing a crucial member of my team. Jean told me to have somebody strong on my side, someone to be in charge the day of the event to manage all the details so I can focus. Normally that person would be Peggy, but I can't ask her to do it. I'll need her support that day, but as my family. Then I remember Colonel Peters.

At ACS, we receive resumes from people all over who want to work for us. A little while back, one really caught my attention. It was beyond impressive. The guy was a fighter jet pilot and a retired colonel from the US Air Force. He went to Top Gun. *The* Top Gun. We didn't have anything for him at ACS when he sent us his information, but judging by his credentials, he'd be the perfect person to help me. I call the number on a Friday, and on Monday morning, Colonel Peters—a big, redheaded pirate of a man—arrives in an army-green pilot suit covered with military patches. It's love at first sight. I hire him on the spot.

There are a few things about Peters that make me nervous, though. One day we're checking over the machines when he asks me how much power the engine has. Normally it wouldn't be an issue, but when he asks, he's not pointing at the engine; he's pointing at the main transmission. Next, he tells me he has everything set up with the Fédération Aéronautique Internationale to certify the record, and I discover a week from our departure date that they haven't heard from him at all. By that time, it's too late and too expensive to send an inspector. I'm pissed off and confused, but the reasons I'm going for the record are personal, and I'm not going to blow our schedule or our budget to get some fancy paper. Peters dresses great, but the guy is a little shifty and doesn't seem to know much about flying at all. I remind myself over and over that he went to Top Gun and put the worries out of my mind.

On March 19, 2002, Peters and I show up at a military base in Johannesburg with all my equipment for testing. In my black pilot suit, I feel like a man on his way to the moon.

One of the biggest dangers of the record will be the hypoxia. Any lack of oxygen to my brain could affect my ability to make decisions and possibly cause permanent damage. Hypoxia is one reason why airplane cabins are pressurized. Since helicopters aren't typically operating at altitudes that would cause any problems, they are not. I'll be relying entirely on my equipment for the mission. In the pressurized chamber today, they will simulate a decrease in oxygen, putting my equipment and my body through the conditions I'll be facing.

I shake hands with the doctors and engineers operating the chamber, and they tell me they're honored to take part in the mission. Instantly, I remember the military therapist telling me more than twenty years ago: *"It will be impossible for you to become a pilot . . . ever."*

The chamber is a big metal cylinder with small windows, some benches, and a table. The air is still and cold when I walk inside. Rudi Britz, a reputable physician, explains that the first test will make me feel early signs of hypoxia: headaches, confusion, rapid breathing, anxiety.

No problem, I think.

He tells me to write my name on a piece of paper over and over, and they'll slowly suck the oxygen out of the chamber.

"Sounds good."

He shuts the door and I begin writing.

Fred North

Fred North

Fred North

Fr . . . e . . . d

I can't control my pen. My brain is saying one thing. My hand is doing another. The paper looks crazy. The writing is totally illegible. I start to get a headache and a tickling feeling in my stomach. My breathing is fast and shallow. A few seconds later they correct the pressure and I'm fine. It's a scary experience but exactly what I need.

Next we do the same test while I'm wearing my equipment. No more scribbling. Everything is working. I'm ready.

The next morning we fly to Cape Town, where Peggy and Thierry Ranarivelo are waiting. Together, we strip Dave's perfect, mint-condition A-Star of all unneeded weight. That night I sleep exactly eight hours. No tossing or turning. No bad dreams. I'm focused. Mentally, I'm already in the helicopter.

At six thirty in the morning on March 23, I'm sitting in the helicopter at Cape Town International Airport under an intensely blue sky. South African Civil Aviation authorities are standing in a little huddle near the tarmac. Dave, Thierry, Peggy, and Peters are gathered next to the helicopter door, which is still open. Everyone is smiling. My stomach is upset. Honestly, if Peters hadn't already dressed me in my gear and hooked me up to the oxygen, I'd be running into the terminal and getting on the first plane back to Paris. I've never been part of something so enormous. It doesn't feel real.

"Did you check everything?" I ask Peters. He's in his full pilot uniform looking like an extra from *M*A*S*H*. "And I mean triple check. Did you?"

He nods and shoots me a thumbs-up.

Peggy kisses me. I can't tell if she's nervous or not. If she were, she'd never let me know.

"You're strong" she says. "And you're ready. No matter what happens, everything will be fine."

Dave and I do a final check on the handheld VHF radio, and everyone steps away from the machine. The sun is shining bright. Every single muscle in my body is tense. As soon as I start the helicopter, my entire life will change.

I inspect my instruments and press the starter button like I've done a million times before. I call the tower on the radio, the voice that will be in my ear for the next hour or so. He clears me to go up.

The skids lift, the cabin fills with bright light, and I rise above the Cape of Good Hope. It takes me eight minutes to climb to twenty thousand feet, but it has taken me my entire life to get *here*.

My focus is deep and comfortable, the way it always is. Then suddenly, I feel a tickling in my stomach. I see strange flashes and my head aches. I'm going to pass out, and I'm not even halfway there. Something's wrong. I call down to the tower.

"I don't feel well. I can't breathe."

"Romeo Hotel Alfa," the tower answers back. "I am relaying from your team. Have you checked your oxygen?"

My breath is getting shallow.

"Yes . . . I did . . . something isn't right."

"Romeo Hotel Alfa, do you want to declare an emergency?" he asks, concerned, deadly serious.

"Stand by," I tell him.

I don't want to quit. I grab at my mask, jacket, and helmet. I can hardly move.

In the right corner of my eye, I notice my counter pressure jacket is completely inflated and deformed. I can't breathe because my lungs are being compressed. Something is wrong with the valve.

That idiot Peters!

I remove my harness seatbelts. Nothing changes, so I start to mess with my parachute straps. The valve that regulates the jacket is stuck underneath them. It's supposed to stay clear at all times. Instead of gradually inflating, the jacket was continually triggered, squeezing me like a giant fist. I pull down the zipper, open the valve, and take the biggest breath of my life. I call back down to the tower.

"Cape Town tower for Romeo Hotel Alfa. I found the issue, all good. I will keep climbing."

"Romeo Hotel Alfa, so happy to hear your voice again," he answers back. He sounds like he was holding his breath too.

I'm going to break the record. Then I'm going to fire Peters.

Without the Jaws of Life crushing my rib cage, I'm able to refocus. I don't love what I'm doing or hate it. I'm just lost in it. At twenty-five thousand feet, the machine is performing well, but all I can feel is the pressure.

I go higher. And higher.

Thirty thousand feet—

Thirty-two thousand feet—

Thirty-five thousand feet—

At almost 38,500 feet, I hear a new voice on the radio.

"What's *that*?"

A South African Airways 747 is talking to the controller, confused by the small target not moving on his radar.

"It's just a crazy Frenchman trying to beat a world altitude record with a helicopter. Don't worry about it," the controller calls back to him, laughing.

"Oh, wow. That's amazing! Let me do a flyby," he says back.

Sure enough, an enormous plane comes by to my right, waving his wings on a turn. The sky is the clearest I've ever seen, and everything is going well. But I'm losing my connection to the helicopter.

As the plane disappears from my field of vision, the machine starts acting strange. I go a little higher and the chopper starts stalling, going up a few feet, then down, then up, then down. It's like I'm flying in a big bowl of soup. At this altitude, there is no oxygen, no density, no power. My movements are exaggerated. I'm trying to find a little extra lift somewhere, but it doesn't exist. The machine isn't responding to me. At 40,500 feet, I've lost total connection with the helicopter. I'm surprised by how lonely it feels.

Suddenly, a fifty-mile-per-hour wind kicks in from the north, dragging me toward the Atlantic. I only have seventeen minutes of fuel left, so it's not a great time to fly over the ocean.

I check my altimeter. I'm at 41,500 feet. Boulet's record was 40,820 feet. I did what I came to do.

But I want to climb higher. I want forty-five thousand feet.

The wind is pushing me away from the shoreline, and I realize all at once how cold I am. My body is shivering. My hands and feet have gone stiff and numb. I want to push further, but I can't feel anything. My low fuel indicator is on. It has been for a while. I only have five percent left. I can't even stand to have less than a quarter tank in my car.

The altimeter says 42,500, and all at once, I know I'm done. I reached my limit. I'm ready to come down.

"Cape Town tower, I reached 42,500 feet. Can you confirm on your radar?" I ask.

"Romeo Hotel Alfa, yes—I confirm, 42,500 feet. Congratulations!" I hear applause in the background.

Just then, there's a massive amount of turbulence. The helicopter is thrown sideways. I panic and lower my collective too fast. Like Turbomeca warned me, the engine flames out and I'm dropping ten thousand feet per minute. It's totally insane.

Time stops and the world feels quiet. I feel almost like I'm underwater. I can't restart the engine until fourteen thousand feet, so I fall and fall. There is nothing but bright blue around me. I'm alone. There's too much to think about, too much to do. *Now! Think!* My altimeter gauge is spinning like a top. Adrenaline takes over.

I pull the collective up a bit to try and control my RPMs. I'm worried I'm going to lose a blade. I'm fighting the controls and losing, trying to manage my ground speed, my rotor speed, get back toward the shore, and manually deflate the counterpressure jacket. My muscles are on fire. My head is throbbing. I can feel my pulse in every inch of my body. I'm way past the point of panic, if I was ever even there. Each breath feels sharp, final. *I don't want to die.*

At eighteen thousand feet I begin the restart procedure (helicopters take longer to start than cars) and wait to press the engine start-up switch. I only have six percent fuel. I've never started an engine midflight before. I don't even know if it's possible right now.

Sixteen thousand feet—

Fifteen thousand feet—

Fourteen thousand feet—

Like a miracle, the machine comes back to life.

But at ten thousand feet, the fuel indicator is hovering just above zero percent, kissing the red line.

"Cape Town Tower, it's Romeo Hotel Alfa. I was able to restart the engine, but I have no fuel left. I am coming in for landing. I might flame out again."

"Romeo Hotel Alfa, we are clearing the runway for you," he answers back. "It's all yours."

I wait for the engine to die, bracing myself, feeling every second as it passes. One minute before landing, my whole body starts shaking, breaking down.

The skids come down hard. There's just enough fuel.

It takes me seven minutes to descend from 42,500 feet, the longest seven minutes of my life. Like always, the landing is the hardest part.

Dave is the one who turns off the helicopter. Peggy helps me out of my equipment and straps. I'm crying. I don't stop for forty-five minutes. I hit my limit—as a pilot and a human being. I saw everything I needed to see, every single part of myself in an hour and a half. And I don't want to see it ever again.

The Cape Town tower stamps my logbook with the altitude recorded and gives me a certificate, which is good enough for me. I go home with Peggy.

It takes me a few days to get my strength back, but as I do, I fire Peters. He never attended Top Gun and was never a colonel in the Air Force. He just looked good in a pilot suit.

x émis par : 013956/989
Fax reçu de : +27 0219443292
25/03/02   17:00   Pg: 1/1

WORLD RECORD ATTEMPT ALTITUDE HELICOPTER

CONFIRMATION

I, John J. MITTELMEYER, confirm that on Saturday 23rd March 2002, at 9:15AM, in Cape Town International Airport, the helicopter Astar AS 350B2 ZS-RHA piloted by Fred NORTH has reached an altitude of 42 500 Feets after take off and landed at destination Cape Town International Airport.
This altitude has been confirmed by transpondeur mode C.

Signed
John J. MITTELMEYER
Radar Room

ATNS COMPANY LTD

2002 -03- 25

PRIVATE BAG X17
D F MALAN AIRPORT
7525

19

Nothing Is Impossible

SOMETHING IN ME CHANGES after the altitude record. Suddenly, everything is clear, and nothing is impossible. If I have a dream, I have no reason not to live it. ACS France is somebody's dream, but it isn't mine. I'm a pilot, not a CEO. No amount of paperwork or cool office furniture will change that. I don't know exactly what my next step is, but I know who will be walking beside me.

In summer 2002, Peggy and I decide to take a road trip from San Francisco to Los Angeles, through Yosemite and Sequoia National Park. I haven't spent a lot of time in California, but it's always felt a bit like the promised land. All the big movie studios are in California, and so are all the people who make them. In my head, we are just taking a vacation. We need a break, a different kind of adventure. All we really want to do is explore, be in the wild, and visit Larry in LA. On paper, nothing is special—but for some reason, I feel it will be.

We fly into New York and spend a week checking out the city before heading west and into the wilderness. Peggy has spent weeks on the phone with a woman named Barbie from Cruise America arranging a rental RV, laying out our itinerary, and reviewing an assortment of class C motor homes outfitted with stoves, small Formica tables, and sleeping platforms covered in foam mats. She decided on a huge tan box that somebody has had the audacity to call "the Chateau." We pick it up from a suburban car lot decorated with metallic streamers and an inflatable tube-shaped man that dances in the wind. Chip, the guy at the dealership, hands us an operating manual, a map of California, and a pair of latex gloves. He tells me they are for cleaning what Peggy calls *la boite à caca*, the tiny tank of black wastewater from the toilet positioned on the Chateau's belly. Neither of us has driven anything larger than a minivan, certainly nothing with a *boite à caca*. It has gray racing stripes down the side and handles like a mastodon.

After rolling (slowly) along I-5, we spend our first night at a campground somewhere between San Francisco and Yosemite. Over the course of the day, the temperature has dropped about twenty degrees. There's snow sitting on top of the Sierra Nevada Mountains in the distance, and as soon as the sun sets, we can see our breath. Peggy says we should plug in. I have no idea where or how to plug in the RV. When we rented it, I figured the entire thing was fully self-sustained, a perfect little house on wheels. Eventually we get hooked up and go to sleep.

About thirty minutes after we shut our eyes, something beeps. It's loud and sharp, like a little bird on steroids. We don't think too much of it and try to rest again. Ninety seconds later, it chirps again. And again. And again. By about the tenth beep, we're both up madly pulling open the fake wood cabinets, searching underneath the table, and peeking behind the stove. We have no idea what it is or where it's coming from. The noise is impossible to isolate.

Sometime after midnight, still jet-lagged and having seen too many action movies, I grab my nail clippers and cut the wires behind the stove like I'm disarming a bomb. For sixty seconds, we stare at each other in perfect silence.

It chirps again. We give up and fall asleep with thin RV pillows over our ears.

Peggy is lying on her back staring up at the ceiling the next morning when she notices a round box with a flashing red light. She jumps out of the bed, removes the plastic cover, and takes out the battery inside. The beeping stops. We don't have smoke detectors in France. Neither one of us has ever even seen one. Peggy starts laughing, and I fall in love with her all over again.

With a now-broken stove and bruised egos, we leave Yosemite and head south past wind farms, cow farms, and oil fields in the low desert. Peggy sings and I do a lot of thinking. I realize how much of my life has been lived above the world, and how little actually *in* it. Approaching Bakersfield at a blistering sixty-five miles per hour, overtaken by Toyota Tercels and PT Cruisers, I feel free, as free as I ever have, maybe more so.

After another sleepless night in a campground that reminds us a little too much of *Deliverance*, we arrive at Lake Isabella in the Sequoia National Forest. We park the RV and stand at the edge of the water, which is blue-green and freezing. Suddenly I'm full of hope, overwhelmingly happy and connected.

"I want to live here," I say.

"Me too." Peggy smiles back at me.

And that's it. We never say, "We're moving to California," but both of us know we're home. At forty-one years old, feeling more like twenty-one, I decide I'm going to take my career as a film pilot all the way to the top, to Hollywood. The first person we call is Larry Blanford.

Larry Blanford walks into the lobby lounge of Shutters on the Beach in Santa Monica in his jeans and aviators, tanned as a cowboy boot, still looking cool as can be. We wave him over to a table facing the ocean and the infamous boardwalk. He hugs us and slides in next to Peggy on the banquette. They've been working together for two years. Peggy loves Larry as much as I do.

He grins. "So, what have you kids been up to out here?"

"Larry," I begin, "we made the decision. We want to move to Los Angeles."

It's the first time I've said it out loud to anyone other than Peggy.

"But we can't do it without you," I go on. "We don't know anyone else here."

Larry looks at us with a big smile and claps his hands. He starts laughing. Peggy breaks into a smile too.

"Heck yeah!" he says. "Fred, you know I'm happy to help you find work. It won't be easy but buddy, you can do this."

Larry knows as well as I do that nobody is waiting for me in America. I'm an established film pilot in Europe. I've made plenty of movies. I have the world record. I've flown Brad Pitt through the Austrian Alps. But no one in LA knows who I am. I'm gambling a twenty-year career on the gut feeling that I can make it. The circle of film pilots in Hollywood is closed, and they're not welcoming new members. Even with Larry's help, it will be hard to get my foot in the door.

For a few minutes we strategize about when to move, where, how we'll get visas, and what projects Larry has coming up. Before he leaves, he looks me straight in the eye (this is the only way Larry bothers to look at anyone) and promises me I'm doing the right thing. I believe him.

"Call me anytime, whatever you need," he says, then disappears out the door onto Pico Boulevard. With Larry's blessing, it starts to feel real. We celebrate over tea.

A big beam of sun comes through the window, and Peggy sets down her Earl Grey. She looks at me with a smile, her head tilted slightly to the right, raising her eyebrow the way she does when she gets an idea.

"Do you want to get married?" she asks.

I'm not expecting it. We'd never even discussed marriage before, but of course I want to marry her. She's my soulmate, my best friend, my family.

I smile. "Of course."

We call Larry Blanford and tell him we need one more favor. The next morning around ten thirty, he meets us at Los Angeles City Hall and serves as our witness as we—wearing the same clothes we camped in—exchange standard-issue vows written by a city officer. The ceremony is simple, funny, and totally perfect. We fly back to Paris husband and wife and sell ACS to an old school friend of Peggy's.

We want to be in Venice for two reasons. First, Venice is the part of Los Angeles where Larry lives, and he's the only person we know. Second, we can walk everywhere. We've heard about the traffic on the 405 and don't want anything to do with it. Venice has the right amount of art, culture, grunge, canals, and bridges. Really, it's about as close to Paris as we can get. There's even a little French Lycée for Naomi who will be coming with us, since Stefi lost the custody battle, prioritizing her night life over taking care of her daughter.

In spring 2003, after flying back and forth from Paris all winter, Peggy finds us a typical California beach bungalow from the 1920s that needs a little love, some remodeling, and the Parisian touch. It's not far from the beach and has several smoke detectors, so she puts in an offer. I work on getting my US commercial pilot license.

My examiner at the Long Beach Airport is a gray-haired man in his fifties named Tim Tucker. Everyone who has ever flown a helicopter knows who Tim Tucker is. He used to be a test pilot and chief instructor for Robinson Helicopter Company. He's worked all over the world and has evaluated thousands of pilots. Philippe Lesourd, a French pilot who covers the always terrible highway traffic and has a school based out of Van Nuys Airport, lets me use his JetRanger. We land on the grass outside Tim's office.

Tim shakes my hand and looks at my paperwork.

"Wow. Ten thousand hours," he says, laughing a bit. "Well, Fred, I think you're the most experienced student pilot I've ever had. I'm not going to ask you to hover or anything like that, but I need you to show me that you know what you are doing."

He thinks a little bit longer, staring out at the runway and a grass area with some random equipment and debris.

"OK," he decides. "I'll have you perform a 180-degree autorotation. Turn the engine off, use the wind to keep the rotor spinning, and land as close as you can to that plastic beacon on the grass. If you can put your skid less than three feet away from it, you're done."

The beacon is small, about the size of a traffic cone.

"No problem," I tell him. I would put my skin on top of a mouse if he asked me.

We go up in the JetRanger, and ten minutes later, my skid is touching the beacon. Within the hour, I have a license in hand. All I need now is a work visa.

The visa doesn't really worry me. The O-1 permit is for people with "extraordinary skills." I would say putting your skid on top of a traffic cone is the definition of an extraordinary skill. I'm a world record holder. I've done plenty of television interviews and been the subject of newspaper articles. Really, they should make me the poster boy for the O-1 visa. We hand our case off to a well-known immigration attorney in Los Angeles, and through late summer, we focus on getting the house ready (not easy from across the Atlantic), shipping our furniture, and teaching Naomi some basic English— things like book, school, beach, and baby. Baby is an important one because in August, the day we close on the house, Peggy discovers she's pregnant.

By October, all our things are in boxes and we've purchased three plane tickets to Los Angeles leaving December 27.

On December 26, our immigration attorney calls to deliver the news that my visa has been denied. He'd handed the application off to an associate who forgot to translate several documents from French to English. Appealing the decision could take months. We can't afford to wait that long. We bought a house. Our daughter is enrolled in school. Visa or no visa, there's no turning back. On December 27 we get on the plane.

For the first two months, I commute back and forth from Los Angeles to Paris, leaving Peggy, who is seven months pregnant, alone to figure things out in California. And she does.

"We can get the E-2 visa," Peggy yells into the phone.

It's just past ten a.m. in Paris, which means it's somewhere past midnight in Los Angeles. I'm on set, about to shoot a commercial. I don't know what an E-2 visa is. I'm just glad she's not in labor.

"What are you talking about?" I ask. "Why are you still awake? What kind of visa?"

She explains that she took Naomi to a little birthday party in Santa Monica for one of the kids in her class at the lycée and met an immigration attorney there who specialized in helping French citizens get their green cards. When Peggy explained our situation, the two of them stayed up until midnight putting together a plan to resubmit our application under a different category. She tells me that if we start a business in LA with the proper funding, a business that will provide jobs and positively impact the economy, we could be eligible for approval. I'm not a CEO, but my wife is.

I fly back to LA, and for two weeks we do nothing but work—gathering all the documents needed, purchasing equipment for the helicopters, hiring a couple people to help run the company, and writing up a detailed business plan combining all the projections and numbers. We submit the application and get an appointment at the US Embassy in Paris at the beginning of March. Peggy will be almost nine months pregnant.

I had pictured our meeting at the embassy to be something kind of classy and exciting: a plush office with leather chairs, a portrait of an American eagle or Abraham Lincoln, a passionate discussion of my business, and a detailed presentation on how we were going to run our operations. There isn't even a watercooler. It's more like a visit to the DMV. We sit in a long, gray hallway lined with a dozen gray chairs, which I'm sad to say are plastic, and wait to be called up to a service window. Peggy is uncomfortable. The baby is kicking constantly, and she's fanning her face with a stack of paperwork.

"North!" calls a tall, bulky blond guy from the window at the end of the hall. He's maybe thirty years old and looks like a football player. We walk up holding hands. Both of us are shaking.

I try a couple of jokes on the officer, whose name tag just says "Burns." Maybe it's his first name or maybe it's his last. Normally, stuff like this goes over well for me, but Burns doesn't react at all. Burns isn't looking to make friends.

He asks a couple of questions, which Peggy and I answer as straightforwardly as possible.

He thinks.

"I'll give you two years, not five," he says, "because I don't believe in your business."

He pounds our application with a giant stamp.

"Thank you," I say. At least, I think that's what I say.

Peggy and I leave the embassy in shock. We're relieved, exhausted, and terrified to have to build a profitable business on a two-year timeline. Peggy feels the baby kick again. I feel the sword of Damocles hovering above our heads.

On April 5, 2004, Tom North is born at St. John's Hospital in Santa Monica, just four days after my first paying job in America. We have to negotiate the cost of the delivery with the doctor because we have no insurance. In France, health care is free, but in America, having a baby costs as much as a Fiat Panda.

Of course, Larry Blanford comes to the hospital as soon as Peggy goes into labor. He stays by our side for a few hours after the birth.

"Hey, Fred," Larry whispers.

We're in the recovery room seated on either side of Peggy. Baby Tom is sleeping on her chest. His face is pink and mostly cheeks, and he already has more hair than I do.

What? I mouth back at Larry.

Peggy shoots both of us a look.

"I've got a commercial for you," he whispers again. "Sikorsky Helicopter."

"Are you guys serious?!" Peggy asks.

The Sikorsky commercial is shooting on a lake with a fake roof peeking out of the water. The premise is that the always reliable Sikorsky is going to rescue a woman from the rooftop during a flood. I'm flying the camera helicopter, and I'm pretty excited to go air-to-air with this monster machine. The rescue chopper circles around the roof over and over. I film it from the front, from the lady's vantage point, and from way above. Finally the chopper goes down to rescue the woman, and I think my work is done. But Larry decides he wants footage of the pilot inside the helicopter too.

"Fred, we're going to get you instead of the other pilot, OK?" Larry tells me.

Larry thinks I'm better looking than the military pilot, so he wants to put me on camera instead. The military pilot looks like an impressive guy to me, but whatever works. Larry films me sitting in the chopper on the ground with the door open. I try to look as handsome and as "G.I. Joe" as possible.

I don't think much of it at the time, but appearing on camera is a big deal. It ends up being my first Screen Actors Guild contract, and SAG is the strongest union in town. There's no way you can book any job as a helicopter stunt pilot on a movie or TV project without membership. I'm mostly interested in filming, not acting, but I'm not above flying around with an itchy wig on my head if the price is right. By the end of summer, I'm booking commercials in Europe and in the US as a stunt pilot and a film pilot. It pays the bills, but it's no big break. That comes after.

In the fall, Larry is hired by Fox Studios to be director of photography for the second unit of *Fantastic Four*, a high-octane superhero movie starring Jessica Alba and Chris Evans. The second unit is responsible mainly for the shots in the movie that don't have principal characters: landscapes, stunts, things like that. The movie has quite a lot of complex aerial work and will be shot in New York and Canada. There's nobody in Canada specializing in aerial filming, and American licensed pilots aren't allowed to fly on Canadian registered aircraft. Larry wants me for the job *if* I can figure out a way around the licensing requirement. It's late October when he calls. The first day of filming is December 8. I don't have a lot of time, but I'm sure I can it make it work.

Steve Flynn, CEO of Blackcomb Helicopters, is the one to deliver the bad news. He's the guy running operations up north. I call him after talking to Larry to start planning for the movie. He brings up the licensing issues right away.

"It's no problem," I tell him. "I'm planning to get my Canadian commercial license within the next month."

He takes a long breath.

"Fred," he says, "I'm sorry. Canada is different. There's no way you can do your commercial in a month. It doesn't work that way. Let's talk about a plan B. We can hire a Canadian pilot—"

"Steve," I cut him off, "there's no plan B. Just tell me: If I succeed with my license, can I fly your helicopter for the job?"

"Yes, but Fred, your timeline is . . . extremely ambitious." He sighs.

"I have to try," I promise, hanging up the phone.

As it turns out, Steve Flynn is not kidding around. The Canadian licensure process takes months of prep. It's more extensive than the French and US protocols combined. *And* I'll have to go back to school to do it. *Merde.*

Aéroport Saint-Mathieu-de-Beloeil is a small airport east of Montreal that offers a three-month prep course for the written portion of the Canadian exam. I call and ask if they can condense it to two weeks for me, given my experience.

The instructor's answer is direct and final:

"Absolutely impossible, M. North. It's a three-hour written test with ninety-percent success required to pass. It takes three months of study, *minimum.*"

"But are the three months of study *required*?" I ask him.

He laughs.

"No. You can choose to study on our own, but no one has ever done it that way."

"But I *can*?"

"You can *try*," he replies. "But you shouldn't."

The Beloeil airport is a small collection of orange-roofed hangars and administrative buildings not far from a town on the Richelieu River. The land around it is cold, flat, and brown. Montreal is forty minutes away. There are no distractions here. I'm sure some people would love it if there were, but it's just small planes, helicopters, cold weather, and fields. I arrive there in early November.

I walk into the flight school, and someone directs me to a classroom full of twenty-year-old aspiring pilots. I take a nervous breath and find a spot at the front. The instructor passes out a thick outline for the next three months and begins to explain the coursework. It's difficult for me to pay attention. I don't have time to talk about studying. I need to *actually* study.

At lunch, I corner the teacher and explain my situation, asking if there's any way he can teach me faster. He says no, just like the first guy.

That afternoon, I skip class. I start asking around and figure out that there are two young guys at the airport who have just completed their written exams. They are not hard to find.

Laurent and Pierre, two friendly looking kids in brand-new pilot jackets, are having a cigarette outside of a hangar when I spot them. They're working on their flying and basically living at the airport, just like I used to.

"Hey, guys!" I walk up to them waving. "My name is Fred North. I'm a film pilot, and I need to get my Canadian commercial license for a movie I'm doing in British Columbia. Any chance you could help me study for the written exam? I'll pay you, of course. I have more than ten thousand hours. I've been flying for twenty years. I just need to pass the test. What do you think?"

Laurent's eyes go big. Pierre's eyes go bigger. They look like they could be brothers—both have sandy-colored hair, freckles, and are built like telecom poles.

"Are you kidding?!" Pierre yells. "We would love to help you! You should be our mentor!"

Laurent stubs out his cigarette. "When do we start?"

"Right now," I tell them.

For the next ten days, we study from six a.m. to midnight in a crappy rented room next to one of the hangars. It's gray inside and gray outside, and the air is so dry that we all get sick. The only time one of us leaves is to get lunch and dinner. Pierre drills me about minimum flight visibility, wind forecasts, Bernoulli's principle, and when to turn my lights on. Laurent brings a massive stack of books and sort of reads them for me, pulling out the important facts, writing out and color-coding his notes.

Memories of school and testing come back to me as we work—the results of my IQ test, the smack of the ruler against my forehead, the awful look in my father's eyes when he wondered out loud what to do with me—but I push them away. By the end of our time, I'm sleep-deprived and overwhelmed, equipped to write the exam and do nothing else, not drive a car, not wipe my own butt.

That day, Pierre and Laurent pick me up from my hotel in a mid-nineties Ford Explorer with bad brakes, then drive me to the testing center like a pair of proud dads. I pass with almost ninety-eight percent. The next day, I pass my flight test and the medical.

A few crazy weeks after arriving in Montreal, I have my Canadian commercial license. Steve Flynn doesn't believe me until I fax him the document and he sees it with his own eyes.

Fantastic Four begins shooting in December. The aerials, as promised, are totally epic.

Six months ago, if you had told me a Canadian helicopter license would be the key to making it in Hollywood, I would have said you were crazy. But over the next couple of years, Canada becomes a hot spot for filming. There's some special tax rebate for moviemaking, and as the productions move north, so do I. The industry in Canada still doesn't have many film pilots, and not many film pilots in LA have the proper credentials to fly in Canada. But I do, and some of my other credentials end up coming in handy too.

My work at ACS France left me more knowledge than I ever wanted about cameras and film equipment in general. Suddenly, productions don't just see me just as a pilot. I'm an aerial coordinator, too, a turnkey solution. I can source machines everywhere from Morocco to Moscow, and I know what gear is right for the footage needed. I can get permits and negotiate with civil aviation in a way most pilots can't or won't. Sure, I'm competing with amazing talent, but I'm offering more. Also, since I spent so many years covering the rallies, doing medevacs for the Raid Gauloises, and landing on top of hotels in Cairo, stunt work comes easily to me. I'm a fish in water. There is nobody better at flying sideways.

Cover Your Ass

"FRED! WHAT ARE YOU DOING this afternoon?"

It's January 2005, and Larry is on the phone. He's excited about something. I can't guess what.

"Nothing much," I answer. "Why?"

"I just got a call from Steve Wynn. I'm assuming you know who that is?" he asks.

I don't.

"Steve Wynn!" Larry yells. "Steve. Wynn. The billionaire."

Still no idea.

"Well, the short version is that this Wynn basically built Las Vegas. Steven Spielberg gave him my number, and he just called me out of the blue. You do know who Steven Spielberg is, right?"

He laughs. So do I.

Very funny, Larry.

"Anyway, Steve Wynn made a commercial for his new hotel, and the aerials are a mess. Just awful, Fred. He needs to redo everything fast. Are you available to meet with him today?"

I shrug. "Sure." I'm still not entirely sure who the guy is or what I'm signing up for, but if Larry is involved, it's got to be good.

"Great!" he says. "Wynn is sending his jet to pick us up from the Santa Monica Airport at two p.m."

"You're not serious." I'm laughing now. "Larry?"

Three hours later I'm in a boardroom with floor-to-ceiling windows overlooking Las Vegas, seated across from the most powerful man on the Strip.

Steve Wynn is an intimidating guy. He's got black hair and he's dressed like he's going to a funeral. I think the identical German shepherds sitting on either side of him are probably overkill, but since they're the size of small dinosaurs and haven't broken eye contact with me since I sat down, I keep my opinion to myself.

There are about a dozen other people at the table. I'm never introduced to them, but I can assume by the looks on their faces that they're executives from the ad agency. They're pale and exhausted, just waiting for the guillotine to drop. The funeral Wynn dressed for is probably theirs.

After a beautiful woman fills our water glasses, Wynn claps his hands together.

"Let's begin," he says.

The lights dim, a projector screen drops down from the ceiling, and the commercial begins to play. It's a disaster.

Right away I can tell they shot at the wrong time of day and didn't get low enough. The light and the angles are all wrong. The hotel looks boring. There's no sense of excitement or anticipation—all things Wynn reminds us of as the footage plays. His hotel looks like crap, he looks like crap, the entire thing is just . . . crap!

The advertising people are shrinking in their Brooks Brothers and looking like they want to hide under the table. It's enormous, so there would be plenty of room for all of them.

The screen goes black and the projector folds back into the ceiling. Light fills the room again. Everyone is quiet but my mind is buzzing with ideas.

Even though the commercial is a train wreck, the building is extraordinary, like a giant bronze fin sticking out of the sand. Larry and I can make something great. I know it.

"Thoughts?" Steve Wynn looks at us.

Larry does most of the talking because Larry is the Director of Photography (DP) *and* because he speaks much better English than I do. He's brutally honest. The agency hired someone who didn't know what they were doing, and the commercial needs to be totally reshot.

"Yes!" Wynn says. "New ideas! Vision!"

He goes on for a while about how important the hotel is, how important he is, how he's *Steve Wynn*, dammit, it's Vegas, dammit—that kind of thing.

The ad executives played it safe. Steve Wynn owns casinos and attack dogs. He's not exactly a "play it safe" kind of guy. I elbow Larry. I know exactly what we need to do.

"Ask him if he's afraid of heights," I whisper. He looks at me, intrigued. Then smiles.

Wynn is still ranting when Larry interrupts him.

"Mr. Wynn," he says, "do you mind me asking if you are comfortable with heights?"

He looks confused and not thrilled to have been cut off.

"No, I don't have any problem with heights. Why?"

Larry nods at me. It's my turn to jump in. Larry has always told me to fight for the right shot, so that's what I do.

"Sir, if you have the balls to stand on top of your hotel, six hundred feet above the Strip, right on the edge—I mean *really* on the edge of the building—we can make something incredible. We'll hover in front of you with the helicopter. The blades will be maybe ten feet from your head. We'll have the camera full frame on your face while you do your speech. Then we'll zoom out, pulling back and dropping down at the same time to reveal your building and the massive Wynn logo."

I stop for a moment, remembering Peggy's father standing on the rock ledge looking out over the Gobi Desert in China.

"It will just be you in the middle of the sky. The shot will be totally epic . . . *if* you've got the balls."

Steve Wynn is silent. I'm either German shepherd dog food or his new best friend. The guys across the table from us are shifting, clearing their throats, messing with their pens.

Wynn stares at me and Larry, eyes darting back and forth. Then he turns his head to the executives.

"You! You! You! You! You! Get out!"

Without a word, they stand up and leave the room. Quickly.

Wynn stands up, leans over the table, and looks at me.

"And who are you exactly?" he asks.

"Sir, my name is Fred North. I am the helicopter pilot."

"Well, George," he says to me, "yes, I do have the balls."

I don't know whether it was my accent or whether he has me confused with someone else, but for the next several days of planning and communication, I'm George. I get the feeling that to Steve Wynn, I always will be.

A couple of weeks later, against a blue sky, Steve Wynn (and his balls) stand on top of his forty-five-story hotel facing the Strip. He's wearing a cool black suit and a safety harness, and he's just as intimidating and powerful without the huge dogs. The guy doesn't flinch. He just fixes his hair, walks straight to the edge of the building, and delivers his lines, looking like he's done it one hundred times before. I'm hovering just over ten feet away from him, and he's staring straight into the camera. We're zoomed in, so as far as the audience can tell, he's standing on the corner of Las Vegas Boulevard and East Desert Inn Road. When he's done talking, I drop down and go back, revealing how massive the hotel is. The audience discovers that Steve Wynn is standing on top of the most magnificent building in Las Vegas like a superhero. After the first take, we all know it's going to be a hit.

"Larry, George," Wynn says to us at the end of the shoot, "you did it."

He looks proud. I can see how much it means to him.

He's on his phone right away, saying, "George was *this* close to me! It was crazy!"

When the commercial comes out, sure enough, it's a monster. People love it. Donald Trump calls Wynn, refusing to believe it wasn't a green screen. Every time I see him on TV standing on the edge of the building, I think, *Man, that guy is living his dream.*

I'm living my dream too.

Little by little, my name gets out there. I make a commercial that people like. Larry recommends me for a film. More directors are willing to hire me, even though I'm not the most well-known pilot in town. US Citizenship and Immigration Services agrees to extend our visa by five years. The travel is almost constant, the money is tight, and the work is hard, but I'm happy. We all are. Peggy, Naomi, baby Tom, and I are settling into California life, making friends, going to the beach, and not exactly hating 290 days of sunshine a year.

On May 31, 2006, my second son, Cooper North, is born in Santa Monica. At the time, I'm in New Zealand with a camera hanging from a long line, shooting Roland Emmerich's movie *10,000 BC*. When we found out Peggy was pregnant, we thought about moving the entire family to Queenstown, but we wanted our baby to be born in the US—mostly so the baby would never, ever have to go through the visa process with godawful "Burns" or anyone like him. Of course, I felt conflicted about missing the delivery, but Peggy insisted. She said she'd done it before, so doing it again wouldn't be such a big deal. The truth is, she'd probably rather have her girlfriends around her during the birth than me and Larry.

Sure enough, she has a perfect delivery. The baby is healthy and adorable, and of course, Larry shows up at the hospital. I meet Cooper in mid-June as soon as my work on the movie wraps. He has dark brown eyes and starts smiling (mischievously) very early on. By nine months he's walking, and soon after that he's trying to skateboard. We both think he's a little stuntman.

In 2007, with several major movies and commercials under my belt, the

Motion Picture Pilots Association grants me membership, and the exclusive, unofficial Hollywood film pilot club makes room for one more. I work a ton, as much as I can. Even though I'm a family man and not ferrying helicopters across the Java Sea or longlining horses anymore, Hollywood is definitely not short on action.

The Incredible Hulk shoots in Rio de Janeiro in late fall. I've spent a lot of time in Central and South America, but most of it has been flying over the jungle to get rainforest footage and chasing Gérard Fusil's competitors up the sides of mountains and across rivers. The cities are new to me, and honestly, after watching my engineer's throat get sliced open by a hairy stranger in Middle-of-Nowhere, Venezuela, I'm more than happy to be closer to civilization this time.

The first day we'll be flying over the *favelas*—busy shantytown neighborhoods that are home to the city's poor and working class. Rocinha, where we're shooting, is loud, busy, and so densely populated that from above it looks like a blanket of concrete houses on the hillside. In the script, this is where Bruce Banner has been hiding out, doing jiujitsu and trying to find out which Amazonian plant will make him less likely to transform into a green monster.

Just as I'm getting in the chopper, a local pilot runs up to me.

"Take this." He smiles, handing me a rusty piece of metal the size of a cafeteria tray.

"Why?" I ask.

"To cover your ass! Sometimes they shoot." He shrugs, making little guns with his fingers.

Apparently Bruce Banner isn't the only one hiding out in Rocinha; the local drug lords like it here too. What they don't like, according to my new friend, is police helicopters flying over their turf.

With a smile still on his face, the guy assures me that the new leader of the cartel is much better and less violent than the last one, whom he murdered. *Merde.*

I thank him, stick the metal on my seat, and take off thinking that if I manage to deflect stray bullets, fly a helicopter, and get aerial footage at the same time, Marvel studios should make a movie about me.

"Just smile and wave," I tell the camera operator.

The two of us fly over the favelas sweating bullets, trying to look as harmless and friendly as possible, smiling like we're in the Miss America pageant.

Thankfully the drug gangs are too busy for target practice that day. Maybe they're out trying to get a selfie with Ed Norton like everyone else?

Maybe it's because I'm a helicopter pilot, or maybe it's just because I'm laid-back, but the people I work with assume I'm universally equipped to handle dangerous situations. When I'm flying, sure, but on the ground, I'm going to crap my pants just as quick as the next guy.

"Fred, there's a situation in the lobby. Lock your door. Do not open it for anyone. Pack up your bags and get ready to leave."

The producer calls me in the early evening sounding terrified and deadly serious. We're somewhere in the Tianmo Desert in China shooting a Rob Cohen movie, *The Mummy: Tomb of the Dragon Emperor.* The aerial unit is small, maybe twenty people. We've spent the day getting lots of panoramic desert shots and flying over a fake Ming village that I'm told will eventually be blown up. There aren't really any hotels in the area, so we're staying in a basic apartment building that does short-term rentals.

I do as I'm told, grabbing my clothes and stuffing them into my suitcase.

Someone knocks on my door. I stay still and don't answer. There's screaming, lots of fast, tense conversation, banging on doors and walls. *Holy shit.* Crouching down on my stomach next to the bed, I take a deep breath. This, whatever it is, is a first for me.

I call Peggy, very quietly, and tell her what's happening, even though I don't really know what's happening at all.

"What the hell, Fred?!" Peggy yells into the phone.

"I love you," I whisper back to her. "Tell the kids I love them. I have to go."

My phone rings again. It's the producer.

"Fred, it's a hostage situation. We called the army and requested their help. You need to wait longer. *Please* do not open your door. I'll call you back when everything is in place."

I call Peggy back with the update. The fact that I'm a hostage does nothing to make her feel better. She wants to stay on the phone, but I need to keep the line open. For three hours, I lie next to the bed filled with adrenaline and feeling like actor Jason Statham. Another call from the producer comes in.

"Fred, a soldier is coming to get you. He's going to knock three times on your door. When he does, you need to get out fast," he says. "When you do get out, keep your head down. Don't look at the people, just follow your escort."

"OK," I agree, thinking that if *The Mummy: Tomb of the Dragon Emperor* is halfway as good as this shit, it will win an Oscar.

Two minutes pass slowly, and I hear three knocks on my door. I open it, and a soldier in a Kevlar vest and fatigues rushes me out.

"Go! Go! Fast! Fast!"

I run down what feels like the longest hallway on earth and into the elevator. We go down, passing each floor with a beep, until we hit the lobby. When the doors open, hundreds of Chinese locals are there, yelling at each other.

The soldiers, fully armed and looking mean, create a narrow pathway for us to exit and push us into military vehicles. We spend the night on cots at a base.

Apparently the company managing the building had failed to pay the owners of the units for renting them out. When the owners heard there were Americans on-site, they decided to hold us ransom until they got their money. Too bad Brendan Fraser wasn't with us.

With every single job, whether the challenges are technical or political, I get better, more confident, and more creative. Sometimes the stories behind the movies are as good as the movies themselves.

21

Go Higher

FOR MORE THAN FORTY YEARS, I have been told to do things by the book, think smaller, act the way people expect, fly the way people expect. I have not been able to do it. Not everyone has liked me. Not everyone has understood me. Not everyone has believed in me. But I have believed in myself. Be the first person to bet on yourself, and you will not be the last.

In early 2008, I get a call to work with Tony Scott. I'm speechless.

I actually reach down and pinch the skin on my arm to make sure I'm not dreaming.

Tony Scott is a legend, a master, the god of all action movies, one of my favorite directors of all time. He is responsible for one of the most captivating, influential pieces of American art ever produced: *Top Gun.*

I remember watching Maverick and Iceman take on the MiG-28s in the movie theater near Champs-Élysées at twenty-four years old, frozen in my seat, consumed by adrenaline, unable to think or move. I can't be sure, but I was probably wearing an Avirex suit at the time.

I agree to the project before the producer can finish explaining it.

The commercial is for Dodge Ram, and it's basically an alpha male's dream come true: something between reality TV, an adventure race, and an action movie. The toughest guys in America—teams of cowboys, firemen, soldiers, and construction workers—are going head-to-head driving pickup trucks in a four-day race. They'll speed through fire, crush buildings, put up bridges, dodge swinging trucks suspended over the desert like wrecking balls, and tackle crazy terrain.

The set is a couple of hours outside Los Angeles in the Mojave. There's nothing around us but dust, scrubby bushes, and a fake ghost town Tony Scott has set up for the competitors to demolish on the last day of filming. The crew is massive, like eighty people. There are cameras and cars everywhere.

When I see Tony Scott, he's standing by a monitor in his signature red baseball cap with a huge smile on his face. I introduce myself and we quickly go over a few shots. Because it's a competition, not many of the scenes are blocked. I'll have to react to the trucks, focus, find the angles myself, and respond to Tony's feedback.

"It's going to be great," he says, excited. "You and I will be working together for the next four days."

I pinch myself again. A French guy and British gentleman are at the wheel of the ultimate macho American fantasy.

We start shooting around nine a.m. The competitors get into the trucks. We get into the choppers. The starting gun cracks.

People have misunderstood my connection to the machine for a long time. I never want to be perceived as careless, so normally when I'm flying, I limit myself. I never want people, especially directors, to think I'm taking uncalculated risks or doing something dangerous. I hold back, even when I know I have more, and take the cautious approach. But Tony Scott doesn't want "cautious." He understands my flying right away and pushes me to go faster, fly closer, and get creative. Nobody has ever pushed me like this.

"This is brilliant, Fred! Give me more, I love it!"

I follow the military team across a long stretch of gravel and through a two-hundred-foot-long fire line. These guys, who have no stunt training at all, are essentially going straight into a giant fireball at sixty miles per hour. They're bold with their driving, so I'm bold with my flying.

"Yes, Fred! This is great! Let me see more!"

So I give him everything. It's four days of pure action and extreme flying: going superfast sideways, diving down to counter the trucks with really close face-to-face scenes, maximal flaring.

On the last day of flying over orange balls of fire and dust, chasing the trucks through the finish, and having Tony Scott yelling in my ear, I realize that the dream I've held onto my entire life—the hope that has grown and changed as I have—can't compare to the reality.

The "Ram Challenge" wraps early, and after the wildest commercial shoot of all time, Tony asks me to work with him again on *Unstoppable,* a movie about a runaway train starring Denzel Washington, Chris Pine, and Rosario Dawson. It's two straight months of intense explosions and train scenes in rural Pennsylvania. When I'm not trying to catch the 777 train in a pretend news chopper, I'm getting a master class in leadership, collaboration, and communication.

Every morning, in the drizzle, Tony gathers the crew over a long table outside next to the tracks to map out critical shots using children's toys: a train, plastic helicopters, and matchbox cars. Illustrating the scenes this way gives us all a chance to see what's going on in his head and to figure out what we need to do to achieve it. He never tells us how to do anything; he just shows us what he needs. When we make it happen for him, he's not shy about his feelings.

"Brilliant, Fred!"

"Brilliant, Christopher!"

"Brilliant, Monica!"

Tony Scott uses *brilliant* more than any other word in the English language, but really, there is no word that describes *him* better. The shoot is challenging; we're derailing a train, dealing with not-so-great weather, and sorting through conflicting ideas, but he still gets the best from all of us. At the end of each day, he grabs the radio from the coordinator to say thank you. The whole thing is perfect. *Almost.*

When the shoot is nearly over, I'm flying between the train and a pine forest when one of the effects guys triggers an explosion late. The helicopter is close to being totally engulfed in flames. The heat is fast but incredible. Everything smells like burning hair.

"Are you OK in there, French Toast?" Tony calls over the radio.

French Toast is not exactly *Iceman*, but when Tony Scott gives you a call sign, you wear it proudly.

The movie wraps, and I never go to another set without a toy helicopter in my pocket.

Right at the beginning of my career as a film pilot, Larry made it clear that the aerial shots were my responsibility. Directors and DPs know what they want to see, or what they *think* they want to see, but they don't always know what's possible from the helicopter. Normally, it can give you even more than what you expect. It's my job to help the creatives see that.

"Speak up! Give them ideas! Fight for the right shot!" Larry would say.

Gaining the confidence to advocate for the best images takes time, but once I start doing it, my career takes off. Five years after moving from France, I'm working on the biggest action movies coming out of Hollywood, and I'm known for being the one thing no one ever imagined I would be: professional.

The more work I do, the more work I do. I prep each film project like a rally race, studying the director's body of work; memorizing the angles, the lighting, and the framing; researching the filming locations; and communicating with the different departments. Really, with anyone on the team who wants to share ideas. I show up to set ready. I have to show up that way. It's not like Michael Bay is going to meet up with you at Starbucks and explain the nuances of his process. At least, he's never offered to.

The first time I worked with Michael Bay was in 1996 on *Armageddon.* I was still living in Paris and just starting out. On day one, just as I was getting into the chopper, he called me on the radio with an important message.

"Fred, this is the opening of my movie. Don't screw it up."

No pressure. At the time, I legitimately *was* worried about screwing it up. Thankfully, I didn't. The guy means business. All the time.

In 2009, he hires me for *Transformers: Revenge of the Fallen*, and I make a point of showing up every single day overprepared, knowing exactly what he wants.

Michael Bay is an artist, and I treat him like one. Just because a guy likes to blow things up and drive fast cars doesn't mean he's not an artist. There's choreography involved and Bay is like the Baryshnikov of action sequences. He doesn't even need to have video on the ground to know what we're shooting or how we are doing it. He sees the helicopter and where the camera is pointed, and when we're finished, he knows if we got the shot or not.

Working together is natural. Pretty soon, the only direction he's giving me is: "Fred, go do your thing."

The prep is everything, but when something happens that I can't prepare for, I adapt. Or at least I try to.

In summer 2010, Peggy and I go to Tokyo to work on Christopher Nolan's *Inception*. It's a sci-fi action movie about dream-sharing technology with tons of effects, huge aerials, and moving parts. We rent two helicopters there and collaborate with local pilots since our licenses aren't valid in Japan. Sometimes we must adjust to different aviation and film cultures, different languages, and different levels of comfort. It isn't always easy for me.

I'm flying the camera helicopter with Abe-san as copilot, and the "picture helicopter," the one you see on-screen in the movie, is flown by Tanaka-san with Peggy as copilot. She's still my favorite person to work with. Neither of the guys speaks English, and we're too heavy with passengers and camera equipment to bring translators on board. Everything was set at a meeting the day before. The pilots had a chance to ask questions through the translator, so we had one chance to deliver instructions.

The scene isn't complicated: The picture helicopter will land on top of a skyscraper. Leonardo DiCaprio and Joseph Gordon-Levitt will walk toward it. They'll get on. The picture helicopter will take off from the building with the actors on board. It's easy. The pilots didn't seem worried about it, and it's something Peggy and I could film in our sleep.

Tanaka-san and Abe-san arrive at the airport in full captain suits topped off with pristine white gloves. Peggy and I are in shorts. The uniform is just a cultural difference, but an unfortunate one considering the weather. It's eighty-five and humid.

When we're still on the ground waiting inside our helicopters, Peggy calls me on the radio. We have our own radio system. For us, this is normal.

"Fred, how much is your guy sweating?"

"What do you mean?" I answer.

"This pilot looks like he just got out of a sauna. And his hands are shaking. Should I be worried?!"

I look over at Abe-san. There's sweat pouring from his temples, and his gloves are soaking wet. It's hot, sure, but I get the feeling there's something else going on too.

Peggy and I go back and forth on the radio. Our best guess is that they're nervous. Who wouldn't be nervous with Leo on their chopper?!

Abe-san looks over at me and my radio, and all of a sudden, his face goes red. The veins in his neck pop out, and the guy just snaps. He's yelling and spitting into his radio and glaring at me like I'm a Russian spy. The next thing we know, ten people are circling the helicopters—airport personnel, cops, all in various uniforms and all sweating their balls off.

"You can't use your radio," Riku, the translator, runs up to explain. For us, air-to-air or air-to-ground communication on a movie set is primordial. Without direct contact, we can't do our jobs properly. After a good ten minutes of back-and-forth with the pilots and probably six other people, I still don't understand the problem. Then Riku says in a serious whisper, "North Korea can hear us."

Peggy and I look at each other and laugh. Hard.

I wasn't so far off with the Russian spy stuff.

We try to explain that there was no way "North Korea can hear us" because our radios have a maximum range of one mile. Unless Kim Jong Un is hiding in the control tower, we're perfectly safe. Our reasoning makes no impact. Their response is final: Cut the radios.

It's an unpleasant surprise, but we do our best to figure it out and hope flying together will smooth everything over. But there is nothing smooth about it.

Abe-san does our takeoff, going forward instead of up, using three full miles of runway like a Boeing 747. Peggy's pilot isn't much better. Tanaka-san refuses to land back on the roof of the building between takes, saying in broken English that they must wait thirty minutes for the turbulence to dissolve each time. The downdraft created by a helicopter at takeoff lasts for less than ten seconds, but here, waiting thirty minutes is the protocol and these guys are *sticking* to that protocol. Not surprisingly, it's a long day. By the end, we're tired and frustrated. We've been smelling pilot body odor and arguing all day. I must admit, though, their commitment to the rules is impressive. The temperature climbs to almost ninety, and they don't ever take their white gloves off. Not once.

By 2011, the kids are all in school and busy. Peggy is busy too. She's running our business and our household, making sure all of us have everything we need. She's a great mother and I love watching her with Naomi and the boys, who—no surprise—are total daredevils. Whether they're running into the ocean, doing backflips into the pool, or rolling around the skate park, she's with them every step, the same way she has been with me. I am travelling more than ever but missing home more than ever as well. My family is proud of me; they encourage and believe in me. It means everything. There is no possible way I can thank them, but I do always try to come back with a few good stories for the kids.

In 2012, I film *G.I. Joe: Retaliation* and come face-to-face with a nine-hundred-pound grizzly in Canadian bear country. I lie in the fetal position on the forest floor while it smells my neck and decides whether I'm dinner or not. In Thailand that same year, after getting some super close, dynamic shots of the principal actors on a boat for *The Hangover Part II*, there's a knock at my hotel room door. The concierge hands me a paper bag. I look inside, see a pair of men's underwear, and assume it's something of mine from the laundry service. I reach to put them back in the drawer and feel something. It's sticky and brown. *Merde.*

Thankfully, it's just Nutella.

Underneath it is a note from Zach Galifianakis:

"You made me shit my pants! Come meet me at the bar."

I guess they didn't brief the actors on just how close the helicopter was going to be.

In Gabon, I'm nearly charged by an elephant. In Puerto Rico, I film *Fast Five* with second unit director Spiro Razatos and an extraordinary team of stunt actors led by Jack and Andy Gill, who are blowing up and flipping cars on the Teodoro Moscoso Bridge. With the trust and support of the studio's risk management team, especially John Harris from the transport safety division at Universal, we're able to push the envelope, play a little part in a franchise that will go down in action movie history. Truly, no day is the same as the last.

I am not a great scholar or a surgeon or a banker, but I am one of the best at what I do. I am a leader in my field. And though my parents still don't really understand me, according to my mom they have seen *Fantastic Four*, *The Jaguar*, and *Clash of the Titans*. They never come out and say they're proud, but they don't need to. I have my suspicions.

Late in summer 2012, I get the news that Tony Scott has taken his own life. I'm devastated. The entire industry is gutted, totally in shock. *Unstoppable* was his final feature film. And it was "brilliant." I promise myself never to settle for anything less than that. His work continues to shape mine. His enthusiasm continues to inspire me. His teaching continues to reach me in everything I do. It takes a special teacher to do that. His death was a tragedy, but his legacy is a triumph.

Every time I set up a shot, I remember the sound of blades in the sky, the dust coming up in a giant, golden cloud, the sting of sweat collecting on my neck and in my eyes, the feel of my heart pounding all over my body, knowing that a dream can take you as high as you want to go.

So go higher.

Epilogue

I'M AWAKE BEFORE THE ALARM rings and showered by five thirty a.m. Sleep was nearly impossible; I had too many thoughts. After months of prep for Sam Hargrave's *Extraction 2*, we're finally filming "the most epic train scene in moviemaking history," *but* we're filming it in Prague, not Sydney. International pandemic restrictions shifted, and so did our production—by around nine thousand miles. Three months of work went straight into the trash. We had to start over. I'm exhausted from living and breathing every detail of a single scene, from months of nothing but focus, and from moving our operation from summertime on the Gold Coast to November in Eastern Europe.

Finding a helicopter company willing to let me land one of their machines on a moving train was not easy in Australia. In Europe, it was even more complicated. Over the last few weeks, I've had more phone calls than I can count with Civil Aviation, the studio, and the helicopter company, answering specific questions, going over every second of the scene, reassuring everyone that we're ready. And we *are* ready. Our plans have plans. I have spent twelve hours a day for the past several months preparing for a scene that will take fifteen minutes to shoot.

I wipe the steam from the mirror in the hotel bathroom and shut my eyes, picturing the scene in my mind. I'll come straight for a sexy, epic approach, landing only one skid on the edge of the train. The five stuntmen will exit the chopper aggressively but safely and begin going after the lead actor. I don't remember how I decided on one skid, but it will add even more movement to the scene. The top of a train is not as roomy as you'd think, but in practice, it went well.

For the past two weeks, under the guidance of my fellow film pilot and friend Ben Skorstad, we have been practicing the scene the best that we can: landing the chopper on a shipping container being hauled by a flatbed truck down a decommissioned runway; trying to figure out how the machine will react; deciding if I'll need to put some fabric on top of the train to give some grip to the skid or whether I should let it slide; calculating the weight and balance of landing on one skid with one thousand pounds of bad guys on board going fifty miles per hour. We have answered many questions, but there are still so many variables—so many questions with no exact answers. How we were able to get the scene greenlit by the studio, I'll never know. They weren't thrilled about a one-camera sequence involving the lead actor on a moving train with three helicopters flying a couple of feet from his head. If there's no Chris Hemsworth, good luck with *Extraction 3*.

I look in the mirror and take a deep breath.

What am I doing here?

What am I thinking?

What if it's just impossible?

Peggy texts me:

How are you feeling?

It's around nine p.m. in Los Angeles. Honestly, I'm not sure how to feel. This scene is now much bigger than me. I have twenty-seven seconds to land a helicopter, one skid, on a moving train and get five guys out before I hit the trees. We did it in twenty-two seconds with the truck, but it was tight.

Excited, I text back.

I arrive on set and have a quick meeting with Sam, the director. It's freezing out, cold enough that both of us are struggling to talk without shivering. The scene was delayed by five days thanks to a string of snowstorms, and this is our first chance to do it. I'm worried my team has lost momentum. Since we got to Prague two weeks ago, the safety and stunt teams have done nothing but live and breathe this scene. We started from square one, landing the helicopter slowly on the train, practicing the weight transfer with the guys on the ground with the engine off, and adding on one component and one stuntman at a time until everything was running perfectly and had been made permanent in our brains. Every day we rehearsed, and every night we debriefed. By the end, we don't just *want* to shoot the scene; we *need* to.

Sam says he wants to film the rehearsal, which is normal for a big, expensive sequence. But I push back: This big expensive sequence is not normal. Things are going to be crazy on top of that train. It's important for him to experience one pass without the camera on his shoulder. Even though he used to be a stuntman, he needs to be out there, seeing and feeling it all—the wind of the chopper, the downwash, the action on the train—without worrying about footage. It's the only way to do it safely.

"OK, Fred." He nods. "I trust you."

He pats me on the back, but I hardly feel it. It's thirty-one degrees. We're both dressed like Bond villains from Siberia.

Sam climbs up on top of the train with the actors and stunt team. The guys look relaxed. They know what to expect. They know to exit horizontally to minimize the weight transfer and to jump one by one, leaving a half-second in between them. They know to be sure their rifles aren't in the way, so they don't shake my seat too much on the way out. They know there are nets on the side of the train just in case something does go wrong. But Sam is a first timer. He's watched the scene dozens of times, but the stunt coordinators, Noon Orsatti and Shane Habberstad, quickly brief him on the action.

The train moves fast along the tracks through a field of dead grass bordered by pine forest. As soon as I get the cue, I begin to chase it down. I spot my fabric landing marker and set my skid onto it easily. The guys start to exit. The wind created by the helicopters throws Sam off balance from the train and into the net. He's fine, but anyone without his level of experience would have been hurt. He pops up looking exhilarated and tells us he's ready to go. I love this guy.

For the second pass, which will be filmed, we have a system in place with the stunt coordinator. My ground pilot will be staged at the back of the train to give me a cue once all five stuntmen are out of the chopper and it's time to bail out. There's no way for me to turn my head and check on the guys; I have too much to deal with keeping the chopper steady. For any stunt operation, I always have safety ground pilots. They're fully licensed commercial helicopter pilots who stay on the ground to give me all the information I need to perform properly and safely. They act as a liaison between me, the crew, and the director, communicating any changes on timing or approach, intervening on safety, confirming the distance of the machine to obstacles, wires, cables, or cranes.

I get the cue to approach the helicopter and I go for it, flying with intensity and precision, setting the skid on my mark. I feel the guys exit and the helicopter shift. The ground pilot gives me the signal to bail, and I get out of there fast, giving it everything. But as I pull away, I realize the fifth guy is still in the chopper. He jumps out as we're hovering above the train and somehow manages to stick the landing. It will look cool on camera, but it's a close call. Too close. We change the cue and hand the responsibility to Noon. It's hard to keep focus with everything going on, but there's no room for error. The next pass is the real deal.

The train is moving across the half-frozen meadow at exactly fifty miles per hour. I'm hovering nearby. Waiting. Ready. It's freezing, but I feel sweat on my palms and the back of my neck. I take a breath. *This is it.*

Action.

All at once I'm focused. The guys are totally silent. We begin the approach, direct, aggressive, hard-hitting. My skid touches down, kissing the top of the train. I feel the guys begin to exit. One, two, three, four, and five. Lighter, lighter, lighter, lighter, and lighter. Noon gives me my cue and I bail, flaring like crazy. The helicopter lifts sharp and quick. I can feel my breath again and the weather. In the corner of my eye, I see the train.

"Cut!" Sam calls.

We got it.

I can hear people cheering from the ground. It really is the most epic train sequence in the history of moviemaking.

The tension lifts from my body as I land in the field, stepping out onto the yellow grass and wondering how anything will ever feel exciting ever again.

I'm flying close to the back of the train the next day for another shot. It's much simpler. Chris Hemsworth shoots at me, I pretend to crash, there's an explosion, justice prevails. It's started to snow, just lightly.

We discussed the timing with the special effects lead a couple of days before. As soon as I clear the back of the train, I'll call "Boom" over the radio. Then, to be sure I'm out of the way, there will be a count of two before special effects will detonate the explosion. The effects lead is in Vienna scouting a location, so there's a new guy today. No problem. I'm sure he's got it down. As far as I'm concerned, the hard work on *Extraction 2* is over for me.

Sam calls action and I fly around to the back of the train. Hemsworth shoots at me. There's smoke everywhere and I pretend to crash, making it look erratic but flying with extreme control. Suddenly there's a rush of heat inside the cabin. Less than three feet from my open door is an orange wall of fire. *Merde.*

Everything is quiet.

Noon and Shane check in. I take an inventory of my body parts. It's all there (except for the hair). I'm OK.

"All good," I call back. "Let's go again."

ENHANCE YOUR EXPERIENCE *by scanning the QR codes on the next pages and dive into Fred's world. Watch video clips, movie trailers, helicopter scenes, commercials and behind the scenes.*

CHAPTER 9
Paris to Dakar Rally, 1988

CHAPTER 12
Raid Gauloises in
Costa Rica, 1990

CHAPTER 13
Raid Gauloises in
New Caledonia, 1991

CHAPTER 14
Paris Dakar Rally to
Cape Town, 1992

CHAPTER 14
Dakar Rally Mitsubishi
Motors TV, 1992

CHAPTER 14
Paris/Moscow/
Beijing Rally, 1992

CHAPTER 15
*Raid Gauloises
in Oman, 1992*

CHAPTER 15
*Ferry from Egypt to
Madagascar, 1994*

CHAPTER 16
The Jaguar
Trailer (French)

CHAPTER 20
Steve Wynn

CHAPTER 20
*Encore Las Vegas Commercial,
Behind the Scenes*

CHAPTER 20
10,000 B.C. *Trailer*

CHAPTER 21
Dodge Ram Challenge,
Behind the Scenes

CHAPTER 21
Unstoppable *Trailer*

CHAPTER 21
Transformers *Trailer*

CHAPTER 21
Inception *Trailer*

CHAPTER 21
The Hangover 2 *Trailer*

Prologue
Extraction 2 *Trailer*

Photo and Illustration Credits

Fred and
Peggy North

About the Authors

FRED NORTH

Acclaimed stunt film pilot Fred North was born in Tunisia in 1961 to French expat parents and began his journey to becoming a pilot at eight years old, the very second he saw and set foot in a helicopter. From the jungles of Costa Rica and Madagascar to the Eurasian Steppe and the Swiss Alps, Fred has flown in some of the world's most perilous and demanding conditions, serving as Camera Helicopter Pilot and Chief Pilot for world-renowned rally car races such as "Paris-Dakar" and "Paris-Moscow-Beijing" and as coordinator for the famous sport trek "Raid Gauloises." At 41, determined to use his skills as a pilot and his natural eye for the camera to tell stories, Fred moved to Los Angeles, making the transition to from "pilot who films" to Film Pilot.

Specializing in the film industry for more than 30 years, Fred is an expert in aerial cinematography, having accumulated more than 15,000 hours shooting feature films and commercials, and more than 20,263 total flying hours. He has over 200 film credits including *Inception, James Bond: Spectre, Mission Impossible, Transformers*, and several movies in *the Fast and Furious* franchise, and has worked with such acclaimed directors as Roland Emmerich, Michael Bay, Tony Scott, Peter Berg, Damian Chazelle, Doug Liman, Joel Schumacher and more.

At age 40, Fred achieved the World Record for "Altitude with a Helicopter," climbing to 42,500 feet in South Africa. At age 60, after years of encouragement, he attempted his most terrifying stunt yet: a memoir. With his partner and collaborator, Peggy, by his side, he looks forward to sharing his story and imploring others to dream big, fly high, and believe in themselves without compromise.

Fred is a member of the SAG – AFTRA, the Motion Pilot association, and the HAI (Helicopter Association International). He was nominated at the SAG stunt awards for his work on *Xmen*.

PEGGY NORTH

Peggy North (1976) was born and raised in Paris, France. She grew up in television studios and on set with her dad, famous sports announcer Bernard Père, and her mother, Renée Père-Champagne, a celebrated TV director. She graduated from La Sorbonne in Arts and Communication in 1998 and met Fred North while interviewing for a job at his company shortly after. They have been together at work and home ever since. A helicopter pilot herself, Peggy has been Fred's stunt coordinator for more than a decade, accumulating over 50 film credits and running the couple's companies. In 2012, led by her passion for design, she created Fire and Crème, a luxury event production company that serves major Hollywood studio executives, politicians, and celebrities.

Following the births of their children, Peggy felt a strong urge to write Fred's story as a legacy for their family. She wanted their daughter and sons to know where their father came from, why he is who he is, and how against all odds he managed to follow his dream in a world full of doubt. She had no plans to share her writing with the world, but when Fred started his social media account and his community began to grow, it became clear that the story was bigger and more impactful than either of them could have imagined. In 2022, Peggy put her business on hold to immerse herself in the story that captured not only her heart but also the hearts of hundreds of thousands of fans around the world.

Countless hours of interviews, chapter drafts, and several international flights later, the foundation of *Flying Sideways* was laid.

Fred and Peggy live in Malibu, California, but spend most of their free time on the island of Kauai. They are avid surfers, but when they're not in the water, they're riding their motorcycles, spending time with their children and friends, enjoying life as much as they can.

Acknowledgments

We want to share our deepest thanks to Roda Ahmed who planted the seed for this book, laid out the map for us, and made the impossible suddenly possible. With the magic words, "Write five hundred words per day, just five hundred words per day," what looked like Everest became the Santa Monica mountains.

Shannon Miller, you are an angel on earth, a woman with so much positivity and genuine kindness, your talent is beyond, working with you was pure joy.

Jennifer Grey, thank you for listening, brainstorming, and helping us find our way to the perfect title. "What is it that Fred does best?" you asked. Well, flying sideways!

This book would not have been possible without the help (and memory!) of family and friends: Joel Bastien, Philippe Tondeur, Francois Serie, Jean Pujol, Gérard Fusil, Vincent Regnier, Thierry Ranarivelo, and Larry Blanford. Going back in time with you all was an adventure of its own.

Thank you to Michael Bay, Gerard Butler, Shawn Levy, John Harris, Sam Hargrave, and Patrick Newhall for reading through our first sample chapters and giving us precious feedback.

Charlize Theron and Jason Statham, thank you for always trusting Fred with your life, it means the world.

Jonathan Spano, you are the best partner anyone could wish for. We are grateful for you.

Fred's team: Ben, Dylan, Garett, Ryan, David, Peter, James, Luc, Michael, Bethany, Cliff—you guys make it all possible, every single time. Philippe Lubrano, you're a rock star. Thank you.

Michael O'Donnell—let's be honest, Fred wouldn't even have a job without you.

Keyvan Taheri, our brother from another mother, your friendship is pure gold.

Becky Bayne, thank you for listening, believing in our vision, and designing this beautiful book.

A special thank you to our publisher Matt West, editor Morgan Rickey and the amazing team at Dexterity, we are grateful for your hard work and eagle eyes.

To Fred's online community, the pilots, the enthusiasts, the film buffs, and yes, even the trolls, we are indebted to you. Thank you for constant support and for helping us think bigger with this project. We hope it was everything you hoped for and then some.

AND last but not least, thank you to our children, Naomi, Tom, and Cooper for being part of our crazy journey, we love you. This book is for you.